SBF

How the FTX Bankruptcy Unwound Crypto's Very Bad Good Guy

Brady Dale

WILEY

Library of Congress Cataloging-in-Publication Data

Names: Dale, Brady, author.
Title: SBF : how the FTX bankruptcy unwound crypto's very bad good guy / by
    Brady Dale.
Description: Hoboken, New Jersey : John Wiley & Sons, Inc. [2023] |
    Includes bibliographical references and index.
Identifiers: LCCN 2023004682 (print) | LCCN 2023004683 (ebook) | ISBN
    9781394196067 (cloth) | ISBN 9781394196081 (adobe pdf) | ISBN
    9781394196074 (epub)
Subjects: LCSH: Bankman-Fried, Sam. | FTX (Firm) | Cryptocurrencies—United
    States. | Financial services industry—Corrupt practices—United States.
    | Bankruptcy—United States. | Fraud—United States.
Classification: LCC HG172.B36 D35 2023 (print) | LCC HG172.B36 (ebook) |
    DDC 332.092 [B]—dc23/eng/20230210
LC record available at https://lccn.loc.gov/2023004682
LC ebook record available at https://lccn.loc.gov/2023004683

Cover Design: Paul McCarthy
Cover Images: © Getty Images: Michael M. Santiago / Staff;
Antagain; Shutterstock: Respiro
SKY10044062_031623

to Michael Lewis,
he leveled up business storytelling.

Contents

Prologue

O ne of the things I've learned as a journalist is something I can't quite explain, even really to myself. It's a thing I know, but putting it in words is harder.

But it's something like this: Sometimes I will try to report a story, based on the fact that I know something has happened. What I want to know is the how and why of that event.

The thing, the happening that broke into public view, is maybe 5 or 10 percent of the story. And from that little piece, I think I know two or three ways that it could possibly be explained. It doesn't *seem* like it could be explained by anything else.

But then you learn maybe 30 or 50 percent of the story. You're still not all the way there, but you realize that there was so much that you just couldn't see when you only had 5 to 10 percent. It looks now like you were blind then.

That's not the part that's hard to explain.

This is: Now that you know more than you knew then, you also can't even identify with yourself and the way you once saw it. It's hard to even see how you ever thought those explanations could be right. Maybe you can't even remember them. That simplicity slips from the set of possibilities.

So here's my point: this book is a reel of film from late 2022. It's an attempt to capture what we think we know about Sam Bankman-Fried, the FTX conglomerate, and the crypto industry, up through to the point of his indictment, arrest, and extradition back to the US, when facts were still fuzzy and emotions were running hot.

Honestly, even that was such a turning point that the whole prior set of feelings and impressions have already vanished.

But it looks like there will be a trial, and when that happens it will layer on so many new facts that this time, this way of understanding will be washed out as if it never was. But it is part of the larger story, and this book will preserve some portion of that, because this is a crucial moment in this still nascent history. If cryptocurrencies persist, people are definitely going to wonder what it looked like from now.

So here goes.

There's a lot I still don't know as I finish this.

But we do know a lot, and I hope putting it together and adding some new pieces of it here can help all of us see more clearly what we can know about it so far. We don't know everything yet, nor even close to everything I suspect we will.

Some notes on the reporting before we start.

First, Sam Bankman-Fried is our subject. In these pages, he will be familiar to you, so I'm going to call him SBF or Sam. That's not because I'm his friend or ever was, but it's how he's known.

I have never met Sam in person, but we talked a few times on the phone. I used to ask him for comment on stories I was working on via email or over Telegram regularly.

Much of this story is a story I know from covering the space since 2015, full time since 2017. Nonetheless, I can back up my own knowledge with actual reporting at the time from news organizations. Quite a bit of that reporting has been my own.

After each chapter, I note accounts that I either referenced or used to double check my memory. They are listed in roughly the order they show up in the chapter (though some are used more than once, obviously).

I also did a lot of interviews for this. In a few cases, I agreed to keep people's identity out of the story because it makes a lot of people nervous in various ways: legally, reputationally, etc. See more details about interviews in the notes.

Many comments in the story come from Twitter. A lot of crypto culture, discourse, decision-making, and even dealmaking happens on Twitter. That's the way we live now. The addresses of all the tweets are shown in the chapter notes. Similarly, when I have had to use the Internet Archive for sources, the full address is given.

In general, I have left internet-speak as is, unless I really felt like readers wouldn't get, for example, an abbreviation. In those cases, I spelled it out or added a footnote. I also fixed some obvious misspellings in comments found online.

In quotes, I've removed filler words, such as "like," and "umm" and pointless repetition that bought the speaker time to think. Sometimes such words, especially "like," seemed more important than other times, as if there were some meaning there. This has been subjective, but the essential meanings of the statements have been unchanged by including them or erasing them.

This book uses the complaints from the Securities and Exchange Commission and Commodity Futures Trading Commission extensively (less so the Department of Justice indictment, because it said the least though probably matters the most). It's important to note here that these are all still allegations. Evidence hasn't been presented, and a court hasn't weighed in.

Complaints aren't always right, and evidence can come to light that clears defendants, but these complaints in many ways support the account of prior sources.

However, SBF and his colleagues are all innocent until proven guilty. Everything presented here that seems inappropriate or criminal should be considered allegations. There is a lot that no one seems to know yet.

And crucially, this book isn't an attempt at a trial in prose. The courts will decide what they decide, undoubtedly concerning a narrow set of questions. Storytelling considers broad questions, to help us all grow our understanding of how humans relate, coordinate, and resolve disputes in an ever more abstracted world.

Much of this book concerns cryptocurrency, which raises perennial questions of style. The standards around how to write out the names of cryptocurrencies are still being debated. To me, cryptocurrency is money, so when I'm talking about tokens or coins as money, I write them lower case as I would any currency: bitcoins and dogecoins are treated just as I would dollars or euros.

Cryptocurrencies all have ticker symbols, like stocks do. So on first mention I will write the name and the ticker in parentheses, such as ether (ETH), dai (DAI), terra usd (UST).

All cryptocurrencies run on a blockchain or protocol of some kind, so when I'm referring to the blockchain or smart contract itself, I will use uppercase: Solana, SushiSwap, Yearn, Ethereum.

Sometimes the name of the protocol and the token are the same, so this should help show the different sense being used. Example: Bitcoin the blockchain versus bitcoin the asset that makes that blockchain work.

Inevitably, these things become muddled in places. The way to write clearly and consistently about cryptocurrency remains a work in progress.

As I wrote this entire book, I was waiting to actually speak with SBF. Every day I worked on it, I became more and more convinced that his guilty plea was inevitable, that the evidence was too overwhelming.

The day of my deadline to Wiley, December 30, 2022, I had completed what I thought was my final draft of the book, but then I got a chance to speak with SBF. When I asked him about the fact that complaints from various agencies seemed to confirm that Alameda and FTX had collaborated in using customer funds inappropriately, he said:

> It's interesting that they seem so confident in claiming that, given that I'm pretty confident that they have extremely little data to go on right now as evidenced by the fact that none of it was in the various complaints.

He then reiterated points he's been making thus far about what went wrong. His story hasn't shifted since the complaints came out, so I'll get to what he told me about all of that when it's appropriate. But he also said this:

> In terms of facing the future, I think I'm just gonna tell the truth and see what happens. And I certainly don't agree with the public narrative, but that's not for me to decide at the end of the day. I think, like, my biggest concern is that the incredibly toxic media environment will mean that there's no way for me to have a fair trial. And that no matter what happens, there will be too much political and public pressure to find me guilty. And that it won't matter what really happened.

I did not have much success reaching other executives from FTX and its related companies, for reasons that are probably obvious. It's been a surprise to everyone that the founder has said as much as he has.

Source Referenced

Interview, Sam Bankman-Fried, phone call interview with spokesperson, Dec. 30, 2022.

Timeline

*F*rom media accounts that have not been disputed by FTX or its affiliates. *Where it's from allegations in CFTC or SEC complaints, that's noted.*

2017

- Jan. 1. Bitcoin price breaks $1,000 for the first time since 2013.
- Oct. or Nov. Alameda founded in Berkeley (CFTC). Gary Wang and Tara MacAulay are early leaders.
- Dec. Nishad Singh joins.
- Dec. 17. New bitcoin all-time high, $19,783.

2018

- Jan. SBF presents Alameda to notable crypto investors in San Francisco.
- March. Caroline Ellison joins Alameda (SEC) from Jane Street.
- April. MacAulay and many other associates from the EA movement leave and take a large amount of capital with them.
- Late. They begin work on a derivatives exchange that would become FTX (CFTC).
- Dec. 15. Bitcoin's nadir, at $3,236.

2019

- Early. Team moves to Hong Kong.
- May. FTX begins. Deposits to FTX are made into an Alameda Bank Account opened in the name of "North Dimension," accounted for manually into customer accounts at FTX.
- July 19. FTX launches the ftt token (SEC).
- Aug. $8 million series A for FTX (SEC). Code is written to allow Alameda to have a negative balance on FTX (SEC).
- Nov. Binance gets 20% stake (CFTC) (could be the same terms as August)

2020

- Jan. FTX US established (CFTC)
- March. Solana launches beta.
- May. Negative balance code is updated (SEC). FTX US goes live.
- Aug. FTX acquires Blockfolio. FTX finally has its own bank account, but never moves prior FTX deposits to Alameda over to that account, leaving $8 billion behind (CFTC). SushiSwap announces vampire attack on Uniswap.
- Sept. SBF steps in to steward the migration of Uniswap deposits to SushiSwap, becoming a public face in DeFi for the first time.

2021

- Jan. Maps.me whitepaper lists SBF as an advisor.
- Feb. Ren, a bitcoin derivatives start-up, joins FTX.
- May. Brett Harrison starts at FTX US.
- July. Binance and FTX break up; Binance receives large stake of ftt as part of its buyout. CZ and Sequoia invests in Series B, $900M in at $18B valuation, with a $1 billion investment (SEC)
- Oct. Oct. FTX US acquires LedgerX (CFTC). SBF hands over control of Alameda to Sam and Caroline. Meme round: $420M from 69 investors.
- Nov. 10. Bitcoin all-time high of $69,044.
- Dec. $719 billion in spot trading volume on FTX.

2022

- Jan. Bitcoin falls below $40,000 for the first time. $500 million series C for FTX. FTX Ventures is announced, led by Amy Wu, from Lightspeed Ventures.
- Feb. DOJ announces arrest of couple holding stolen Bitfinex bitcoin. Solana blockchain bridge to Ethereum, Wormhole, exploited for over $300 million.
- Mar. Federal funds rate increases for the first time since Dec. 2018.
- April. Groundbreaking of new FTX HQ in Nassau. Crypto Bahamas, in collaboration with SALT.
- May. The Terra stablecoin unravels. The gradual correction in crypto markets becomes more acute. Alameda draws on its secret line of credit at FTX to meet margin calls from lenders. The line of credit is hidden in FTX's accounts. (SEC). FTX appears at CFTC hearing to discuss its request to offer derivatives in the US. Bitcoin falls below $30,000 for the first time.
- June. BlockFi spared from insolvency by $250 million line of credit arranged by SBF. Coinbase announces layoffs. Alameda research offers financing to Voyager Digital. Bitcoin falls below $20,000 for the first time.
- June to late July 2022. Alameda still the largest depositor of stablecoins.
- July. Crypto hedge fund Three Arrows Capital files for bankruptcy. Crypto lender Celsius declares bankruptcy.
- Aug. The first version of the Digital Commodities Consumer Protection Act (the SBF bill) is introduced in the Senate. Treasury sanctions the Tornado Cash smart contract on Ethereum. Sam Trabucco steps down as co-CEO of Alameda Research.
- Sept. Brett Harrison steps down as president of FTX US. SBF circulates a memo on shutting down Alameda internally (CFTC).
- Oct. Jonathan Cheeseman leaves FTX as head of overt-the-counter trading. Mango Markets' smart contracts exploited for over $100 million. SBF releases his "Possible Digital Industry Standards" blog post, setting off a bitter controversy.

Nov.

- 2nd. CoinDesk posts its story about Alameda's balance sheet.
- 6th. Binance CEO announces plans for it to liquidate its holdings of ftt from FTX's buyout of its original stake. Customers begin leaving FTX.
- 7th. SBF tweets that FTX's assets are "fine" and that FTX does not invest customer assets.
- 8th. FTX announces Binance will acquire FTX. Election Day in the US.
- 9th. Binance cancels acquisition. $5 billion leaves FTX that day. Ryan Salame tips off Bahamas regulators that client funds had been misused to cover Alameda debts. Ellison tells Alameda staff about misuse of FTX customer funds and most resign.
- 10th. SBF tweets, among other things: "I'm sorry. That's the biggest thing. I fucked up." Nishad Singh resigns.
- 11th. FTX declares bankruptcy, SBF resigns.
- 17th. New CEO submits the bankruptcies "first day declaration" to the US bankruptcy court in Delaware.
- 18th. Gary Wang and Caroline Ellison end their employment with FTX (SEC).
- 19th. Bitcoin hits its lowest price of 2022, $15,742.
- 28th. Crypto lender BlockFi declares bankruptcy.

Dec. 2022

- SBF is arrested in the Bahamas and charged with multiple crimes, and the CFTC and SEC bring civil suits against the companies he ran.
- SBF agrees to be extradited to the US, where he is released on bail, without a passport, and with an ankle bracelet.
- Wang and Ellison agree to cooperate with prosecutors.

Chapter 1

I Want to Believe

I am drowning in Sam.

He's everywhere, and unlike any other CEO after a comparably colossal unwinding, he's not coming at me indirectly, via journalists searching out his history.

No, this deluge is him. *He won't stop. It's as if he can't stop. I want to get the story of FTX down, but how can anyone discern it through all the noise that is him: that is Sam Bankman-Fried? That is SBF. That nasally, excessively informed voice that just won't stop offering his version of events in his extra-qualified statistically tinted mysticism.*

These words are coming to you from somewhere around the halfway point of writing this book. It's December 1, 2022. Tonight, as my workday at Axios, the internet-native news site, was ending, I was trying to make some time to do a little bit of research on companies that one of his companies, Alameda Research, has backed, but then I got a message on our Slack that SBF, the boy wonder who lost several billion dollars in crypto wealth, was doing a Twitter Spaces.

For those blessedly adrift from the gravity of Twitter, Spaces are where a few people can go online and talk with each other, no video, just voice, while dozens or hundreds or thousands of others just listen, interacting only with a few emoji. Spaces has become a big way for big accounts to broadcast. And SBF, since late November and here in early December 2022, was all about broadcasting.

This was after SBF had made a morning show appearance with George Stephanopoulous, which I haven't then watched yet. And after a New York Times internet broadcast with Andrew Ross Sorkin, which I also haven't watched yet. I am the only person I know in the media who hasn't watched. I am too busy writing this book to watch a thing I knew would be that will there when I am ready. I plan to watch it later. But now he is talking again, to some random faux-investigators on Twitter in a wannabe Barbara Walters grilling I just have the misfortune of hearing.

I listened to a little of the Spaces, but it was more aggravation than information. There was too much of him. I'm drowning.

Sam will not stop coming. People say this deluge is the masterpiece of public relations plotted out by warlock-level flaks inducted into issue control dark arts. But this view comes from mere witnesses of PR, perhaps its clients. This was not PR. PR is the sandstorm in which I've built my home. It's pointless pellets of banal sameness, a maelstrom in which I heave to inhale a few breaths of trustworthy observations. PR has a taste and a smell of risk aversion. What SBF was doing was not that.

This was him. This torrent sprung from his need. This was all Sam.

So much Sam.

I am drowning in Sam.

— Dec. 1, 2022

★★★

Sam Bankman-Fried offered a story that you wanted to believe. The talkative boy billionaire who would turn the wealth creation engine of cryptocurrency into a robber baron's war chest with which he could fix the world.

He would be like Andrew Carnegie with his libraries, and who doesn't like those libraries? There was one in my tiny little hometown in Southeast Kansas. It's beautiful.

But Andrew Carnegie paid for those libraries in part by—for example—hiring thugs to bust unionized workers trying to negotiate a better contract. Not great stuff, as it goes. Some of our grandparents paid for those libraries in lost wages.

But SBF wouldn't spin up a war chest from anything nasty like air pollution–belching factories and life-threatening working conditions. SBF's war chest would be created off the internet, scratching wealth off like solid gold paint flecks from space money bouncing around something called a blockchain. Far from creating industrial scars in people's backyards, blockchains don't even seem real!

So if a good guy could come along and make his wealth off that and then help a whole lot of people with that money, where would the harm be?

It was an appealing way to see SBF. A lot of people got sucked into it. I got sucked into it—I believed that he believed the story he was telling. Bonnie Tyler sang it out in 1984, and we all feel today just as she did then: we're all holding out for a hero.

Let me ask you this question: What if we are all in fact better off for the fact that SBF never got a chance to take a crack at really going to town saving the world?

What if he was the very last hero anyone needed?

What if, in fact, the lesson of SBF is this: the last thing anyone needs is a hero.

Chapter 2

The Third Turn: CZ

There are three turning points in the story of Sam Bankman-Fried. In each one, his project started to go in the wrong direction. This one, the last one, turned so hard and so fast there was no saving it.

SBF's empire fell apart because the crypto news site CoinDesk got a look at something that looked much like a balance sheet. Its report, by reporter Ian Allison, ran only a few hundred words, but it ended up being the most high-impact single dispatch in all of business news in 2022. Maybe in all of news?

FTX, the cryptocurrency exchange he founded, was created based on the experience of running Alameda Research, a trading firm SBF started with others in 2017. Theoretically, FTX and Alameda were separate companies, but every indication suggests that the borders between them were much fuzzier than they should have been.

The balance sheet Allison got his hands on belonged to Alameda Research, and he presented it that way. He wrote:

> The financials make concrete what industry-watchers already suspect: Alameda is big. As of June 30, the company's assets amounted to $14.6 billion. Its single biggest asset: $3.66 billion of "unlocked FTT." The third-largest entry on the assets side of the accounting ledger? A $2.16 billion pile of "FTT collateral."

By "ftt" he meant an exchange token that FTX had spun up in order to make using the exchange more addictive. We'll go more into how this worked later, but for now, think of it like this: ftt was like a loyalty card at a coffee shop, only this loyalty card also pays a little bit of the coffee shop's profits, above and beyond the free cup they get every sixth visit. But! The twist: Users have to buy the exchange's loyalty cards. On the other hand, that means they can have as many of them as they want, and the more customers had the more they shared in FTX's profits.

To most people, the passage quoted above from Allison's post probably reads as so much accounting gobbledygook, but one very important person read it and became alarmed. He is probably the most powerful single person in the whole cryptocurrency industry, the billionaire Changpeng Zhao (or just "CZ"). CZ himself had a big pile of FTX's ftt token. Binance is the biggest crypto exchange in the world, but some believed that FTX had a shot at unseating it one day.

The story hit like a howitzer shell, but when you look back at SBF's tweets over the weekend following Allison's Wednesday post, he acted as though he wasn't worried. And, in truth, it wasn't really Allison's story that brought FTX down. It was CZ's reaction. In a reversal of the biblical story, Goliath would be the one to land the critical hit.

On Sunday, November 6, CZ tweeted, "As part of Binance's exit from FTX equity last year, Binance received roughly $2.1 billion USD equivalent in cash (BUSD and FTT). Due to recent revelations that have come to light, we have decided to liquidate any remaining FTT on our books."

Then he wrote, "We will try to do so in a way that minimizes market impact."

CZ's team did not succeed in minimizing market impact.

In fact, Binance's founder kicked off a wave of contagion across the industry that will likely make the 2018 bitcoin and cryptocurrency downturn look like a boom year. It's so bad that even Binance will feel it.

The morning after CZ's promise to dump FTX's exchange token, another crypto news site, The Block, reported that withdrawals from FTX's platform seemed to have been halted. One of The Block's researchers had looked at one of FTX's addresses on the Ethereum blockchain and found out that funds just weren't moving. Meanwhile, on Twitter, customers were complaining. They wanted out.

It was Tuesday morning. Election Day in the United States. Events would start moving very quickly.

My fellow reporters at Axios heard of the stoppage and started hitting our crypto channel on Slack asking in what possible world halted withdrawals could not be very, very bad. For my part, it was hard to believe that FTX could have serious trouble. I had come to see it as a responsible actor run by a bunch of upstanding geeks.

But after three hours passed without withdrawals, the worst seemed possible.

Exchanges have complex approaches to security, but the basic idea comes down to this: cryptocurrency deposits are held in what is colloquially called "wallets." Really, these are pieces of software that keep track of how much cryptocurrency a person or entity has.

They are digital lockboxes, and their keys are just data. They are very easily copied and therefore stolen if someone manages to get a look at them. It's hard to steal such keys from someone. On the other hand, if someone does get a copy of the keys, they can take someone's wealth much more quickly than a thief with the world's fastest getaway car.

So exchanges have to strike a balance between customer convenience and security. To that end, the bulk of customer funds are kept in what's called cold storage. Basically, wallets that aren't connected to the internet. This means that moving funds out of a cold wallet is more cumbersome, slower, even for the exchange's staff.

They also store some cryptocurrency on a wallet that's actively connected to the internet to speed up withdrawals. That's called a hot wallet. Exchange staff makes a guess about how many withdrawals customers will make on a given day, and that's how much crypto an exchange will keep on a hot wallet.

When an exchange underestimates how much crypto it will need for its hot wallet, there can be a lag on withdrawals.

I thought maybe with so much demand for withdrawals that day, the 23-year-olds who must be running FTX security over in the Bahamas couldn't keep up as they followed security procedures to move funds from cold to hot wallets as needed.

But then it came.

"Things have come full circle," SBF tweeted that Tuesday morning. "We have come to an agreement on a strategic transaction with Binance for FTX.com."

It wasn't a bottleneck. The problem was deeper.

CZ followed, "This afternoon, FTX asked for our help. There is a significant liquidity crunch. To protect users, we signed a non-binding LOI [letter of intent], intending to fully acquire FTX.com and help cover the liquidity crunch."

Once I managed to reattach my lower jaw back inside my head, I read a Reuters report that people had attempted to draw $6 billion worth of assets in 72 hours, only to force FTX to admit that it didn't have enough crypto on hand.

More on this in Chapter 11, but this simply shouldn't happen. It was described as a bank run at the time, but . . . *crypto exchanges aren't banks*. They should have all their deposits *all the time*.

I wasn't the only one who had erred on the side of believing SBF when he presented himself and his exchanges as among the most responsible parties in the business. It turned out that that's what he was counting on, that we'd all keep buying this good boy image that he'd done such a good job selling.

In other words: FTX's only real insurance on customer deposits was a meme.

Sources Referenced

"**Divisions in Sam Bankman-Fried's Crypto Empire Blur on His Trading Titan Alameda's Balance Sheet**," Allison, Ian, CoinDesk, Nov. 2, 2022.

SBF, @SBF_FTX, Twitter, Nov. 5, 2022: https://twitter.com/SBF_FTX/status/1588965167827935232.

CZ, @cz_binance, Twitter, Nov. 6, 2022: https://twitter.com/cz_binance/status/15 89283421704290306.

"FTX appears to have stopped processing withdrawals, on-chain data show," Khatri, Yogita, The Block, Nov. 8, 2022.

"Crypto exchange FTX saw $6 bln in withdrawals in 72 hours," Wilson, Tom, and Angus Berwick, Reuters, Nov. 8, 2022.

"Hot wallets, non-custodian exchanges, and smart solutions," SO&SATO Innovation Lawyers, August 27, 2019.

SBF, @SBF_FTX, Twitter, Nov. 8, 2022: https://twitter.com/SBF_FTX/status/15 90012124864348160.

CZ, @cz_binance, Twitter, Nov. 8, 2022: https://twitter.com/cz_binance/status/15 90013613586411520.

Chapter 3

The Second Turn: Unstablecoin

When FTX melted down, the prevailing emotion was shock, but when the terra usd stablecoin (ticker symbol: UST) had fallen apart six months prior, it had been schadenfreude.

For those who didn't lose piles of money on it, the sound of terra usd crashing was the perfect music to dance to as they shook their hate of crypto and its culture right on out.

That story had a different villain, a man named Do Kwon, the Korean cofounder of Terraform Labs, the company behind terra usd and its twin coin luna (technically, "terra," but no one called luna that). But it's a story that's also crucial to FTX and Alameda Research.

What we don't know is this: Were Alameda's debts to FTX already so bad before Terra that both were already doomed? Or could FTX have saved itself by letting Alameda go under with other hedge funds like it in May or June?

So here's what happened: terra usd was an algorithmic stablecoin running on its own blockchain, also called Terra. A stablecoin is a token that is designed to maintain a consistent price in the market. In almost all cases, that price is one US dollar.

Stablecoins are useful, especially for traders. For example, if a trader looks for brief jumps in a certain minor cryptocurrency (known colloquially as "altcoins" or "shitcoins" or "alts"), he or she can keep their cash ready in a stablecoin on an exchange. Then, when opportunity arises, buy an alt quickly and watch its price go up.

Next, when they have made enough, they can sell back into a stablecoin just as fast, maybe turning $100 into $121. If they post a screenshot of the trade on Twitter or in a Telegram channel, fans will call the trader a genius.

Plus, stablecoins make it easy to move between trading venues without passing through a bank account (which is slow and janky). They can withdraw a stablecoin onto a blockchain and move it to another exchange without ever troubling the bank's anti–money laundering team. This way a trader can use six exchanges, but their bank only ever sees one. Plus, it's just faster.

So stablecoins make life easier, at least so long as people still think in dollar terms. And don't let anyone kid you: they all do.

Stablecoins are useful but boring.

Terra had an audacious design. It attempted to use software in order to control its supply (more on this in Chapter 34). That way, it could match up with demand in just the right way that it would tend to trade for $1 on the open market.

That might sound crazy, but it is basically how the US dollar works. *I'm just kidding. It was crazy.*

But it wasn't crazy because its design was wrong. It's really that Terra's *history* was wrong.

The US dollar, today, works through supply-and-demand management. The Federal Reserve uses various levers to increase and decrease the amount of dollars on the market as needed. Or to increase or decrease demand. It *mostly* increases, because it believes a little inflation is good for the economy. But that's changed somewhat, very recently, as I will discuss in Part II.

But it's true when people say there's nothing backing the buck. Well, nothing . . . besides *the whole US economy*. People want access to the US

Stablecoins

When it seems necessary to explain something that there's a very good chance some readers have read about before, I'm going to mark it off in a box like this.

For example, if you read any coverage of the terra stablecoin crash, then you read some version of the following explanation of stablecoins:

Most stablecoins work the same way. Some qualified institutional partner deposits actual bank account dollars with a stablecoin issuer. The issuer then creates a token on some blockchain that stands in for that dollar.

So it's like a coupon that can be exchanged for cash.

Then there are stablecoins created as debts. So someone puts up some collateral (a cryptocurrency), and a percentage of its value is borrowed as a stablecoin. This is good for traders because they can make bets without selling assets they believe will go up in value long term.

Those are the two big models. The first is very safe (but definitely not as safe as a US bank deposit). The second is *usually* safe (see Chapter 19).

Then there was terra usd.

---

market (including folks living in it), and dollars are the language commerce speaks here.

But the dollar is not explicitly redeemable for anything, not like it once was. There is gold in Fort Knox, but it's not for you. There is a level on which dollars are backed by US Treasuries, but the circularity of that is not something you want to contemplate if you want to sleep well tonight.

Here's what dollars are actually backed by: faith. *And that's not stupid. Because the United States has earned it.* The dollar has proved its reliability.

Dollar users have faith that the US economy is going to continue being this *engine* that people want to trade with. Because they want to trade with it, they will want dollars. So that demand for dollars insures the value of dollars.

That sounds like mysticism, but it's really the same reason *anything* has value deep down.

The dollar earned that faith through a process. When the US economy was smaller and the US government was newer, the dollar was backed. It was first backed by silver, and then it was backed by gold. In those years, precious metals stood in for the track record the state didn't have yet. That approach became untenable, and at a certain point President Richard Nixon broke the buck.

On August 15, 1971, President Nixon went on TV and said, "I have directed Secretary Connally to suspend temporarily the convertibility of the dollar into gold or other reserve assets." Well, Nixon never got around to *unsuspending* it, and now he's dead.

So the dollar floats freely still. Except it's not free, because the Fed manages it. It's not algorithmic, though. They do it with data gathered by hand, charts, meetings, and press releases. It's very analog.

But more important than how it works is how it *got there*. It's that history, its track record.

So Terraform Labs came along and tried to do the same thing as the Fed on the blockchain, only they skipped all that pesky stuff about building up an economy first, going through a whole messy period of competing currencies, settling on one, all while mucking about with gold and silver backing for a while (or something like them). You know, *earning faith*.

Terraform Labs just fired up a blockchain and started spitting out tokens and wishing everyone good luck.

It had a good story in the beginning. I first wrote about terra in 2018. One of its cofounders was Daniel Shin, who ran a big e-commerce company in Korea called TMON. At the time, he said he wanted to launch a stablecoin for people to use on his ecommerce sites and all the others as well, because the margins in e-commerce were tiny and credit card fees were killing them. So if people would pay in cryptocurrency, both companies and customers would come out ahead.

Practically, it sounded like a tough sell to me, but I could see the logic.

Terra actually ran on two tokens: terra usd, the stablecoin, and luna. Luna was what we call a governance token, but it was also essential to the stability of the system.

We'll get into this more later, but in short, terra and luna did this dance where the supply of terra usd would expand and contract based on the demand. That way, there was always just the right amount of terra usd in the world so that its price stayed fixed at a dollar. *Unlike the dollar, this was all automated.*

Sometimes terra usd would be created. Sometimes destroyed. Luna holders could get rich as demand for it went up, but if the stablecoin fell below its peg, luna holders would feel a pinch.

So the 2018 story was about e-commerce, but that changed. In 2020, decentralized finance (known as DeFi) had started to catch on with people who were into making money much too fast in the cryptocurrency game. It was the first time in a couple years that it felt like anything in crypto was clicking. Terra's creators moved in fast to grab a piece.

So now demand for terra usd would be driven by investors, not consumers.

In 2021, Terraform Labs launched Anchor, a savings account for terra usd. It offered a 20% yield to anyone who stuck their stablecoins inside.

No limits. No caps. Just a 20% easy annual return. For what?

Anchor did some lending, like a bank. It also got some returns on the stuff people put up as collateral to borrow. But it didn't get to a 20% profit. The truth is: the blockchain just covered the yield out of pocket. That sounds crazy, yes, but that's really how it *actually* worked.

Call it a growth hack. Early on, the terra blockchain had accumulated a giant pile of terra usd through its open market operations. So they were just using it to kickstart demand.

This rickety shotgun shack of a financial system was Kwon's doing. Kwon was Shin's cofounder. Like SBF, he has a huge risk appetite. But he is also completely different from SBF. Where SBF is frenetic, Kwon is cool and calm.

He famously got served by the US Securities and Exchange Commission at a conference in New York and hung around the rest of the day. He was so nonplussed that people weren't sure if it really happened (it did).

In January 2022, Anchor was starting to run out of reserve money to cover the interest on users' deposits. So Kwon posted on Twitter that he'd produce $300 million in assets to refill Anchor's reserves to cover interest payments.

One day, a founder of the fund Multicoin Capital, Kyle Samani, asked on Twitter: "Serious question, where is this 300M coming from?"

Kwon replied, "Your mom, obviously."

On February 7, with a week's worth of reserves left in Anchor, I messaged Kwon on Telegram about it, saying, "You haven't said where the money is coming from."

"No, I said it's coming from Kyle's mom," Kwon wrote back. "Was pretty explicit about that."

Then later that night (for me, morning for him), he sent me a link to the proposal that would authorize moving the funds from Terra's treasury to Anchor's. In other words, yes, they were just paying for savers' yield out of pocket once more.

Anchor's team still didn't know how to earn enough to cover its super-high interest rate.

In May, the wheels would come off terra usd suddenly and take luna with it. The stablecoin would lose all its value as luna hopelessly attempted to clear the market of excess terra usd, only to print so much new supply that the governance token effectively lost all its value as well.

This outcome was foreseen before Terra ever started. It's called the "death spiral." The death spiral is thought of as the inevitable end of any algorithmic stablecoin.

As I tried to report on this period, no one could tell me with confidence what Alameda, FTX's sister hedge fund, was doing during this time. But the Commodity Futures Trading Commission says that it knows. The CFTC alleged in its December 13, 2022, complaint before US Court of the Southern District of New York that:

> By early 2022, Alameda had invested several billion dollars in directional, unhedged, illiquid, and/or long-term investments. To fund these investment activities, Alameda had relied on billions of dollars of loans from digital asset lending platforms, traditional bank lines of credit, and its unlimited borrowing abilities on the FTX, including its access to customer funds.

In other words, the CFTC was alleging that, contrary to everything FTX staff had said, contrary to its own terms of service, Alameda had been using FTX as its personal lender. It could borrow anything it wanted from FTX customers at any time, and no one ever knew.

As 2022 began, Terra was seen by many as something to be optimistic about. Then in May it fell apart. Just what triggered it is a long and complicated story. It's tinged with hubris and conspiracy and bad luck, but the point is this tenuous experiment that Kwon and crew had let go much too far exploded like Mentos in a bottle of Diet Coke.

When things crash in crypto they crash really fast. Everyone knows this, and yet everyone forgets it.

The Terra crash was different than FTX, but Terra had split the industry. A lot of newcomers were excited about Terra. Many old-timers thought its system was doomed from the start, however, and were glad to see they had been proven right.

As FTX went under, the consensus view among observers was that the Terra crash is what put Alameda Research into the hole. If Alameda Research hadn't gone into a hole, FTX wouldn't have needed to paper over that hole. If FTX hadn't papered over the hole, it would have had enough money to cover customer deposits when the market panicked following CZ's tweets.

Who knows if Terra was really the hemlock the boy philosopher-king drank, but it didn't help. It might have already been in trouble.

But the timing is telling. CFTC staff wrote in the complaint, "In approximately May and/or June 2022, Alameda was subject to a large number of such margin calls and loan recalls. It did not have sufficient liquid assets to service its loans. Instead, at the direction of Bankman-Fried, Alameda greatly increased its usage of FTX customer funds to meet its external debt obligations."

Alameda had an $8 billion hole in FTX's accounts, "a staggering amount that exceeded FTX total lifetime revenue," the complaint alleges.

And what did Sam do then? He started bailing out other companies as if he were the one guy left who still knew what he was doing, one of the youngest leaders playing the responsible adult.

When, in fact, as the complaint puts it, "Bankman-Fried stated privately that he was pursuing an aggressive acquisition strategy during this time at least in part to gain access to additional sources of capital that could be used to support his existing businesses and fill the hole in customer funds that had been created."

Sources Referenced

"**Nixon Shock**," Wikipedia, Version: Nov. 8, 2022: https://en.wikipedia.org/w/index.php?title=Nixon_shock&oldid=1120737092.

"**Binance Backs $32 Million Funding for Unicorn Founder's Crypto Stablecoin**," Dale, Brady, CoinDesk, Aug. 29, 2018.

"**Terra Money: Stability and Adoption**," Kereiakes, Evan and Do Kwon, Marco Di Maggio, Nicholas Platias, April 2019. https://assets.website-files.com/611153e7af981472d8da199c/618b02d13e938ae1f8ad1e45_Terra_White_paper.pdf.

"**Anchor Launch Puts UST in the Stablecoin Race Against DAI**," Dale, Brady, CoinDesk, March 17, 2021.

"**Terra's Do Kwon Was Served by SEC at Crypto Conference**," Benson, Jeff, Scott Chipolina and Daniel Roberts, Decrypt, Oct. 24, 2021.

"**Anchor Protocol Burns Through Its Reserves as Deposits Pile Up**," Dale, Brady, The Defiant, Jan. 26, 2022.

@KyleSamani, Twitter, Jan. 28, 2022: https://twitter.com/stablekwon/status/1487106588263743489.

"**#880 The $10 Billion Stablecoin Bet on The Bitcoin Standard w/ Do Kwon**," The Pomp Podcast, March 24, 2022.

"**Abracadabra's MIM Stablecoin Briefly Lost Dollar Peg as FTX's FTT Token Tanked**," Godbole, Omkar, CoinDesk, Nov. 8, 2022.

"**CFTC Charges Sam Bankman-Fried, FTX Trading and Alameda with Fraud and Material Misrepresentations**," press release and complaint before the US Southern District of New York, Commody Futures Trading Commission, Dec. 13, 2022.

"**Billions of Luna minted as supply grows 20-fold in four days**," Copeland, Tim, The Block, May 12, 2022.

Chapter 4

The First Turn:
The Miami Conceit

In March 2021, FTX signed a deal for the naming rights of the Miami Heat Arena, taking over a branding position once held by American Airlines. They agreed to pay $135 million over 19 years.

In November 2020, The Miami Heat and Miami–Dade County announced that they would be looking for another sponsor. So FTX got to be the first crypto company to buy naming rights on a major sports stadium.

This was a weird moment.

Sponsoring a stadium in the middle of a bubble has a way of backfiring. In the dot-com era, this internet provider called PsiNet put its name in giant letters above where the Baltimore Ravens played. The field where the Astros played once bore the name of maybe the 2000s most notorious boondoggle: Enron.[1]

So in 2021, the Heat deal had the scent of hubris.

---

[1] That name will come up again.

Six weeks after the announcement, SBF told the crypto news site Decrypt:

> It's been a pretty good year for us. To the point where, frankly, we don't need to rely on the other 18 years to have the funds for this.

The Greeks wrote whole tragedies warning against this kind of talk. SBF would have probably called such cautionary tales irrational, and they might be. But they are also lindy.[2] And they look pretty good right now.

But within FTX at the time, the idea was that it's probably reasonable to think that a big company would spend something like 15 to 20 percent of its budget on marketing. Seen in that way, it was a good deal, especially broken out over almost two decades.

The CFTC saw it differently. In its December 13 complaint before US Southern District of New York, CFTC legal staff would drop in an evocative adverb in an otherwise very dry account of financial misconduct. The complaint says that customer funds were "furtively used" to pay for its grandest promotions, such as the stadium deal.

A former FTX insider who agreed to speak with me on the condition that I not use a name told me the Heat deal marked a shift. "It was the beginning of this unstoppable celebrity spending spree," the person said. "It was the beginning of a focus on things that weren't the core business."

FTX also bought rights to a UC Berkeley stadium, became the official crypto platform for Major League Baseball, and got some confusing array of rights that a creative law firm intern must have made up from the Golden State Warriors and also for a Formula One team.

FTX spent the most money renaming an e-sports team (young guys who play video games while fans watch), most likely taking the view that such fans were more likely to be his company's future than the beer-and-hot-dog set found in stadiums.

He definitely got into the heads of his competition. Crypto.com, another exchange working to take the American market, got its own

---

[2]"Lindy" is internet-speak. It means old but not just old. It captures the idea that certain things have stood the test of time and therefore are probably better than the new thing. Coffee is lindy, but Red Bull is not.

stadiums, and a little blockchain called Tezos snagged a piece of the view inside the New York Mets baseball stadium, which meant SBF was right where he wanted to be, living rent free in the heads of his rivals and peers.

And then of course there was the bromance with quarterback Tom Brady, which culminated at Crypto Bahamas (Chapter 32).

"I think he enjoyed the attention," my source said.

SBF would tell Decrypt in a subsequent interview that all these naming deals were having the effect that he wanted them to have. "If you measure it by something like downloads per dollar spent on advertising, it's not going to come out well," he said. "In the last five minutes, new evidence has been brought to my attention that this has had a really big impact. And that evidence is you deciding it was important to ask me about it."

Getting a name up onto a city arena is, no doubt, a way to get that name into people's minds, but when the name is scrubbed off on the cameras of local TV stations, that does something else. That gets that name into people's memories.

Sources Referenced

"**Crypto industry to get first major U.S. stadium with Miami–Dade County approving FTX for Heat home**," Pound, Jesse, CNBC, Mar. 26, 2021.

"**CFTC Charges Sam Bankman-Fried, FTX Trading and Alameda with Fraud and Material Misrepresentations**," press release and complaint before the U.S. Southern District of New York, Commodity Futures Trading Commission, Dec. 13, 2022.

FTX insider, interview via phone, Dec. 18, 2022.

"**Miami Heat to cut ties with bankrupt FTX, rename arena**," Windhorst, Brian, ESPN, Nov. 11, 2022.

"**PSINet is coming down from football stadium**," Sentementes, Gus, and Brent Jones, the *Baltimore Sun*, February 13, 2002.

"**Astros stuck with Enron name—for now**," Rovell, Darren, ESPN.com, Jan. 25, 2002.

"**FTX CEO on 19-Year Miami Heat Sponsorship: 'We Don't Need the Other 18 Years to Have the Funds'**," Roberts, Daniel, Decrypt, May 7, 2021.

"**UC Berkeley's $17M FTX Stadium Naming Deal Dead After Just 450 Days**," Nguyen, Kevin, the *San Francisco Standard*, Nov. 18, 2022.

"**FTX Becomes Official Cryptocurrency Exchange Brand of MLB**," Kelly, Liam, Decrypt, June 23, 2021.

"**Cryptocurrency platform FTX will pay Golden State Warriors $10 million for global rights**," Young, Jabari, CNBC, Dec. 14, 2021.

"**A Pro E-Sports Team Is Getting $210 Million to Change Its Name**," Browning, Kellen, the *New York Times*, June 4, 2021.

"**Mercedes F1 Team Suspends FTX Deal Amid Company's Collapse**," Hayward, Andrew, Decrypt, Nov. 11, 2022.

"**Sam Bankman-Fried Says FTX's Huge Sports Marketing Push Is 'Clearly' Working**," Roberts, Daniel, Decrypt, Jan. 29, 2022.

PART I

ACQUIRE

Chapter 5

A Portrait of Sam

SBF has a curly mane, a high-energy affect, a certain jitter in his body language, and he is definitely not actually awkward as everyone portrays him—not really.

He's a geek, but a geek with swagger. He is not a nerd. A geek is someone who sees something super-interesting in topics that other people don't. A geek can still be cool. Or at least charismatic, because a geek can still relate to others on a human level. A nerd obsesses on uncool topics as a substitute for social acumen. Those obsessions are the means by which nerds relate to other nerds. So a nerd can never be cool.

Sam's a geek.

But if people say he's a nerd, an autist, an awkward turtle, they do it largely because SBF wants them to. He constructed that image because he knows that there's an allure to those characterizations. But listen to him on any of the gazillion podcasts or interviews he's taken part in, and it's obvious that all kinds of people *enjoy* talking to him. He sucks people in, and he knows what he's doing when he does it.

That's the opposite of awkward.

Mr. Bankman-Fried at a speaking engagement/conference in 2022. (Photo by Craig Barritt/Getty Images Entertainment/Getty Images)

SBF is the son of two Stanford professors. Their family is said to have been supportive and intellectual. He went to college at MIT, where he studied physics. He worked for a time at Jane Street in New York. Then he left and got into crypto trading. The stated plan: make a lot of money and give it away.

There's a tremendous literature of SBF, but one of the most justly maligned pieces was published by Sequoia Capital (and unpublished following the implosion of his firms). You can still find it on the Internet Archive, however.

In that post, there are two moments in which, in my view, he's presented incorrectly in just the way he wanted.

In one, he does an all-hands staff meeting over Zoom, despite the fact that about half the people in the meeting are in the room together. Regardless, 100 percent do the meeting online. Second, when the writer finally gets some face time with SBF, he conducts the whole interview playing the video game Storybook Brawl (one that FTX announced acquiring in March 2022).

The writer rather credulously interprets these as the behavior of someone who doesn't know how to interact with people unless it's mediated by a screen.

However, I suspect that the reason everyone went on Zoom for the staff meeting was in fact about equity. This wouldn't be obvious, maybe, to someone who hasn't spent some time hanging around the sort of people SBF hung around with. He knows that being in the same room together makes for a higher-bandwidth meeting, but that advantages all the people who are together to the detriment of everyone who doesn't have a choice but to join over Zoom.

Much has been made of Sam's allegiance to Effective Altruism (EA), a philosophy that pushes people to do as much good as they can. What's less commented on is that EA emerged from rationalism. Modern rationalists are big on thinking intentionally about *how* people interact. To a mainstream person, it might seem normal for everyone *in a room* together to sit at one table while others rely on video chat, but rationalists are likely to object that doing so creates an insider-outsider dynamic.

I'm not saying that I know this is the explanation, but I do know EAs were conscientious about such matters as their meetups moved online during the pandemic. Requiring everyone to use Zoom if anyone has to use Zoom is the kind of thing a company grounded in this way of thinking *would* do.

If there is one characteristic that defines rationalists, it's that they are critical of everything. *Everything.*

Then what if the second move—playing the video game—was just the opposite? What if that was a flex, a bit of theater? What if SBF played the video game the whole time he talked to the interviewer because he knew the interviewer would write that he spent the interview playing a video game?

A strategic insouciance is the pose of someone who's already on the path to winning the game of life. It really seems like everything SBF was doing was geared toward that much larger goal.

For example, his great wealth came up in almost every interview he gave. He talked about how much money he had, more than anyone in crypto. Full stop.

Crypto people don't talk a lot about how rich they are in general, because doing so helps cyber criminals decide how much they should prioritize attacking one versus another. But also, it's not like crypto people come from another planet. They might flash some expensive stuff, but they don't tend to drop numbers into polite conversation. That's gauche everywhere.

But SBF would always go right into talking about his billions. He loved it.

And maybe that's what made him so media friendly. Reporters want to talk about this stuff. Every human is curious about the lives of the very rich, but they're seldom frank about it.

SBF was.

In fact, in general SBF was adept at finding out what an interviewer wanted to hear and giving that to him or her. He seems to have been a little addicted to it.

Case in point: in an infamous 2022 interview that SBF gave on Bloomberg's Odd Lots podcast, the hosts asked SBF to explain something that had been a very hot topic two years before: yield farming.

This conversation has been misread by everyone who's listened to it and misreported on by anyone who's covered it. And that's too bad, because those misreads mask a nuanced view into SBF's mind at work.

SBF begins by saying, "Let me give you sort of like a really toy model of it," he says. "Maybe for now actually ignore what it does or pretend it does literally nothing. It's just a box."

Those last two sentences are really important, and Odd Lots, Joe Weisenthal, Tracy Alloway, and fellow guest Matt Levine do not hear them or heed them.

Sam is making a rhetorical move here that's not uncommon to anyone who explains things regularly and is very common among the sort of people he hangs out with (people who blog about utilitarianism online and/or know what it means to describe something as "Bayesian"—more on this in Chapter 18).

The move is this: someone has just asked about a very complicated thing that is—in practice—connected to many other things. So to explain just that thing, strip away all those other things and simplify it to the point of absurdity. Simplify it in a way that would never be found in the real world. That's what makes it a "toy." It's too simple, really, but it's just the key bits.

If you took macroeconomics, your professor did this when he talked about comparative advantage. That's the idea in economics that everyone is better off if nations (or companies, or people, or whatever) specialize in making what they are really good at and trade for everything else.

It is very likely that your professor taught the example given by the famous economist David Ricardo. Your professor probably described a model in which there were two countries, England and Portugal. They both made cloth and they both made wine. The basic example shows that however the costs of production change, there is always an advantage to both countries with at least some specialization and trade.

Obviously, the world has more than two countries, and people want more than two things. But it's a helpful place to start. It's also a *toy model*.

But this notion of oversimplification for the purpose of illumination just zooms right past all three of the folks SBF's talking to on that episode. They take SBF's box as a serious explanation and they have talked about it that way ever since.

So then SBF starts explaining yield farming in this oversimplified way (I will explain it in a fuller way in Chapter 20). He says this box is a place for people to put their digital money and then, when they want, to take it back out. That's all this fictional box in his toy model does.

Yield farming, he says, is when the creators of something like the box give people a new token, a new crypto asset, spun out of thin air, for putting funds somewhere the creators want them to put it. In the case of the box, that's making pointless deposits. Creators of similar, non-toy boxes typically give out such tokens pro rata, based on deposits, distributing them on a predictable schedule over time.

It's a scheme that rewards getting in as soon as possible (as we'll see in Chapter 22).

People with that token, SBF says, "can vote on what to do with any proceeds or other cool things that happen from this box. And of course, so far, we haven't exactly given a compelling reason for why there ever would be any proceeds from this box."

In this model, the box's token has no inherent value, but in the world of crypto, if enough money went in the box, the hype alone would give it value, SBF explains.

To this, Matt Levine (who is, incidentally, probably the most famous business writer in the world right now), cuts in to say, "I think of myself as like a fairly cynical person. And that was so much more cynical than how I would've described farming. You're just like, 'Well, I'm in the Ponzi business, and it's pretty good.'"

Except yield farming would only actually be a Ponzi if the world's real boxes didn't do anything, but they do. Or at least they try. Because they aren't toys. They are real.

But like I said, they all completely missed the fact that he'd called it a toy model, and SBF sees that and he almost pulls out there and turns his toy model into a more real model. He says, "So on the one hand, I think that's a pretty reasonable response, but let me play around with this a little bit. Because that's one framing of this."

But then Levine cuts in and asks him if he can explain more how any of this is sustainable with a joke about how Ponzi schemes have been outperforming bitcoin, lately.

That's when, to my ear, SBF realizes: *Oh they are enjoying this story*. And that's why this story is less a vignette about three reporters who should learn to listen more closely to what their guests *are saying* and less to what they *would like to hear them say* (it's also that) and more an illumination of SBF's priorities.

So he says, "Right. So let me, okay, cool. I'll stay on the cynical route, think about—like—cynically, what could happen here?"

Hosts Weisenthal and Alloway are audibly delighted by this version of yield farming, because—as Sam's fellow rationalists might say—it confirmed their "priors" (Chapter 18).

But here's where, in my reading, SBF *really was* cynical. As soon as he saw how much his description delighted his interlocutors, he rolled with it.[1] It mattered more to him to charm these tastemakers than it did to make the case that the industry that turned him into a billionaire might be experimenting with something real.

If the trading pair on offer was cred for SBF vs. blockchain cred, he was dumping his blockchain cred bags in a hot minute. For his own cred, he was a buy at any price.

---

[1] In November, Weisenthal would revisit this episode on the *Bloomberg Crypto* podcast, with host Stacy-Marie Ishmael. In that episode, they would double down on Bloomberg's interpretation that this had been an admission of some kind. That said, Weisenthal would concur with this reading: what threw him off wasn't so much the model itself as Sam's decision not to push back once it was clear he had stunned them. On Twitter in April, SBF would try to explain to his followers that "the box" had only ever been an intentional oversimplification.

What really drove Sam? Did he want to do good or did he want the power to make change? I think this book will make the answer to that clear, and the answer also helps explain why he let it go wrong.

In early 2021, SBF and I had a couple long interviews. In the first one, he said something to me that stands out now. We spoke at the time when Elon Musk first showed real interest in bitcoin (rather than doge-coin), briefly allowing it to be used for payments to Tesla.

SBF reflected on that by saying that the world had changed in a way that most people think they understand, but they really don't. The change he pointed to was that "the impact that one person can have on social media is unbelievably massive and the sets of people that could have that impact is way larger."

Elon Musk, he said, is one of those people. And he seemed to think Musk had earned that power, but he also said that he didn't think most people understood that other massively important people would be "a little weird and random and contingent."

It used to be that only, say, the US President and the very top celebrities or artists had that kind of reach, but that's all different now. "That impact can be massive and world changing," he said. And seems now as if he was telling me, without telling me, what he was really going for.

So here's a question that's worth considering as you go through the rest of this book:

> Do you think that if someone came to SBF and said, look, there are two doors you can walk through. Through one door, you will create heaven on earth, but you will get no credit for it. It will take your whole productive life, and, at the end, you will know you did it, but no one else will.
>
> Through the other door, you will be one of the biggest and best philanthropists ever. Andrew Carnegie? Bill Gates? You will surpass them both by far. But the world will still be full of disease, war and that general sense of "things sort of suck for a lot of folks" will remain. Some lives will be improved, sure, but it won't be a step change for humanity.
>
> Which door do you think he would go through?

It's a good question when considering SBF. It's the question at the heart of this whole story. And there's really an even deeper question: Should anyone go through either door?

But with regard to SBF, his wealth, and his intentions: yes, he had an expensive apartment in a gated community until his wealth turned into ashes, but penthouses full of hookers and blow were probably not in his future.

Personally, I have no doubt that SBF had every intention to give piles and piles of money away, and I also suspect he would have micromanaged that giving optimizing for a variety of outcomes.

The question SBF's story raises is if even doing good can become dangerous if someone sets out to do it at a certain scale. Does it become especially dangerous when the scale is really more important than the good?

Sources Referenced

"The Parents in the Middle of FTX's Collapse," Yaffe-Bellany, David, Lora Kelley, and Kenneth P. Vogel, the *New York Times*, Dec. 12, 2022.

"Most Influential 2021: Sam Bankman-Fried," Wilser, Jeff, CoinDesk, Dec. 7, 2021.

"Still the Face of Crypto," Wang, Tracy, CoinDesk, Dec. 5, 2022.

"Sam Bankman-Fried Has a Savior Complex—And Maybe You Should Too," Fisher, Adam, Sequoia, on Archive.org: https://web.archive.org/web/20221027180943/https://www.sequoiacap.com/article/sam-bankman-fried-spotlight/.

"'Storybook Brawl' developer acquired by crypto exchange firm FTX," Wilde, Thomas, GeekWire, March 22, 2022.

"Sam Bankman-Fried tries to explain himself," Piper, Kelsey, Vox.com, Nov. 16, 2022.

"Sam Bankman-Fried and Matt Levine on How to Make Money in Crypto," Alloway, Tracy, and Joe Weisenthal, *Odd Lots* podcast, Bloomberg.com, April 25, 2022.

Sam Bankman-Fried, @SBF_FTX, April 25, 2022: https://twitter.com/SBF_FTX/status/1518676208657092609.

"Comparative advantage," Policonomics, https://policonomics.com/comparative-advantage/.

Interview, Sam Bankman-Fried, via videochat/Telegram call, Feb. 8, 2021.

"FTX Pulls a Fast One," Kharif, Olga, Yugeqi Yang, and Hannah Miller, Bloomberg Businessweek, Nov. 21, 2022.

"Tesla buys $1.5 billion in bitcoin, plans to accept it as payment," Kovach, Steve, CNBC, Feb. 8, 2022.

Chapter 6

Crypto

In the beginning Satoshi created the Bitcoin protocol. And Satoshi said, "Let the input of unspent transaction outputs create new unspent transaction outputs, and let the verifier be rewarded in fresh bitcoin added to the coinbase." And it was, and Satoshi saw that it was good.

Let's step back before we really get going.

An explanation of why people are excited about cryptocurrency, blockchains, and all they enable is needed for the rest of this book to make sense. My guess is that you've seen some before, and they didn't stick or you didn't find them convincing.

So this explanation will be different. This explanation isn't about money or speed or the banking system. It's about what *actually* secures crypto networks, the layer of security that's really more important than that provided by the technology.

It's the layer no one talks about because, if you don't know about it, it sounds too crazy. And if you do know about it, it seems too obvious. That's the part I'm going to talk about here: the culture that forms around a cryptocurrency.

So the metaphorical firmament on which SBF and his cohort stood was the industry that rose up around bitcoin and other cryptocurrencies, which all began with a whitepaper by some pseudonymous fellow going by the made-up name Satoshi Nakamoto published on Halloween 2008. Since then, thousands of cryptocurrencies have trick-or-treated around the global economy. They did it first by throwing costumes on what was really just bitcoin with slightly cuter names, and then by actually coming up with all new looks.

The first bitcoins were issued on January 3, 2009, and the industry began that day. No one really cared about it for a while, though. It was just a collective experiment that people calling themselves "cypherpunks" ran on their computers.

Bitcoin has a bunch of interesting features, but there are two worth highlighting.

First, it has a fixed supply and a predictable inflation schedule. Bitcoin was created amidst the 2008 financial crisis, and its creator seems to have meant it as a comment on government-controlled money supply. Such supplies have tendency to change based on the anxieties of the folks in charge.

Satoshi thought that was a bad approach, so he created a kind of money that demands that users adapt to it, not the other way around.

Second, no one has ever busted Bitcoin, as far as we can tell. This is quite a feat because Bitcoin sits right out in the open, all its bits and pieces on display, and all the smartest cybercriminals in the world would love to rob this wide-open bank. So far, though, they haven't.

People get robbed of their bitcoin all the time, of course. But Bitcoin proper has yet to be manipulated. There are exactly as many bitcoin out there as there should be, no more, no less. That's really something.

And the nice thing about bitcoin is that you don't have to take my word for it. You can check. That was in the design from the start. Anyone should be able to verify that bitcoin's books balance, and anyone can, to this day.

Bitcoin seeped into the real world on May 22, 2010, when Laszlo Hanyecz was able to arrange to buy two large Papa John's pizzas for 10,000 bitcoin, through a convoluted hack.

How Bitcoin works

Honestly, it doesn't matter.

Not for you. Not for me, either.

You know how sometimes when you make a phone call the sound is terrible, but then if you hang up and try again, it's fine. Why does it do that? Do you know? Someone does. I don't. I bet you don't, either. And neither of us care.

If Bitcoin takes off, people will just use it, and they won't care why it works. In fact, there's a decent chance they won't even know they are using it. It will just be in "the stack" of how payments work. It's one of those things people think they want to understand, but what they really want to understand is why they would want to use it in the first place.

Bitcoin is a cool system. If it succeeds, then, one day, no one will care any more about how it runs than they do about how refrigerators work.

Anyway, reading won't really help. The best way to wrap your head around bitcoin is to buy a little (say, $50 worth), figure out how to get it onto a wallet you control, and then send a little bit to someone else. I promise, if you do that, you'll get further than I can ever get you in these pages.

But people don't really use bitcoin for buying and selling that much. People mostly use bitcoin for betting on bitcoin. That is, if you zoom out enough, bitcoin has consistently gone up in value over time. Most people buy at the wrong time and sell at the wrong time, but for those who (mostly) just sit, there's been a lot of value gained by just waiting.

Many of those people assume there will be more value gained by sitting even longer. These people call themselves "hodlers" (from "hodl," a misspelling of "hold," which has also come to mean "hold on for dear life"). The upshot of this is that using bitcoin, for a lot of people, looks a lot like doing nothing. But they are doing nothing *with intention*.

The name bitcoiners have given this is "store-of-value." You can just call it a bet if you want. Either way.

Many people say that this is a waste of money, a bad trade, and anyone in it is a fool. That could be right, but a lot of people are doing it. Similarly, I think Porsches are twerpy toys for men who can't get over their receding hairlines, but I don't write frantic op-eds about the fact that people buy them.

Glassnode estimates that there's about 4.5 million active Bitcoin addresses per week as of the time of writing (it varies). It's not huge, but it's not nothing. It's a decent little city. In the global economy, Bitcoin is Philadelphia—not great or anything but probably here for the foreseeable.

The other blockchain that actually matters is Ethereum. Ethereum is the original smart contract blockchain, and it has its own cryptocurrency called ether. A "smart contract" is just a computer program, but that terminology caught on. It makes sense, too, because—unlike most computer programs—the main work smart contracts do is move digital money around in different ways.

This is all done autonomously on the Ethereum blockchain. A smart contract runs without any human intervention. If a developer wants to, they can finish the code and publish it in such a way that no one can ever turn it off or change it ever again.

Here's an example of a very simple smart contract someone could write. Say someone wanted to hold their ethers over time, but he didn't trust himself not to sell them in a downturn. That person could write a smart contract called Savebot, and Savebot would not let him sell.

Savebot would have its own Ethereum wallet, just like a person's. The user could send it, say, 1 ether (ETH) and tell it not to let him withdraw it for three years. Then anyone would be able to open it up from time to time and check, "Hey Savebot, do you still have that ETH?"

Savebot would look and report back, "Yes, I have it. It's right here."

Then the user might be like, "Hey Savebot, can I have it back? I know it's only been a year, but . . . I want it."

Savebot: "No."

When the three years were up, however, Savebot would give them the all-clear.

This is a crucial bit, however. In order to actually get the ether transferred back from Savebot the user would need to *pay a little bit in ether* to run the code on all the computers in the world that keep copies of the Ethereum blockchain.

Savebot isn't on any one of them. It's on *all of them*.

It shouldn't cost much. This should be a fairly small calculation, but it wouldn't be nothing. Savebot just needs to verify the date has passed, and, if it has, execute a simple transaction. To run it today, it would probably be a few dollars' worth of ether, much, much less than the value of the ether held inside. But the user isn't paying Savebot to run the transaction. It's paying the Ethereum network itself.

This is a really important idea. Blockchains need a coin because the coin serves as the coordination mechanism. They only work, they are only safe, if so many people are running copies of them that it would be too much work for a group to collude and manipulate people's accounts.

In order to achieve that, people need to earn something for running those copies. They need to get paid to do work. So coins (like bitcoins and ethers) are inherent to blockchains.

Smart contracts are neat, too, because once something like Savebot is up and running, anyone can use it. A developer can give Savebot to the world, and it becomes a public good.

Smart people can look at the code and see if there are any risks. If it looks safe, they can say: "Hey this is smart. You should feel safe using it if it seems helpful."

The world seems to want Ethereum, and it seems to want Bitcoin. Other blockchains are trying to be wanted, but none of them have become indispensable, though Dogecoin might be getting there.

So now I'm going to go one level deeper: it doesn't really matter what blockchains *do*. It's who uses it and how those users come to relate to each other.

What makes some blockchains win and some blockchains lose is the same thing that makes some nations win and some nations lose. They have a narrative that unifies a group of people. The technology, the coins, give those people a thing they can hold and own and make bets on and use that puts that idea into the real world and allows it to interact with other things.

But it's not the technology. It's the idea.

Use cases are some of the trees. Culture is the forest.

This is the truth, and the truth is the way. So this is also the way.

So! People who like Bitcoin and people who like Ethereum are both in the blockchain industry. But that's also like saying Carly Rae Jepsen and the Rolling Stones are in the music industry. They both do arena shows with guitars and amplifiers, yet a very, very different crowd attends each.

No doubt there are people in every major city who have attended both Carly Rae Jepsen shows and Rolling Stones shows, but they are outliers. You will not be able to pick them out in the larger crowd.

Fans of each buy into the notion of live music. Fans of each are probably more likely to prefer either act over, say, Burt Bacharach, but (still) each kind of fan sees a distinctly different path to perfect musical ecstasy. The fact that some people can see both doesn't make the two options any less distinct.

It's the same for Bitcoin and Ethereum and any other blockchain that eventually clicks with people. It isn't really the blockchain. It's the culture that rises up around it that actually secures each network. The technology needs to reflect the culture, but it's still the culture.

And that is why, peering into the future, I can imagine a day when Bitcoin gets broken.

For Bitcoin to break, first, Bitcoin has to win. It becomes this channel that everyone uses to move value around the globe. Maybe not the only channel, but people aren't fighting it anymore. It's a path.

Maybe no one buys coffee with bitcoin, but transfers between banks (or whatever replaces them) run on Bitcoin. It's deep in the guts of society. At that point, people have largely forgotten about Bitcoin's ideas. Those have become cute notions from the early days, like people who thought the internet would break up big publishers and enable a million independent voices to flourish on stand-alone websites.

By that time, Bitcoin will be operated by people who speak strictly in terms such as "profit and loss" and "EBITDA." No one will talk about Bitcoin mining anymore. It will just be "the consensus network" or something even more buzzwordized.

They could do it once bitcoin was no longer an idea and it just became infrastructure. Something normal people no longer felt part of but something they felt beholden to. And—as with all such things— eventually, its controlling stakes could become concentrated until some entity or entities controlled enough of its security system that they could cheat in some very clever, very subtle way.

Maybe they would reclaim long-untouched coins? Or they could order transactions unfairly to scrape a little edge off trades in each block. In other words, they could use their power for black-edge, financial dark magic.

Some way that goes on for so long that eventually everyone would just get used to it and say to themselves: that's the way the system works now.

In that future, Bitcoin will have gone the way of all things (which isn't death but corruption).

And years after that, one day, some anthropologist or academic philosopher will come along and look at the story of the blockchain, and they will write a very good thesis that tells it like it is now and it still will be then: that it was never the technology that really secured Bitcoin. It was always actual human consensus. It had been culture all along.

When that layer of consensus erodes, that's when it breaks down, at a moment no one is likely to notice until it is too far gone to see.

This is what people see once they've gotten in deep enough and looked long enough and have taken enough in. This is how the world has always changed. Once upon a time, we thought we needed kings. Now we don't. It's just as hard to imagine we ever did need kings now as it once was to imagine a world without them.

But before most people get this far, they get to this point: okay, maybe crypto is a little bet worth making? So they buy a little of . . . what? Something.

For those who cross that threshold, the first decision most of them make is deciding which team they want to play on. Am I an Ethereum guy? Am I a Bitcoin guy? Maybe I want to swing for the fences with Dogecoin? What the heck is *Algorand*?

In crypto, people can hedge cultures. Maybe someone chooses to primarily focus on Ethereum, but she holds some bitcoin. No reason to be crazy. Maybe those guys are right?

Most people hedge a little, but they also mostly choose a team on which they are going to play. People want to be in a thing with others. They want to believe. But that's not what SBF and the FTX complex was about. They didn't believe in any of it, but they took hedges on all of it.

It's easy to point to FTX's unraveling and say (as many have): "See, obviously crypto was always a sham."

Except, the whole FTX megalith was a short trade on crypto's core thesis, against the one thing the bitcoiners and the ethereans and the doge-stans and all the rest believe in.

FTX lured people into trusting it and not themselves, to give up control of their assets, turn them over to strangers and *just play for gains*. Crypto has never been about trusting anyone but yourself.

So the fact that FTX came crashing down around SBF, if anything, was evidence that the truly old-school bitcoiners had been right all along: *don't trust, verify*.

Sources Referenced

"**Bitcoin: A Peer-to-Peer Electronic Cash System**," Nakomoto, Satoshi, Bitcoin. org: https://bitcoin.org/bitcoin.pdf.

"**What Is Bitcoin Pizza Day?**," George, Benedict, CoinDesk, Aug. 5, 2022.

"**Bitcoin: Number of Active Addresses**," Glassnode: https://studio.glassnode.com/ metrics?a=BTC&m=addresses.ActiveCount&resolution=1w.

"**Ethereum: A Next-Generation Smart Contract and Decentralized Application Platform**," Buterin, Vitalik, 2014, Ethereum. org: https://ethereum.org/669c 9e2e2027310b6b3cdce6e1c52962/Ethereum_Whitepaper_-_Buterin_2014.pdf.

Chapter 7

The Asia Trade

The early days of SBF in crypto, the beginning of Alameda and all those many billions, are behind a veil of something like myth.

It's this story about the trade he was said to be doing in Asia, starting in 2017.

The story SBF told (one he even told me once) was that he graduated college and went to work for Jane Street. Jane Street is a 23-year-old quantitative trading firm. It's said to be a nice place to work. SBF told me he had been happy there.

If you listen to his version of this decision he always takes forever telling it, savoring the details of the options he considered and his game-theoretical approaches toward estimating what would have the highest impact.

Here's what matters for our purposes: giving away lots of money well is high impact. He had already made good money at Jane Street. He was pretty sure he could make a lot more.

And the truth is, SBF liked trading.

In his version, he took some time off from his job to try a few things. When he first started going walkabout he says he went home from New York City to the Bay Area, where he was from, and hung out with the Effective Altruist (EA) community there. He realized that he really liked being part of that.

The Bay Area was the heart of the EA scene, in his view. He told me that he hadn't been crazy about the New York EAs. He found himself not showing up to meetings there. On the *80,000 Hours* podcast, though, he said he liked hanging around San Francisco. And that's what made him decide to leave Jane Street and try some other things.

He told me he worked a little for the Center for Effective Altruism (CEA) in October and November 2017, but he was also curious about crypto trading.

"My quote-unquote night job was trading crypto, but in fact I was spending most of my time on my night job," he told me in February 2021. He said he had gotten a bit hooked.

He tells a similar story in many interviews. If he was at CEA in late 2017, he would have been working with his Alameda Research cofounder, Tara MacAulay, who went from being chief operating officer to CEO of CEA that year. One of my sources, who asked to remain nameless, said that because SBF had told Jane Street he was leaving to work for a non-profit they let him take a more languorous departure. Usually, the firm makes people leave as soon as they offer their resignation, for security reasons.

Jane Street never replied to a request for comment on this point.

I've never heard him mention MacAulay when he tells it, but that doesn't mean he never has. His LinkedIn only shows him at CEA for two months, and that's how he describes it in podcast appearances as well.

However, CEA did not respond to a request for comment to confirm that he was actually ever on the payroll there.

His LinkedIn says he served as "Director of Development." But he's not mentioned in the organization's year-end report on the Effective Altruism forum, published on December 19, 2017, though MacAulay's promotion is cited. Beyond mentioning where readers can give, the report doesn't address fundraising for CEA.

This is what he told me when I asked if he'd ever been on the payroll at CEA. "I'm not sure whether I got set up on payroll, because among other things I would not have been trying to make it urgent to get set up on payroll. I was going to donate whatever payroll I got to the Center for Effective Altruism. So there was no urgency in that happening."

He says he really did work there. He joined the CEA Slack, but he never really got to the point of doing much in the way of real work. "I started coming to the office, but not that long thereafter I started basically just working on Alameda full time," he said. "I basically sort of admitted to myself that it was dumb to be splitting my time, and I should just come to terms with the fact that I was gonna be trading crypto."

On SBF's second appearance on the FTX podcast, he spoke to the work itself. "I really like trading," he said. "I don't know that I'll find another role that I enjoy at the sort of object level as much as that."

("Object-level" is a philosophical concept popular among Effective Altruists—it roughly means "the thing itself" rather than what the thing represents; in other words, he liked trading itself, but he shifted to entrepreneurship because it enabled him to generate more money and power, which gave him more satisfaction, which would be the "meta-level"— more on all this in Chapters 18 and 29.)

The host asked him to describe his "seminal crypto trading" moment, and SBF said, "Doing my first arb on Bittrex versus Poloniex[1] back in the day. There was like 10 percent or something. I just did a round trip in complete there and was like: 'Wow I didn't think it would work.'" He doesn't remember for sure which minor cryptocurrency it was. By round trip, he means he bought the asset in question in dollars on one exchange. Moved it to another. Sold it for dollars and transferred those back to the first exchange. At the end, he had more in dollars than he started, even despite exchange fees.

He continued, "I just assumed, this arb can't be real, but it did turn out to be real."

That was late fall 2017. He tried some more, a few worked, a lot didn't, but if you could just get some of them to work, "It could be pretty big," he said.

He invited his old friend Gary Wang, who was at Google, to join him. Wang moved to the Bay Area, and they started actually building out systems.

"The best trade we ever found, there was an arbitrage in Japan, and it was just worth an obscene amount and every week earlier that we

---

[1] Two once-popular crypto exchanges, neither very prominent today.

Arbitrage or arb

Arbitrage sounds like a difficult concept, but it's simple.

It's just the idea of making a profit off different prices for the same thing in two different places. It's usually used to describe trading away the difference in price of a commodity or a security in two different markets.

In a super-connected world, arbitrages are rare, tiny, and fleeting. New, inefficient markets have more of them, though, like crypto did early on.

---

could've figured out how to do it would've been worth so much," he said on the FTX podcast.

This is the famous trade where, as he tells it, bitcoin sold for more in Japan than it did in much of the rest of the world, and there was a lot of demand. The way to exploit that trade was all about operational problems. Seeing the price difference, as he's told many people, was easy.

To profit off it, a company needed bank accounts in both countries. It needed citizens in both countries. It needed bank staff who would let someone make large deposits on a regular basis and believe the person when he said he wasn't a money launderer. Then a company needed to be able to move between yen and dollars.

If it could get all these parts working, though, it could run the trade as long as it lasted. At least, that's what Sam said made it work.

And of course that's the trouble with the arbitrage business, in the end. Arbitrageurs trade their own advantage away.

He talked about those early days on the *80,000 Hours* podcast, and the host noted that when he heard about SBF's company back then, it always seemed like they were making big plays that they might have a very serious chance of going bust.

SBF agreed. Here's how he explained its risk-taking: "Whatever is the highest net expected value thing is what we should do," he told the host, Robert Wiblin. "I do think those are probably the right choices, but they were scary. I think even more so than some chance of going bust, what they sort of entailed was that we had to have a lot of faith in ourselves almost—that they really would have had a significant chance of going bust if we didn't play our cards exactly right," he said.

So maybe that's it, really? Maybe the answer is that they were able to grow their capital quickly because on many trades they were taking near-existential risks that they would make it to the next trade. A company that's willing to bet everything to maximize returns now has a shot of pulling way out ahead of everyone, after all.

But it also might go broke.

But the Alameda Research team was made up of a lot of really young people, folks without much in the way of obligations, from supportive backgrounds, and who already knew they could support themselves quite comfortably. Sure they could risk the company, but at that point, that was all they were risking.

Why not go for it?

Not everyone saw it that way. Several of the people who had joined Alameda because of MacAulay had left shortly after it launched, in April 2018, precisely because of risky behavior, both financially and operationally.

"He didn't want to feel constrained," Naia Bouscal told the *Wall Street Journal* in November 2022. Bouscal was a former software engineer at Alameda who left with Ms. MacAulay and the others. "But as a result we ended up not really knowing how much money we even had."

Bouscal did not reply to my request for further comment.

The earliest staffers worked from a house in Berkeley, California, until eventually moving into an office and then later to Hong Kong.

MacAulay would go on to start Lantern Ventures, a proprietary trading firm that has been in operation but under the radar since 2018. In November, she would say on Twitter, "I am shocked, appalled, and frankly, angry. BTC was birthed from the trauma of 2008. Sam's actions are a perversion of everything crypto stands for."

MacAulay declined to speak further about her time with Alameda, via a spokesperson.

I asked SBF in December why he never includes her in the origin story of Alameda, and he said, "I don't think it's well defined who the cofounders of Alameda were. I . . . we never had an official company-blessed designation of that."

Expected value (EV)

In short, expected value, or "EV," is decision-making with two components: a guess of how valuable something will be (even if it doesn't have a dollar value associated in fact, *make one up*) and a guess about its probability.

For example, let's say you have a job that pays you $1,000 every week. Your boss likes you. You like it. You've never been in trouble. Your expected value for any given week in the future then is 99% × $1,000. So your expected value for that job is $999 per week, or $51,948 per year.

Whereas, let's say someone offers to sell you a lottery ticket with a jackpot of $1,000,000,000. You estimate your odds of winning at 0.0001%. Your expected value is $1. So if the ticket costs a dollar or less, you should buy it. If it's more than a dollar, you shouldn't.

A true aficionado like SBF would apply this in unconventional ways. Say you were offered a job that paid $20,000 more per year than your current job, but you have to move cities. You have a girlfriend or boyfriend in your current city, however, and if you move, that will likely end the relationship. So ask yourself: Does that relationship bring an additional $20,000 in value to your life (in contentment, pleasure, etc.)? And is it likely to last another year so that full value is realized?

If you only saw a 50/50 chance of it lasting a year, then it needs to bring you $40,000 or more in value in order to outweigh the job offer.

And so on.

Here's the most important aspect of it to understand (and this will be important later). To truly think about expected value the way SBF and his fellow travelers do, it's crucial to think of it as *actual money*.

If someone offers a coin flip to give you $1,000, that's worth $500 to anyone who accepts. If a person accepts the offer, they become $500 richer in that moment. Further, it would be rational to pay as much as $499 to make that flip. Do you see?

> Take this a step further. Imagine someone had $1,000, and someone else offers to pay them $100 for a coin flip. But if the person accepts the offer, they have to turn over the $1,000 if they lose the flip. This is a terrible deal. The upside is $100. The downside is $900.
>
> Risk actually goes on the decision-making balance sheet as if it were a real liability.

That said, he admitted that "one could totally reasonably have listed her as a cofounder. Like there was a time at which I think that would have felt appropriate." Yet he confirmed that MacAulay never got to own any part of the firm. "Although, it's worth noting that, frankly, we were still figuring out details of who was going to own what, when things started imploding and she left."

Bouscal said that she and her departing cohort "came to the conclusion he's not a person we wanted to be in business with or associate with."

Bankman-Fried was offered a $1 million buyout, the *Journal* reported, but he refused. At that point, many investors pulled their capital, but Alameda carried on.

The risk-taking disposition the firm was born with never went away. The problem was, at some point it seems like its leadership didn't notice that—later—something changed.

Whereas, early on, the only people at risk were the staff and investors, eventually, the customers of a technically separate firm were gradually, silently brought along on the ride, with no disclosure and, for that matter, not even any upside.

Sources Referenced

Interview, Sam Bankman-Fried, via videochat/Telegram call, Feb. 8, 2021.
"Sam Bankman-Fried on taking a high-risk approach to crypto and doing good," Wiblin, Robert, and Keiran Harris, *80,000 Hours* podcast, April 14, 2022.
FTX insider, interview via phone, Dec. 18, 2022.

"**Episode 3: Sam Bankman Fried discusses altruism**," Yver, Tristan, *FTX Podcast*. Date unknown (podcast unpublished).

"**Episode 91: Sam Bankman-Fried founder of FTX and Alameda Research**," Yver, Tristan, *FTX Podcast*, published Nov. 30, 2021.

"**Centre for Effective Altruism (CEA): An overview of 2017 and our 2018 plans**," LarissaHeskethRowe, Forum, Effective Altruism.org, Dec. 19, 2017.

"**Early Alameda Staffers Quit After Battling Sam Bankman-Fried Over Risk, Compliance Concerns**," Zuckerman, Gregory, *Wall Street Journal*, Nov. 30, 2022.

Tara Mac Aulay, @Tara_MacAulay, Twitter, Nov. 16, 2022: https://twitter.com/Tara_MacAulay/status/1592985305556074497.

Interview, Sam Bankman-Fried, phone call with spokesperson, Dec. 30, 2022.

Chapter 8

Early Alameda

In January 2018, Juan Benet decided to help convene a group to talk about investing in Alameda Research.

Benet is one of the industry's big brains. He created two distributed ways of managing data storage: the Interplanetary File System and Filecoin. They break up data, encrypt it, and tuck it on hard drives all over the world, with people who have no idea what they are keeping safe. These systems create an alternative to huge, centralized data centers. Benet also had a hand in launching CoinList, a straightlaced token launching project.

Benet had closed the largest initial coin offering to date a few months before, $257 million for Filecoin. He couldn't do the meeting, but he wanted to get some of the best folks in San Francisco's crypto scene together to meet this guy who had made an impression on him: Sam Bankman-Fried.

Benet did not reply to my request for comment on this arrangement.

Benet asked Polychain if it could put together a meeting of potential investors. A knowledgeable source told me that in the room was Olaf Carlson-Wee, Polychain's founder; Ryan Zurrer, on the team; Richard Craib, CEO of Numerai, a hedge fund that had a token; and Fred Ehrsam, a cofounder of Coinbase. It was a nighttime meeting, at 8:30 p.m. local time.

My account of this meeting comes from Craib, a source familiar with the events, and SBF. This meeting has not been previously reported.

Craib immediately thought the whole arrangement was unusual. Typically a founder meets with investors one-on-one, he told me. This felt like some kind of summit. It interested Craib because, at that point, there were not many crypto-focused funds, especially not ones that could hold liquid assets. Craib had backed Polychain, and he told me he was curious about SBF because he was game to back others.

All of these players would go on to be some of the biggest king-makers in the nascent industry. Two of them, Carlson-Wee and Ehrsam, brought Hollywood looks combined with the sort of idiosyncratic personalities made for a multi-season Netflix epic.

If the stars were younger, Owen Wilson could have played Carlson-Wee if Wilson could tone-down his goofiness, and Leonardo DiCaprio could be cast as Ehrsam, if it's possible for DiCaprio to tap into any sort of inner geek.

Liquid vs. illiquid and how cryptocurrency complicates funds

Most venture funds focus on an illiquid asset: equity in companies. Equity (i.e. ownership) isn't completely illiquid, but it's hard to sell. Most venture funds have rules that say that they can only hold illiquid assets (or mostly). If a company goes public, such funds generally sell ASAP, paying its limited partners (LPs) back pro rata.

Crypto complicates this, because venture investments often come with tokens that are either immediately liquid or will be much sooner than most equity would ever be. Polychain was one of the first to set up a legal structure where it could embrace tokens on behalf of its LPs and trade them, as necessary, to manage risk in the fund.

SBF handled their grilling gamely. Here was a young guy, brand-new to crypto, up against some of the old guard. They all knew each other, but he didn't know them. Even then he was confident and knowledgeable and sounded like he knew what he was doing.

"The way he speaks is kind of striking. It's sort of obscurantist," Craib said. "He would use all the right jargon, but you'd never quite understand what he was saying. He liked to make you feel like he was the smartest guy in the room."

Knowing Craib was there is thematically interesting, though he told me that was the only time he ever spoke with SBF. Craib is something of the anti-Sam, another geeky super-brain who excels at profiting by abstracting everything and pulling out insights.

Unlike SBF, for whom it was all an ulterior motive for a greater scheme to change the world, Craib is (as far as I can tell) a pure investor.

SBF described Alameda in the meeting as making most of its money on geographic arbitrage, which squares with SBF's own account of that time (like the Japan trade from the prior chapter). It was a lucrative spot to be in, but the idea was that that arbitrage didn't have a lot more life left in it.

Craib doesn't remember specific terms being discussed, but my unnamed source did, recalling figures vastly higher than the traditional 2 percent management fee and 20 percent of returns most funds offered.

I asked SBF about this, and he didn't remember particular terms. He said at that point they had a variety of arrangements that they offered to a variety of different audiences. All Craib remembers was SBF saying a large portion of the profits would go to charity. As soon as Craib heard that part of the pitch, he was out. He told me that he found Effective Altruism off-putting.

For his part, SBF didn't remember anything coming of the meeting. His focus had clearly been on Polychain, which was new at the time, but so was Alameda.

He said, "I think they were very interested in what we had to say. I didn't get the sense that they were close to investing. Like I got the sense that, you know, they were sort of like, 'Oh, that's interesting. We have no idea if it's real.'"

SBF told me in December that after MacAulay left, about 75% of the capital went with her. He estimated that Alameda had about $40 million to work with after the breakup.

"We spent the next year or so making money, and we were making somewhere between 50 and 100 percent annualized returns on the capital," he said. A lot of that went to donations and expenses, so it wasn't as good as it sounded, he explained, but they did, for a while, have a very consistent way to make a lot of money quickly.

When they got all the steps right, they could realize somewhere between 5 and 20 percent each business day running the arbitrage to Japan. It basically took them all day to do it, and if they made any mistakes, they wouldn't have money in their account back at the end of the day to make it possible to do a round trip over the next day.

Eventually, the arbitrage dried up, as such things always do. But there were others.

In April 2022, SBF would appear on the *Odd Lots* podcast from Bloomberg and explain that the arbitrages weren't as good as in the Japan trade days, but there was more money moving around, so it didn't matter.

"I think that so far, the sort of story of crypto has sort of been like spreads are coming in and at the same time volumes are going up such that actually the arbitrageurs are making about as much as they always did," SBF said.

Basically, 20 percent on $1 billion is $200 million, and that's great.

But 1 percent of $20 billion is also $200 million.

SBF can describe lots of different arbitrages it would do in those days, but they quickly became much more complicated and subtle than the simple concept of just getting bitcoin into Japan and dollars back out.

Craib has no regrets about staying away. But 10 months later, Ehrsam would announce a new fund, Paradigm, cofounded with Sequoia Capital alum Matt Huang. It announced itself with a bombshell that got the attention of everyone in the industry: investments from several university endowments, including Yale.

Other big, conservative names like that *might* have bet on crypto before, but if they had, they hadn't been open about it. This marked Paradigm out as playing on a different level than its peers.

Paradigm did, however, ultimately invest $278 million in FTX itself. Then, in 2021 SBF coauthored a paper with one of Paradigm's researchers, Dave White, on "Everlasting Options."

After FTX collapsed in November 2022, Huang would post on Twitter: "We feel deep regret for having invested in a founder and company who ultimately did not align with crypto's values and who have done enormous damage to the ecosystem."

Paradigm's founders declined to provide further comment.

Sources Referenced

"**$257 Million: Filecoin Breaks All-Time Record for ICO Funding**," Higgins, Stan, CoinDesk, Sept. 7, 2017.

Interview, unnamed source, WhatsApp call, Dec. 10, 2022.

Interview, Bankman-Fried, Sam, phone call with spokesperson, Dec. 30, 2022.

Richard Craib on Twitter, @richardcraib, Nov. 10, 2022, 11:13 PM ET: https://twitter.com/richardcraib/status/1590920693293944832/video/1.

Interview, Craib, Richard, via mobile, Dec. 10, 2022.

"**Sam Bankman-Fried and Matt Levine on How to Make Money in Crypto**," Alloway, Tracy and Joe Weisenthal, *Odd Lots* podcast, Bloomberg.com, April 25, 2022.

"**The most influential endowment manager just jumped into crypto with bets on two Silicon Valley funds**," Rooney, Kate, and Ari Levy, CNBC, October 5, 2018.

"**Investors Who Put $2 Billion into FTX Face Scrutiny, Too**," Griffith, Erin and David Yaffe-Bellany, the *New York Times*, Nov. 11, 2022.

Matt Huang on Twitter, @matthuang, Nov. 15, 2022, 2:07 PM ET: https://twitter.com/matthuang/status/1592595243907526656.

Chapter 9

The ICO Era

If you asked almost anyone in cryptocurrency whom they would want to meet if they could meet just one person, I think a lot of them would say Satoshi Nakamoto, the creator of Bitcoin. But not me. I want to meet the CEO of the Useless Ethereum Token.

The Useless Ethereum Token was a gag for cash. The person running it was active on Reddit and Twitter and other such places in 2017, the last time people went crazy for crypto. We did an email interview in those days, but he never told me his name. He only went by UET CEO.

The website is still up. It's worth a look. The logo says it all.

ICOs (or "initial coin offerings") were the second big new way to raise money that the internet created for us. The first big new way was crowdfunding via sites such as Kickstarter, IndieGogo, and GoFundMe. Crowdfunding reflected an optimistic era in the tech industry.

By 2017, the mood had become darker. By then, we all knew Silicon Valley oligarchs had turned us into lotus eaters scrolling mobiles in the gardens beneath the walls surrounding Bezos's and Zuckerberg's cuddle puddles of cash.

The UET CEO, whoever he was, was already jaded and saw a lot of ICOs grabbing money without much actual business. So he offered to sell a token that he promised would be worth absolutely nothing to anyone. He also committed to spending the money completely frivolously and to do no good for the world with it. The disarmingly honest caper earned him 310 ETH in 2017, about $42,000.

That would be worth $350,000 in November 2022.

OK, so what were ICOs? What are tokens? Did this ever make sense?

First let's start with coins. Bitcoin is a coin. Ether is a coin. Coins are the fundamental economic unit of a blockchain. Each blockchain is separate and unique.

A blockchain is basically a spreadsheet, one that has a record of every account that holds a crypto asset governed by that blockchain. A blockchain is also a record of every single prior copy of that spreadsheet, going all the way back to the beginning.

Blockchains use coins to reward lots of people for keeping copies of all those records and checking each other's work. Sometimes those people are called validators. Sometimes they are called miners. Basically, they are all *bookkeepers*.

Coins pay the bookkeepers, so a coin is essential, existential to a blockchain.

Okay, now, some blockchains, such as bitcoin, can only do one kind of asset. Bitcoin only does bitcoin.[1]

Other blockchains can spin up other assets. These additional assets are not essential, but they often enable some of the uses that make a blockchain valuable.

These additional assets are called tokens, technically. But the truth is most people used "tokens" and "coins" interchangeably, although it helps to at least understand the distinction.

A token needs coins. Coins don't need tokens.

Initial coin offerings in 2017 were mostly about launching new tokens (so the name is confusing, I know), but some new coins were launched with ICOs (such as Tezos and Filecoin), although mostly it was about tokens.

So let's give an example.

---

[1] For anyone who ends up going down the Bitcoin rabbit hole, there was something called "colored coins" on Bitcoin for a while. It was an idea that never took off—right idea, wrong tool.

Let's imagine that Netflix had started with a token sale in 2017. Reed Hastings, Netflix's founder, was going to start it from day one as a streaming service, and he was going to raise money by selling a token to pay for development. He calls his token flix (FLIX), and it's going to run on the Ethereum blockchain.

Hastings might make a billion tokens with a smart contract that makes it clear to everyone: once those billion flix are made there can never be any more or any less.

So then he could say that one flix would be tradeable for *one month* of Netflix streaming, once the service goes live. It doesn't exist yet, though, so he raises $25 million by selling 100 million flix (10%) of his supply at $0.25 apiece.

Then strangers on the internet could buy flix and bet that when it goes live, people will be willing to pay more than 25¢ for a month of limitless movies and TV. So they buy it pre-launch, betting on that future success.

Once they have flix, they can trade it, based on whatever news or rumors are going around about Hastings' development efforts. Until, finally, the service goes live.

When it does, the market would find a price for flix. If it turned out that our imagined Hastings launched something roughly as good as what the company really launched back in 2011, then we should expect a flix would be worth about $8. So people who bought it at 25¢ in that initial sale would make a nice profit.

Later on, flix might vary in price based on how good the latest show offerings are or how well Netflix does at securing licenses for the old movies folks most want to watch again. Its price would give its team real-time feedback from the market.

In 2017 and 2018 there was this idea that tokens were like an *arcade token* or a *laundry token*. They were a way to pay to use something.

Around $12 billion was raised in ICOs in those years, according to CoinDesk.

With me so far?

The truth is, initial coin offerings were never really that straightforward, though. They'd sell a bunch of tokens, but it was seldom clear exactly what service the token would be good for or just how much of a service it would be good for.

Looking back, there were a few genuine visionaries from that era and more enterprises that began then have persisted to now than one might expect. But there were also a lot of straight-up thieves. It could be tough to tell the difference. The thieves and the prophets all spoke the same language.

In early 2018 that whole market would come crashing down when American securities regulators started showing the bad kind of interest in ICOs (though surprisingly few companies have faced serious consequences from those days).

A year or so later, tokens would be hot again. In 2019 and 2020, founders came to realize that the way for a company to get value out of launching a token was *not* to sell it—at least not to the public (investors will buy anything).

Selling tokens attracts the wrong people and makes the wrong impression. Strangely, the path to success with tokens now seems to be to give them away. At least, this was the thinking in 2020 and 2021.

So let's go back to flix. Imagine Netflix launched in this era. Hastings might instead sell some tokens to investors to get going and then start getting regular people involved in building up the project.

For example, he might want filmmakers to start putting their movies into Netflix. He might reward them for doing so and reward them even more if people actually watched those movies.

To that end, Hastings gives filmmakers, say, 0.01 free flix for every half hour paying users actually watched of whatever they uploaded.

Giving users a token for something that helped make a new product more healthy came to be seen as a better way to build a culture around one of these new assets.

Tokens ended up being used all sorts of ways for encouraging all sorts of behaviors. More and more, though, teams started to settle on one use case common to most new tokens.

Tokens stopped being arcade tokens, a way to pay for usage. Tokens became votes. They became a way of deciding what would happen with a crypto project as it changed.

And if that sounds just like reinventing finance as we know it, well, *sort of.* The difference, however, was that the "enterprise" normally wasn't a company. The enterprise was a bunch of code that ran autonomously on a blockchain.

That's not something traditional finance can do; banks can't run without staff. Blockchain banks can, however. Plus, they run completely openly, such that everyone can look at all their books all the time. So, sure, governance tokens are like stocks, except they are completely different.

I can imagine how a Netflix could run on a blockchain—in theory, but the truth is people weren't building things like Netflix then or now. So far, they have been mainly building financial tools. They have been building exchanges, banks, and betting markets (more on these in Chapter 17).

So governance tokens have been a way to decide, for example, what kind of assets to support in these new financial products.

For users, these are nice because they are 100 percent transparent. Not only can a user check their own deposit, they can check everyone else's too. They can see if the new product is solvent. If it is and they like how it's working, they might want to own some of its governance token and help it grow.

The final model for the best way to use tokens is not settled yet (and legal and regulatory concerns raise whole other issues). So far, tokens take many forms and they do different kinds of work in different kinds of projects. At their best, though, they give people a way to coalesce around some piece of software that runs on the internet on its own, at least until governance token holders vote to change it.

Tokens also give founders a new business model. Tokens allow a founder to find people to take an early bet on an idea. To reward early supporters. To allow the market to assess the value of the project in real time as it progresses. And they give founders an incentive to drive value to their own stash of tokens and slowly exit over time, as they turn the machine they created over to its users.

That is, of course, the very idealistic vision. How it has worked out in practice is a lot more complicated.

Of course my guy, the UET CEO, skipped all the middle steps. He took the money and ran. I would love to know what he's up to now. I wouldn't be surprised if he took his 310 ethers and started a fund.

If you're reading this UET CEO, call me—let's catch up.

Sources Referenced

Useless Ethereum Token website, https://uetoken.com/.

"**Cryptocurrency Has Its Potato Salad Moment with the Useless Ethereum Token**," Dale, Brady, *Observer*, July 5, 2017.

"**$6.3 Billion: 2018 ICO Funding Has Passed 2017's Total**," Floyd, David, CoinDesk, April 18, 2018.

"**Cryptocurrency Firms Targeted in SEC Probe**," Eaglesham, Jean, and Paul Vigna, *Wall Street Journal*, Feb. 28, 2018.

"**SEC ICO Probe Underway, But Stories Conflict on Size of Sweep**," Hochstein, Marc, and Bailey Reutzel, CoinDesk, Feb. 28, 2018.

"**So Long ICOs, Hello Airdrops: The Free Token Giveaway Craze Is Here**," Dale, Brady, CoinDesk, March 18, 2018.

Chapter 10

Crypto Winter

The cold flurries of Crypto Winter 2018 came in the form of whispers and rumors about "information requests" from the US Securities and Exchange Commission (SEC).

And if "information requests" sound innocuous, apparently they aren't if you're an attorney. Especially if you're an attorney in the financial industry. Especially if you're an attorney in the financial industry working for a company in a really weird new corner of finance that looks *extremely* scammy to almost everyone giving it a sideways glance.

The cryptocurrency market in 2018 froze up like a Hell's Angel wandering into a tea party for 7th-grade suburban girls. The good times of public ICOs were over all at once. Several companies suddenly shut down, leaving little more than a Medium post or a tweet thread to remember them by.

What might have been, Videocoin! We won't soon forget you, Bee Token!

It was as if there was a sense that everyone had known it was more fun than it should have been, floating wild ideas on a whim only for strangers to funnel a few million dollars at four to eight cofounders on the hopes that maybe they would do something real and make the value of these weird crypto tokens go up later.

Meanwhile, SBF was starting to hit the first truly rough patch in his path to riches and global fame. Bitcoin had fallen fast from its all-time high just under $20,000 in early December.

Then came the regulatory letters. That crushed ICOs, the new way of funding start-ups.

I explained ICOs last chapter. Logistically, most ICOs took place on Ethereum. Tokens turned out to be the first real use case of the first blockchain that could do tokens. Because investors needed ether to invest in these things, ICOs drove up ether's price.

In those days, it was very hard to buy ethers with dollars, though, so investors bought bitcoin to buy ether. So ICOs *also* drove up the price of bitcoin.

Exchanges such as Colorado's Shapeshift were doing a bang-up business in trading bitcoin for ether so that wannabe investors could trade that for different kinds of crypto dreams.

The original version of Shapeshift was a very surreal experience for a modern internet user. Basically, once you bought some bitcoin on an exchange, you could move it off the exchange to your own wallet. Then, you would go on Shapeshift and tell it what you wanted to buy. You would put in your bitcoin address and your Ethereum address and then tell Shapeshift how much ether you wanted.

It would tell you how much bitcoin to send and what address to send it to. Once you did, a few minutes later, you would have your ether.

This was definitely not a trustless setup. There was this unsettling moment after you sent your bitcoin where you'd think: Was I just robbed? But then before long your ether would appear. Once you had the coins, it hit you that you had just done a financial transaction without telling anyone your name.

There got to be a lot less demand for services like ShapeShift once the financial inspectors started scoping out the place, though. Without those volumes bouncing around between blockchains, ether and bitcoin prices dropped fast.

That's roughly when MacAulay ran out of patience with SBF. According to the *WSJ*'s account, early staff were concerned that he was imitating the method of high-frequency trading that he'd learned at Jane Street, without imitating its risk management practices.

Another early SBF collaborator, Tamara Frankel, would come along after MacAulay exited, but she corroborated this assessment. "Sam has never had good risk management. In fact I would say his strength was resilience to risk," Frankel said.

The account cites one example of millions of dollars in losses after the firm didn't correctly account for transfers of the cryptocurrency xrp (XRP),[1] from the company Ripple.

SBF *seemed* to speak to just that gaff in 2019, after FTX was launched, when he appeared on the YouTube show *Nugget's News*, talking about Alameda's early days.

"Let me start off by telling you the single biggest mistake we've ever made," he says. He talks about how cryptocurrency transfers between exchanges were a real mess then.

He admits that early on Alameda sent a ton of an altcoin called xrp from Kraken to Bitthumb (two centralized exchanges, like the kind SBF would found in 2019). This was a transfer that a lot of people complained about, he said.

He notes that this terrible trade happened in February 2018 when the price of xrp was tanking. "We sent a lot of xrp, *a lot of xrp* from Kraken to Bitthumb," he said.

A lot got lost. It took a lot of wrangling to get some of it back.

Since then, he said, they had built up a careful system that automated and checked transfers, but he admits the team was being too cavalier at that time.

He was able to laugh it off a year or so later after his companies were in a new era, but by then his earliest partners were long gone.

A little while after his EA allies left, Tamara Frankel would begin working for Alameda on a consulting basis, she tells me. "Sam was interested in me because I had a large network of crypto whales who were my friends," she said.

Frankel is an intriguing character. She keeps a very low profile, but when you speak to her she sounds as excited as any new convert. She currently is a partner in D1 Ventures, a fund trading its own capital.

---

[1] It really doesn't matter what xrp is. It's just a fairly old coin that persists for some reason. People talked about it a lot more back then than now.

By the time she found Sam, she had been in crypto long enough that she had lots of connections to traders and players all over the world. SBF had none of that yet. He was a guy in Berkeley with trading skills and will.

Frankel told me she was struck by his fast-moving mind and his lack of ideology. Up to that point, in 2018, everyone in crypto had an ideology. Blockchains meant something.

But Sam was different. He was just there for the financial upside. She recalled an early conversation with SBF where she was trying to sort him out, figure out where he fit in this weird world. She asked him which cryptocurrency he found really interesting.

His answer? "Tether."

Bitcoin is about busting money out of government control. Ethereum is about a utopian dream.

Tether just copies dollars over to the blockchain. It's a stablecoin designed to make trading more convenient. That's it.

Saying he found Tether interesting was a non-statement. This was like a network engineer who said USB cables were his favorite piece of equipment. Like a mechanic who said his favorite part of a car was the door handle.

But to Frankel, she thought this distance might be good. During the ICO bonanza, there had been so much shilling, hustling, rug pulling, and scamming. That manipulative nonsense was made easier by the fact that too many of the starry-eyed newcomers thought they weren't just making a bet by buying into Paragon or Ravencoin or SpankChain or *whatever*, but that *they were changing the world, man.*

But SBF worked all the time for nothing more than the gains off wild arbitrage trades. "I liked working with Sam because he was kind of crazy and high risk," she said.

It was refreshing to Frankel that SBF simply didn't seem to comprehend the cultural fault lines of the space. The coins were all just a means to an end in his eyes, at least early on.

She said she saw him this way: "He's looking at this through a completely non-biased lens," she told me. "I thought: Maybe this is what the industry needs is somebody who doesn't have these deep-set beliefs."

In other words, he was an Effective Altruist, but blockchain nihilist.

Sources Referenced

"**Cryptocurrency Firms Targeted in SEC Probe**," Eaglesham, Jean, and Paul Vigna, *Wall Street Journal*, Feb. 28, 2018.

"**Bitcoin Drops Below $9K, Top Altcoins Down 16% On Global Regulatory News**," Parts, Helen, Cointelegraph, March 9, 2018.

@Tara_MacAulay, Twitter, Nov. 16, 2022: https://twitter.com/Tara_MacAulay/status/1592985303262072834.

"**Early Alameda Staffers Quit After Battling Sam Bankman-Fried Over Risk, Compliance Concerns**," Zuckerman, Gregory, the *Wall Street Journal*, Nov. 30, 2022.

Interview, Frankel, Tamara, mobile, Dec. 6, 2022.

"**Why Traders, Quants & Whales Are Moving to FTX Cryptocurrency Exchange**," *Nugget's News*, YouTube, Sept. 4, 2019: https://youtu.be/KdRnWQjSuBw.

Chapter 11

The Exchange Business

Imagine you have $500 in coins, right? Actual metal coins.

You've got all kinds of coins. Silver dollars, half dollars, quarters, dimes, nickels, pennies. You've got some other kinds of money, too. Some euro, some Korean won . . . maybe pesos? Whatever! But it all adds up to $500.

You take a shoebox and stack all the coins up inside until you make a very cool replica of downtown Minneapolis. You take a photo, post it to Instagram, and it gets all the likes.

Amazing.

Next, you put the lid on the box, seal it with duct tape, pick it up and shake the living hell out of it.

How much money is in the box when you open it back up?

There is still $500 in the box. Because it was a box. It was closed. It doesn't matter how you stacked it before or how much you mix it up.

That's how money works. It's just a number; no matter how much you move it around there's still the same amount there.

That's how the exchange business works, too. Or it should be.

You could call the shoebox a toy model of the fundamental business of an exchange. It's just that. People put money in the box, and everyone using the box plays with it to their heart's content. The money doesn't even have to move around at all. The money can just sit, the trading happens in a regular old database, like the ones that run Twitter, Facebook, and the terrible software behind your doctor's website.

From a bookkeeping perspective, running an exchange should be dead simple.

Let's imagine an exchange that only trades two things, dollars and bitcoins.

There are only two people on the exchange: you and me.

You have put one bitcoin on the exchange. I have $4,000. Let's say bitcoin is priced at $20,000 where it was for a lot of later 2022 until FTX blew up the world.

Unless you want to cut me some really crazy deal, I can only buy 0.2 bitcoin. That's it. There's no magic system to get more money in the box. The box is lopsided. I buy all the bitcoin I can and I just sit there. And you just sit there with your $1,000 and 0.8 bitcoin waiting for someone else to show up and give you something else to buy.

Is this making sense? Do you see the point I'm making about FTX here? This model scales up to all the people, all the coins, all the cryptocurrencies you want to put in there. It doesn't matter how much you have in an exchange; as long as the business you're doing is *just* an exchange business, this should all be very simple.

And FTX promised it was this simple. As the CFTC (Commodity Futures Trading Commission) noted in its complaint:

> FTX Trading represented, in its Terms of Service and elsewhere, that customers were the "owner[s]" of all assets in their accounts, had "control" over the assets at all times, and that those assets were "appropriately safeguarded and segregated" from FTX's own funds.

In fact, doing the business of the exchange makes it all gradually easier to keep track of everyone's money, because every time someone makes a trade, the exchange gets to shave off a tiny little fee. Each time that happens, the exchange is responsible for a little less customer money and has a little more of its own as a cushion, just in case.

But we know how this story ends, right? We all understand: customers put money into FTX, and it should have just left customer funds alone.

There's really not some Monopoly Money thing going on. Exchanges just provide a meeting place for people who want to trade. They work great as long as no one trades something that they don't have.

The truth is, no one in an exchange is really in a position to trade something they don't have, because the exchange won't let you trade something that you haven't turned over to them.

Oh, wait.

Sorry.

I was wrong.

There is one party that can trade what they don't have. Usually, we expect that party not to trade, but we just have to trust them.

The party that can trade something it doesn't have is the party that runs the database that says what's in the exchange. That party is the exchange itself.

And, look, let's play devil's advocate here for a minute, just to complete the picture.

It must be so tempting for an exchange to misuse its customers' funds. You're sitting there running a company that keeps multiple billions of dollars' worth of assets safe at all times.

As I write this, Nansen, a crypto data company, estimates over $7 billion in assets across wallets it associates with Bitfinex. That's just one exchange, and not even one of the very biggest.

$7 billion!

For someone running such an exchange, he or she knows that 999 days out of 1000, a very large portion of the exchange's funds just... sit there. Sure, to its users, funds are moving all over. But those are just numbers in a database. Nothing is actually moving. The funds are all in fact at rest on various blockchains, doing nothing in the exchange's cold wallets.

There's an amount that comes in every day, and there is an amount that goes out. Usually, the former is a little bigger than the latter. But if you subtract out the size of either, they don't even touch what remains.

Let's say this is a $7 billion exchange and on its worst day ever it saw $1 billion in withdrawals.

That must make it feel a lot like it has $6 billion that it could just play around with. But fine, the CEO is a responsible exchange operator. What if he just played around with, *say*, 1 percent.

What if you just played around with a half a percent? Just $35 million. Like I said, it must feel very tempting. Especially if, for some reason, the company *needs* some money. *Just for a little bit.*

That is, of course, how it starts. That's how it becomes too simple to put a very easy business on the bad road, one where a CEO just keeps convincing himself that he can win it all back.

Of course running an exchange is a ridiculously hard business, one that must first build up an exceptional amount of trust from users. It needs incredible security because cyber criminals will be sniffing around all its accounts constantly. It needs a database that can move faster than Twitter's.

Plus, it needs to think about user experience, trade execution, how to match buyers with sellers, marketing, brand awareness, community, and what sort of financial instruments it wants to offer.

It's really hard.

Various traders told me FTX was really nice to use. It was also fast to list new tokens that the market was excited about.

But all those other complications aside, once an exchange has customers, it should in fact be quite easy to have everyone's money when they want it. If no one can buy something that no one else has deposited, then no one can withdraw anything that's not already there.

So on that level it is simple. FTX should have had all of its customers, deposits because once they were deposited, those deposits should have just stayed put.

But let's go beyond that and talk about exchanges in a world where there are also other exchanges.

Suppose one exchange doesn't have the right proportion of bitcoin to dollars, right? It's not as simple as my example above, but in terms of the people who have dollars and want bitcoin, imagine it's a little out of balance. There's not enough bitcoin on the exchange for all the dollars that want to buy it there.

Well, there would be a local uptick in the price of bitcoin. Bitcoin on *that* exchange would start to tick up just a little bit in price. Maybe only a dollar. Maybe just a few pennies, but it would get just a little bit out of line in the rest of the market.

What would happen?

Somebody would put more bitcoin on that exchange, that's what would happen. A company like Alameda would spot that, deposit more bitcoin, and post a sell order right away. Alameda would capture a sliver of profit, and the difference would go away.

That's arbitrage.

There's one crucial piece of an exchange's user experience that the exchange itself typically doesn't handle. Any time someone goes to an exchange, a remarkable thing happens. For just about any asset that they want to trade, they can basically always find a buyer or a seller.

If you've ever been into collectibles, you know how strange this is. You might go to a collector's show looking to buy or sell one specific item, and it can take you a while to find a taker. If you can find one at all!

But on crypto exchanges, as long as a customer is willing to stick to the prevailing market price, she will almost always find a buyer or a seller for her trade on just about any asset an exchange lists. So is it really true that at any moment there's a person much like her who wants to take the other side of her trade? Are markets really that liquid in crypto?

If not, how is it that exchanges have this great user experience, where a counterparty is always handy whenever a normal person is ready to swap one cryptocurrency for another?

It's because of market makers. That's what they do.

Sources Referenced

"**CFTC Charges Sam Bankman-Fried, FTX Trading and Alameda with Fraud and Material Misrepresentations**," press release and complaint before the US Southern District of New York, Commody Futures Trading Commission, Dec. 13, 2022.

Nansen Portfolio, Bitfinex: https://portfolio.nansen.ai/dashboard/bitfinex, viewed in Dec. 2022.

Chapter 12

Select Heists

Business journalism geeks love Matt Levine. In fact, lately, he's become so popular there's a certain class of journalist who seems to be starting to hate him because too many people like him. So it goes!

The aforementioned Levine is a columnist at Bloomberg who used to be a lawyer. Every weekday he writes a smart and funny roundup of business news. Levine wrote something cheeky about cryptocurrency exchanges in 2017:

> The other reason not to trade bitcoin is that, as far as I can tell, the fate of any bitcoin exchange/wallet/bank/custodian is to be hacked. That is just how bitcoin works: You buy bitcoins on an exchange, and you store them at the exchange because it's a pain to keep your private key yourself, and then the exchange gets hacked and your bitcoins get stolen.

Bitcoin was still very much the main thing on people's minds back then, but a lot of people were also buying bitcoin because they wanted to buy into initial coin offerings.

What he wrote was sort of right, but if he could write this again, I'd hope he would strike "wallet" from his list. When wallets get hacked, it's usually been the user's mistake.

But it's true that basically all exchanges have been hacked, to greater and lesser extents. A third-party exchange is no place to keep cryptocurrency when an owner is not actively trading.

There are four reasons why exchanges are bad places to keep cryptocurrency.

1. Ideological. Satoshi created Bitcoin because he wanted people to actually have full ownership of their money. Cash or gold can be kept in the home, but that can become impractical at a certain point, plus it can be tricky to transport. So he created a bearer asset that takes up no space. So, if someone prefers to trust someone else with their wealth, then why even bother with Bitcoin?

2. Practical. Bitcoin really, truly is a bearer instrument. It is much, much harder to get it back once it's stolen. There's no technical way to get it back. The only way to get it back is to find the thief (hard) and force them, either with force or law enforcement (also tricky—in no small part because many such thieves work for national governments now). So it's better not to risk it.

3. Piratical. An exchange is a giant pile of gold that is very attractive to thieves. They are prowling and poking each one's edges 24 hours a day, seven days a week. One person's little hardware wallet on a keychain in their closet safe with $1,000 or so in crypto on it just isn't worth a whole lot of thinking. Thieves have a pretty good idea of how much is inside each exchange, and those huge numbers are much more appealing than whatever pittance an individual has.

4. Methodical. Crypto on an exchange is too easy to trade. If it's there, a person will probably trade it and later regret it. If it's on a hardware wallet, sending bitcoin there is easy, but getting it back out is harder. So an owner probably won't trade it and they will be much happier for that later.

But in the end Levine is right. A lot of people do keep their crypto assets on exchanges, and most crypto exchanges really do get hacked (eventually, at least a little).

People just don't want to take responsibility for these assets. Exchanges work much more like the rest of the web. They work like an online bank or airline. Wallets are weird, so most people stick with the familiar model.

But centralized exchanges do collapse and get breached all the time. Here's a roundup of some of the great ones:

Coinbase. Super-early on, Coinbase got hit for a $250,000 theft of bitcoin, because a contractor had a password to a system that could reach Coinbase's "hot" wallet (where it kept *some* bitcoins at an interconnected Bitcoin address, ready for users that wanted to make a withdrawal).

The attacker only got a tiny piece of all their bitcoin, because most of it was stored super-securely. This bitcoin was the cryptocurrency it kept ready for customers who wanted to make withdrawals. It could have been a reputational disaster, but they managed to keep it quiet, as Jeff John Roberts reported in his book *Kings of Crypto*.

It's by far the smallest breach on this list, and it wasn't enough to meaningfully impact operations or threaten its solvency.

It's noteworthy because most people would tell you Coinbase has never been hacked. *Not quite* true, but very close.

Mt. Gox. The name is an acronym for Magic The Gathering Online Exchange, because it started as a site for trading cards from the collectible card game *Magic*. Mt. Gox was founded by Jed McCaleb. He would pivot the exchange to trading bitcoin, and it would become the biggest bitcoin exchange in the world—for a while.

He sold the exchange to a guy named Mark Karpelès in 2011.

In 2014, Mt. Gox would file for bankruptcy in Japan after admitting to losing 850,000 bitcoin, which was nominally over $400 million at the time. This was, it seems, stolen, though it took a long time for the firm to even admit there was a problem. It seems like it had been playing a game of fulfilling customer withdrawal requests with other customers' new deposits (which would only make it worse).

Weirdly, after the bankruptcy, they found 200,000 bitcoin staff had just sort of forgotten about. The value of what's left is enough to repay people the cash value of what they lost back then. But most of the booty, hundreds of thousands of bitcoin, has been on the wind for years.

Nothing says crypto oldhead like losing some bitcoin in Mt. Gox.

Bitfinex. The 2016 Bitfinex hack became exciting again in early 2022. A young Brooklyn couple, Ilya Lichtenstein and his wife, Heather Morgan, were arrested for possessing lots of the bitcoin stolen from the exchange, worth $3.6 billion at the time of the arrest (a lot less now, but still way more than the $72 million it was worth when it was stolen).

More on this later, but the couple has not been charged with committing the theft. Fun fact: the Feds found Lichtenstein's private key on a cloud server (like, Google Docs, or whatever) which was not the move.

Unlike Mt. Gox, Bitfinex survived the hack, though the means by which it did so are controversial. That is, however, a whole other story.

QuadrigaCX. The exchange's founder, Gerald Cotten, was declared dead in India on December 9, 2018, and no one had keys to access the exchange's assets but him. It was soon found that his exchange, then the leader in Canada, owed customers $130 million.

As far as anyone can tell, all its crypto assets were gone before he died. Experts have said that if you wanted to go somewhere, fake a death and disappear forever, India would be a great spot.

But no one has ever found any evidence that he's alive, either.

Those are just a few examples. Lots of lesser, forgettable exchanges have been hacked. Generally speaking, the hackers just got away with it. No one got anything back.

Exchange hacks are so common lately that they are barely even news. As I was gathering up details for this chapter, I noticed a $200 million exchange hack at the end of 2021 against Bitmart that I hadn't taken note of at the time.

Which is all just to say that when SBF decided to get into the exchange business, he was setting himself up against a world of dark cyber magic. This was known. So, it is strange how cavalier he became about it.

That said, these stories aren't really about cryptocurrency. They are about the laziness of humans permitting something that is best distributed to be re-centralized. It's about people who want the wealth of bitcoin without using the feature that gives it value. It's like buying gold bricks and painting them black.

As funny as Levine's 2017 adage about the destiny of exchanges is, he repeats a refrain here that's a little specious.

Since then, Levine dove deep into the space and wrote an opus of a crypto explainer in the October 31, 2022, issue of *Business Week*. It's very good, very fun, and after that work, one would hope that he probably would phrase his gag about custody *a bit* differently now.

Seriously, it's not that hard to hold bitcoin or other cryptocurrencies yourself. And it's better.

It's not hard, but it is *weird*. You need to learn to think about an asset and a personal account a little differently. Once it clicks you'll be fine. All it takes to make it click is to play around with the stuff a little bit.

Sources Referenced

Kings of Crypto: One Startup's Quest to Take Cryptocurrency Out of Silicon Valley and Onto Wall Street, Roberts, Jeff John, Harvard Business Press, Dec. 15, 2020.

"**Bitcoin Traders and Index Funds**," Levine, Matt, Bloomberg, Oct. 3, 2017.

"**A $480 Million Mystery: The Saga of Mt. Gox**," Floyd, David, NASDAQ, Aug 10, 2015.

"**Mt. Gox Creditors Inch Closer to Repayment as Bitcoin Dump Looms**," Kharif, Olga, Bloomberg, July 7, 2022.

"**Inside the Chess Match That Led the Feds to $3.6 Billion in Stolen Bitcoin**," Chow, Andrew, *Time*, Feb. 10, 2022.

"**Bitfinex's LEO Token Explodes After US Seizes $4B of Bitcoin Lost in 2016 Hack**," Dale, Brady, The Defiant, Feb. 8, 2022.

"**The Collapse of QuadrigaCX: What We Know (And What We Don't)**," De, Nikhilesh, and Anna Baydkova, CoinDesk, Feb. 6, 2019.

Exit Scam, Lammer, Aaron, May- June 2021: https://www.exitscam.show/.

"**FTX hacker reportedly transfers a portion of stolen funds to OKX after using Bitcoin mixer**," Bannermanquist, Judith, Cointelegraph, Nov. 29, 2022.

"**Chaos and hackers stalk investors on cryptocurrency exchanges**," Stecklow, Steve, Alexandra Harney, and Jemima Kelly, Reuters, Sept. 29, 2017.

"**The Crypto Story**," Levine, Matt, *Bloomberg Businessweek*, Oct. 25, 2022.

Chapter 13

Market Making

Elaine Song used to work at Okcoin, an exchange. New projects would launch and want to be listed, and she would work on making that happen. She was there starting in late 2018, after the wild heyday of the boom that peaked in 2017.

She never met the Alameda Research team or worked with them, but she heard about them. The folks at Okcoin were curious about how this small crew of very young people were doing so well out there.

The company was glad to have them on its exchange. Alameda was the kind of customer that every exchange wants. Scratch that, they were the kind of customer that is basically essential to make any cryptocurrency exchange work. Alameda, by then, had become a market maker.

Market makers serve an incredibly important role on exchanges. They keep trades going.

You can think of market makers as time travel machines.

That is, people need to meet in two different ways in order to make a trade: place and time. Let's say you have a cow and you want money, and I have money but I want a cow.

Someone in the Old West might set up an exchange for us. They would build a big stable where everyone knows to come and meet with their cows or their money. They might be ready to make change and keep order, and whatever else it took to facilitate that kind of thing in the wild days.

But a place isn't enough. We're both busy ranchers, right? Do we want to stand around all day, waiting for the right person to trade with to appear? No, we don't want to do that.

But imagine that there will be other players in the market who *are* willing to hang around. Those players will buy the cow when it first shows up and sell it to the guy with the money when he moseys in later. That person goes to the place (the market) and solves the problem of time.

The market helps us meet in space. The market maker helps us meet *in time*. That's why they are like time machines for trades.

So, odds are, if you go to a cryptocurrency exchange and you either buy or sell, you are almost certainly trading with a market maker. That's why there always seems to be someone around in exchanges ready to trade just about everything. There are people who make just that their whole business.

A market maker uses the platform just like everyone else, endlessly buying when people are making offers and selling that inventory when people want to buy.

The business model is simple: if the bitcoin price is $20,000, market makers buy at, *say*, $19,950 and sell at $20,050. That $100 profit on the spread can add up when making lots of sales a day.

Obviously, the price is going to keep moving around over the day, so the market maker keeps the risk neutralized by buying no more often than they sell. In fact, they probably match these moves up across multiple exchanges at the same time, making sure they have a full picture of the market and a greater diversity of traders to manage their risk.

Market makers also manage risk by how widely they gauge their spreads. A wider spread is less risky than a tight spread. Sure, they might miss some trades that their competitors take, but it also means that the next trade they *do* pick up will be on the correct side of the new price when it moves.

The danger for a market maker hits when the price moves quickly, and suddenly they are selling assets at a discount. The closer they list to the market price, the more likely this is to happen.

Alameda had become a market maker, but, as in so many things, the story goes that they had become something of a different kind of market maker.

Tamara Frankel knew the Alameda team early on, helping it get access to assets when it saw opportunities for trades. As Alameda was recovering from the loss of much of its initial capital when many of SBF's cofounders departed to start Lantern Ventures, Frankel was setting up her own over-the-counter (OTC) trading desk.

As Frankel tells it, they did a lot of work together largely before FTX, when it was still just one firm.

OTC desks are ways that large trades can be made without alerting the open markets. Basically, they happen over a phone call or a website. A person has to be vetted to get access to them.

On an exchange, every bid and ask is posted, and every trader sees the deals as they close, continually updating the market of what's happening with price. But OTC trades can be made without alerting retail traders.

But that story is a bit too simple, because, in Frankel's telling, everything about trading in that era was chaotic, and finding liquidity from one part of the world to another was a mess. In that mess, Alameda saw opportunity.

Many OTC desks seemed to basically operate at a fixed spread around the market price, something like a half a percent. Alameda came in and saw a fast way to start stealing market share: offer a tighter spread.

One of the things Frankel said she liked about SBF was that he was willing to be disruptive. She said that the whole OTC market was agog as SBF just came in and undercut the existing players. There were people out there just trading the difference between Alameda's desk and other desks and turning a profit. There was a decent chance that Alameda was taking a loss on those trades, but it was building up market share.

As Zane Tackett, an alum of several exchanges and, most recently, of FTX, told me, it's not like bear markets are a time when someone can't make money in crypto. It's different, but it can be done. The trading doesn't stop.

In fact, Jason Fang, of Sora Ventures, told me that tight spreads weren't Alameda's only fresh angle. Before they came along, most OTC trades happened on Telegram, the messaging app. You'd get into a private channel with the OTC desk and say what you wanted, and the staff would quote you a price.

Alameda set up an API, he said. You didn't have to talk to anyone, and it was faster. Your computer could talk to their computer, and the deal would get done without a word. Now lots of people do it that way, but Alameda was early to OTC by API.

That said, the tight spreads seem to have been key. At the end of the day, it's all about how much money traders can make, so this idea of keeping spreads narrow as a way to undercut competition would carry through all the way into beginning FTX.

Michael Feng runs a market making firm called CoinAlpha, and he also makes market making software called Hummingbot.

According to Feng, his firm had recently been testing a proprietary trading strategy and "we found if we used FTX as the centralized exchange, it was much better than using any other centralized exchanges," he said. "The reason is because FTX had the lowest fees, it had really tight spreads."

His take: it seemed as though Alameda were subsidizing liquidity for the most active markets (like for bitcoin trades) to make it an attractive place for high-frequency traders. How they made this happen or how they afforded it, we don't know, but during SBF's media tour after the great unwinding, he made it very clear that he was thinking a lot more about FTX's volume than he was thinking about risk.

As FTX launched in 2019, Alameda was crucial to giving new users someone to trade with. Caroline Ellison, the last CEO of Alameda when it shut down, talked about the early days of market making for the new exchange with a tone of remembered exhaustion on the *FTX Podcast*.

"I spent a lot more of my time thinking about providing liquidity on FTX. Just because I knew we basically had to be out all the time or maybe there would be nothing out in the order book. It was a huge challenge and not the most fun thing because the reward was like, yeah. . . if you do well. . . there's liquidity on FTX," she said. "As a trader the most fun thing is to—like—make money."

Later, Tackett told me that even as other market makers started to take up a lot of the volume as the exchange secured a solid customer base, Alameda was more willing to trade in the alt coins. They weren't worth the time for other market makers, but for whatever reason they were for Alameda.

As Feng explained, a new kind of market making business came on the scene in the midst of the decentralized finance boom of 2020.

Normally, there's just not enough business out there for most market making firms to bother with trading new tokens for free. New tokens, from a market maker's perspective, just aren't that interesting, especially after whatever initial hype wave passes. New tokens don't have enough volume to justify the work.

So token startups will hire a market maker and pay them to make markets for them across multiple exchanges. That way, if anyone did want to buy or sell their tokens, there would be a counterparty.

Token start-ups talk a lot about their bold vision for changing the world, but what their backers want to see early on is value increasing for the token price. The first thing that makes that happen is getting the token listed on different exchanges. In 2017 and 2018, that cost at least a million dollars up front just to land on each exchange.

Then a start-up would have to pay at least several hundred thousand for a market maker to provide liquidity on those exchanges.

But a new line of business opened up as Uniswap took off in 2019. I'll describe Uniswap more later, but basically, it was an open exchange on the internet. Traders didn't need to deposit anything to use it, they could just trade on Ethereum.

It was a so-called decentralized exchange. It wasn't the first, but it was the first to really catch on.

Anyone could list a token on Uniswap. It was permissionless. All it took was a deposit of the token and a deposit of ether equal to the value of the token. Then the market would work out the price from there.

This was a way to make a token available right away, so people could use it or trade it. This undercut traditional exchanges. It wasn't nearly as good as being listed in lots of places that had lots of really active liquidity, but it was *a place*. It made a token available to buy. Anyone could get to Uniswap from any internet connection.

So here's the new model that some market makers would offer in this new world: as Feng described it, a market maker wouldn't ask for a payment. Instead, they'd ask for a loan of the token that wanted liquidity and an option to buy that supply at a specific price sometime in the future.

In a way, this aligned the market maker with the token issuer. It gave the market maker an incentive to create a lot of liquidity and trade a lot of places, because that should drive the price up. If it went up, the market maker could close the position at a profit by exercising their option to buy what they had borrowed cheap.

"In practice, token projects are very confused about what market making is and what they should be doing from a liquidity perspective, so they hire market makers more for the advisory part," Feng said.

Alameda wasn't the only practitioner of this model. For example, Wintermute, one of the leading crypto market makers, cut a similar deal with MakerDAO, the scion of the decentralized finance world.

In Wintermute's proposal, it would return either 10,000 of Maker DAO's maker (MKR) token or 50 million usd coin (a stablecoin, each worth $1, pretty much always). In other words, if the maker token's value was more than $50 million by then, it could make a profit.

In Feng's telling, new token start-ups would take these deals because they felt cheap and they seemed easy. Also, in many cases, Alameda was one of their investors, so it was tough to say no.

MacLane Wilkison is the founder of NuCypher, a distributed encryption system that was one of the early ICO projects that came out of the era with a product and their reputation intact. "To the extent that any of my portfolio companies asked, I would tell them to avoid Alameda because of their reputation for abusing their seed round allocations," he told me over Telegram. "The 'Alameda special' of low-float, high fully diluted MC [market cap] projects where they insta-list a perp on FTX to lock in their profit then sell the unlocks into the ground was a common pattern."

I asked him about it, and SBF didn't really dispute this characterization of Alameda's work. "It would be too strong to say it's false. It's more complicated than that," he said.

It's no secret that new tokens often have an early moment in the sun, a brief inexplicable rise. It's just the opportunity for someone with an option to buy cheap. The early 2020s have been rich in new tokens, and Alameda had the perfect perch from which to sell them.

But SBF said they were arrangements that were more mutually beneficial than they are being described now, and that's where he disagrees.

As more sophisticated trading shops entered into the space and ate up the margins Alameda could get on classic market making, was it trying to find some other angle? Was this line of the business the sign of a prop desk that was flailing around for a new model?

For his part, SBF downplayed the importance of this kind of activity. "I don't think it *needed* to seek other lines of business. Like it didn't have to do anything," he said. "It is certainly the case that competition got tougher and, you know, up through 2021, while competition was getting tougher, sizes were also getting larger. And so those more than balanced out, and Alameda made a lot."

We know Alameda was doing a lot of things besides classic market making. And it was, as we shall see, for sure chasing lots of tokens.

Sources Referenced

Interview, Song, Elaine, Mobile, Nov. 29, 2022.

Interview, Fang, Jason, Telegram call, Nov. 28, 2022.

Interview, Feng, Michael, videoconference, Nov. 28, 2022.

Interview, Frankel, Tamara, mobile, Dec. 13, 2022.

Interview, Tackett, Zane, videoconference, Dec. 5, 2022.

FTX Podcast **#36**, "**Caroline Ellison Lead Trader at Alameda Research**," Yver, Tristan, *FTX Podcast*, Jan. 22, 2021 (unpublished, date based on Podtail record).

"**Wintermute Wants to Become MKR Market-Maker Via Governance Vote**," Dale, Brady. The Defiant, Oct. 1, 2021.

Interview, Bankman-Fried, Sam, phone call with spokesperson, Dec. 30, 2022.

Chapter 14

Beginning FTX

In October 2018, Sam Bankman-Fried was thinking about what's wrong with exchanges.

David Gan, then a venture investor on the team at another exchange, Huobi, was crashing at a friend's house during 2018's San Francisco Blockchain Week. His friend hosted a party while he was there for crypto enthusiasts, and that's where Gan first met SBF.

"I think I talked to him for 11 hours straight," Gan said. SBF just wouldn't stop, and he wasn't leaving as everyone else did.

SBF cornered him to talk about crypto exchanges, and what he thought about Huobi in particular. They talked about crypto exchanges and nothing but exchanges till dawn, even though trading wasn't what Gan was responsible for at Huobi. He thought then, and still does, about start-ups.

"I'm not that big of a trader. I didn't understand all the intricacies," Gan said.

But Gan said he found it interesting to hear all this detail about the exchange business and the minute observations about his employer's product from this obsessive trader.

Later, SBF produced a four- or five-page memo on what he thought about Huobi and how it could be better. Gan said he presented it to higher-ups at Huobi, but no one knew who SBF was then. The executives didn't take the memo seriously.

According to the CFTC account, SBF and his cofounder, Gary Wang, must have been already working on the software that would become FTX, with their developer team.

They moved to Hong Kong before launching, making the transition in 2019, because, as Business Insider recounts, the firm's former chief operating officer, Andy Coghan, said SBF thought they were losing out on $50,000 every day the team wasn't there.

Before long, SBF was fundraising to start FTX (the name stood for "Futures Exchange"). He pitched it to Gan, but Gan said that Huobi wasn't in the practice of backing other exchanges. Understandably. Gan said he almost invested from his personal funds but decided not to. At that point, he wasn't convinced he wouldn't be better off just buying ethers and bitcoin to get the upside of the eventual bull market.

Six months later, FTX posted its first tweet on April 16, 2019: "Hello world! We are here because we feel passionately about offering a futures product that can grow with the cryptocurrency market!"

The early tweets were largely about stablecoins. FTX's initial pitch was very much about collateralizing and settling its derivatives with dollars. The stablecoins it led with were true usd (TUSD) and usd coin (USDC).

Bitcoin was trading just above $5,000 when FTX launched. So if you wanted to take a 5X perpetual long on 1 bitcoin, you'd need to post your collateral in usd coin. A bitcoin wouldn't work. For perps, a trader needed that value in stablecoins. Then if bitcoin went up $100, you could close the position and exit with a fresh $500 in usd coin.

"We believe this is attractive to institutional investors as well as newcomers to the asset class," the official account tweeted on April 19.

It turned out that FTX was launching into a fraught environment for the exchange business.

Nine days after that first tweet, the New York Attorney General, Letitia James, would make one of the biggest crypto announcements of 2019: she had an investigation underway into iFinex, the parent company of both Bitfinex, a major crypto exchange, and Tether, the issuer of the world's largest stablecoin (then and now).

Stop me if you've heard this one before, but according to her petition to the court, Bitfinex has lost $850 million and was using Tether's reserves to cover up its losses until it could make the money back.

In other words, the solvent company in a family of related companies was accused of using its assets on hand—assets one could argue it was only stewarding on behalf of others—to cover for its sibling company. At the time, tether's market cap was a mere $2 billion, almost comically low compared to how big it has gotten since.[1]

For its part, FTX had fun with the news. It bought a URL: shortTether.com. It started tweeting it out to people talking about the controversy on May 2, 2019. It even tweeted the link to Bitfinex'ed, the notorious internet gadfly of Bitfinex and Tether.

Alameda would become the biggest holder of tether in the world by 2021, but when FTX started, iFinex still dominated the tether supply according to research by the crypto site PROTOS.

That said, by August, SBF would tell CoinDesk that FTX was processing between $50 and $300 million in tether volume each day across its 10,000 users, most of whom lived in China.

In July, FTX would announce its first seed round, for $8 million, led by Proof-of-Capital, with participation from Consensus Lab, FBG (a major Asian fund), and Galois Capital. Proof-of-Capital was led in part by Chris McCann, an alum of Greylock Ventures and today with Race Capital.

"Proof of Capital is honored to help the company go to market in Asia," said McCann, in a statement.

McCann and SBF would prove to be fellow travelers over the next several years. McCann had also been early into Solana, a blockchain that would power much of FTX's wealth, until it lost steam in 2021.

McCann and I, randomly, knew each other before blockchains even existed. We met in 2008 in Philadelphia. I wrote a little content for this

---

[1] The matter would resolve in 2021 with an $18.5 million slap on the wrist, when tether was pushing a $50 billion market cap.

start-up founded by two young women. He did some business development within an incubator they joined.

I never got paid by the startup. I doubt he did either. But we hung
out a few times. The start-up went nowhere. All that is just to say that I
was surprised to see his name when I started covering crypto full-time
in 2017. We've been in touch off and on over the years, and I messaged
him to get his take on Alameda and FTX in the early days.

No response yet.

Proof-of-Capital rebranded to Race when they brought on two more
partners and were trying to show that they were about more than crypto.

There's a deal memo that's been circulating online from FTX's first
fundraising round, from Race Capital, dated July 24, 2019. It was also
published in late 2021 on The Generalist, with Race Capital's permission.

The memo argued that FTX's key competitor as it entered the space
was BitMEX, the exchange that led in margin trading. BitMEX was
under investigation as the round was circulating, and the memo says that
FTX could capitalize that and also give traders more options.

BitMEX, they noted, was a bitcoin-focused exchange. FTX would
offer new products that would excite traders, such as stablecoin futures
(especially tether) and fun index products (such as its shitcoin index[2] and
the exchange token index—more on exchange tokens in the next chapter).

Somewhat presciently, under "risk factors," the Race Capital team
noted issues related to the Alameda Research and FTX relationship.

"It is unclear how much of the time Sam will dedicate to Alameda
vs. FTX. Given the speed of execution we believe there will be dedica-
tion to FTX; however, it remains to be seen," it says.

Also, it notes, "Alameda will be the initial market maker for FTX
itself. The team intends to bring on more market makers over time;
however, this is a major risk. We have talked to other quantitative hedge
funds who are hesitant to trade on FTX for this reason."

Several investors have said to me or said in the press that they passed
on FTX for this reason.

But FTX touted its ties to Alameda as a competitive advantage. A
sponsored post on CoinTelegraph reports, "The crypto exchange adds
that it is backed by Alameda Research . . . FTX argues that its offering

---

[2]"Shitcoins" is a term for new cryptocurrencies without much of a track record. As the name suggests,
many of these are not very promising.

is hard to replicate because of how many of its unique selling points depend on Alameda's expertise."

Alameda was crucial to the firm for another reason as well: it had a bank account. According to the SEC's complaint against the firm, when FTX started it directed users to deposit their dollars into both an Alameda bank account and, later, into another company it owned called North Dimension.

It kept doing this until sometime in 2021. Customers' funds would go in, their accounts on FTX would get credited, but they would remain at the disposal of Alameda.

The complaint alleges that "in quarterly balance sheets that [Caroline] Ellison prepared, and that were provided to Alameda's third-party lenders, Alameda tracked this liability as a 'loan,' but did not specify that the 'loan' was from FTX."

This would become the notorious "fiat@ftx.com" account that would be later blamed for much of the hole in FTX's balance sheet.

Anyway, FTX's first attempt to raise money was a bit ham-fisted. The Block has reported on a fundraising round where it sought a loan from investors that it would pay back with a 15% rate of return. This document is noted to have said there was no risk, though SBF walked that back at the time of the solicitation, saying they did it too fast.

"Saying no risk was a fuckup, we should not have put that in our deck," SBF wrote in a Telegram group chat where the solicitation appeared. I spoke to one investor who got this pitch at the time but wasn't interested in doing a loan deal.

Though this document has been widely reported on, SBF told me in December that he could only remember one investor taking the deal. Another source told me that they knew of one, which could be the same person. "We did not have the sort of relationships or contacts at the time or reputation that would've made that plausible," SBF said.

A little later, after Alameda had a bit more of a track record, he said the firm would turn to larger lenders, such as Genesis Trading, which has a lending unit, to finance its trading.

We do know about the seed round, but no one really thinks about that $8 million seed round check much, though. On the *Acquired* podcast in early 2022, McCann says that they had trouble getting pickup from other funds. Their co-investors were mostly traders who could see the potential.

"The biggest hiccup that most funds had was they were launching FTX, but Alameda was going to be the market maker in their own exchange. This was like a cardinal sin in the eyes of other investment funds," McCann said.

Whatever support they did get on that loan offering, it was important, but it didn't signal anything. They weren't investments that people took note of.

The first check into Alameda that *really mattered* came at the end of the year, when Binance—now the largest exchange in the world—backed the young company.

"We see quite a bit ourselves in the FTX team and believe in their potential in becoming a major player in the crypto derivatives markets," CZ, Binance CEO, said in a press release posted to the company's blog.

It sounds like this wasn't just diplomatic talk by an investor glowing up a founder in his portfolio. Harry Halperin, founder of the privacy project Nym, told me that he met SBF around this time, at a Binance event in Singapore. SBF was walking around with CZ, looking a bit like a protégé.

"I only remember Sam because of, to be frank, the hair," Halperin said. CZ knew there was a token in the future for Nym, so he suggested to Halperin that he consider Alameda as their market maker.

"CZ was very friendly toward him," Halperin said, as if he "considered him part of the larger Binance family."

CZ didn't announce how much he invested in FTX,[3] but still: this was the round that got the world's attention. It was something like being knighted by the king. Yet, the relationship between the two acronymic CEOs would only last about 18 months.

Three years after investing, CZ would sink FTX with a tweet.

Sources Referenced

Interview, David Gan, video conference, Nov. 22, 2022.

"CFTC Charges Sam Bankman-Fried, FTX Trading and Alameda with Fraud and Material Misrepresentations," press release and complaint before the US Southern District of New York, Commodity Futures Trading Commission, Dec. 13, 2022.

---

[3] The CFTC's complaint said Binance bought a 20% stake.

"**Attorney General James Announces Court Order against 'Crypto' Currency Company Under Investigation for Fraud**," New York Attorney General, April 25, 2019.

"**FTX founder Sam Bankman-Fried gets by on 4 hours' sleep and multitasks on 6 screens. Insiders break down what the 29-year-old crypto billionaire is really like—and the tough questions facing his company**," Huang, Vicky Ge, and Kari McMahon, Business Insider, Dec. 15, 2021.

"**Bitfinex Covered $850 Million Loss Using Tether Funds, NY Prosecutors Allege**," De, Nikhilesh, CoinDesk, Apr. 25, 2019.

"**Cryptocurrency firms Tether and Bitfinex agree to pay $18.5 million fine to end New York probe**," Browne, Ryan, CNBC, Feb. 23, 2021.

"**Tether Papers: This is exactly who acquired 70% of all USDT ever issued**," Protos staff, PROTOS, Nov. 10, 2021.

"**Why Tether Volume Is at All-Time Highs**," Cuen, Leigh, CoinDesk, Aug. 29, 2019.

"**Crypto Derivatives Platform FTX Raises $8 Million in Seed Round**," Shome, Arnab, Finance Magnates, July 8, 2019.

"**FTX raises $8 million for cryptocurrency derivatives exchange and trading platform**," Takahashi, Dean, VentureBeat Aug. 6, 2019.

"**Binance Announces Strategic Investment in Cryptocurrency Derivatives Exchange FTX**," Binance Blog, Binance.com, Dec. 20, 2019.

"**Sam Bankman-Fried: Why I Bought Back Binance's Shares in FTX**," Hamacher, Adriana, Decrypt, July 22, 2021.

Race Capital deal memo, July 24, 2019.

"**FTX Trilogy, Part 2: Speedrun**," Gabriele, Mario, The Generalist, Aug. 8, 2021.

"**Crypto Derivatives Platform Vows to Tackle Socialized Losses Seen on Other Exchanges**," Blenkinsop, Connor, Cointelegraph (sponsored), May 24, 2019.

Securities and Exchange Commission v. Caroline Ellison and Zixiao "Gary" Wang, United States District of New York, Dec. 21, 2022.

"**This little-known firm with a weird website was central to the misappropriation of FTX customers' money, regulators say**," Morgenson, Gretchen, NBC News, Dec. 27, 2022.

"**Alameda promised 'high returns with no risk' in 2018 pitch**," Chaparro, Frank, The Block, Nov. 11, 2022.

"**Race Capital, Crypto Investing, and FTX + Solana's Early Days**," *Acquired* podcast, Jan. 26, 2022.

Chapter 15

For That, This (FTT)

I t's frequently said digital assets don't have any purpose and anyone who buys them is foolishly opting into a Ponzi, but that's not true. At least the first part isn't true, the part about the purpose.

All cryptocurrencies are good for *at least* one thing, and the Samglomerate was institutionally geared for just that thing. They are all good for trading, and trading is something that lots of people like to do.

It's like playing a video game, except some people make money off trading while actual gamers only spend money on video games.

Most people don't make money trading—at least not over time, but some do. But those that don't at least get to play the game of trying to get better, joking around with other traders in text chats, and trying to find their distinctive trick.

As long as retail traders are playing with money they can afford to lose, trading is a quirky corner of the economy, like birdwatching, Instagram influencing, vinyl record collecting, and competitive dog grooming.

It doesn't make sense to most people as entertainment, and it doesn't make sense to me, either. But neither does watching golf on television, and that's worth $700 million a year to the PGA.

The volume of trading is what SBF and his retinue liked about cryptocurrencies. As far as I can tell, this is the only aspect they *actually* liked. New people kept coming in, volumes were going up, and there was free money to be had for teams with focus and a war chest.

And yet, despite the fact that SBF and his cohort didn't actually buy into the message of Bitcoin and the larger crypto world, it was inevitable that they would launch some kind of token.

The opportunity to create something that had real dollar value from nothing would not be one this crew could resist.

★★★

So you've probably heard that bitcoin is anonymous, right?

And then you've probably *also heard* that it's totally *not anonymous.* That any such promises are a myth.

But then you've probably also heard stories of, say, some guy stealing many millions of dollars' worth of bitcoin, and no one can find that guy. Which . . . sounds anonymous? Doesn't it?

It's money on the wind, which seems like it was anonymous? The messages are confusing.

Whether or not bitcoin (and its ilk) is anonymous is kind of like the question of who killed JFK. No one has a decisive answer about it, but anyone with a strong opinion sounds a little crazy once they start talking.

So.

Forget about all that.

Let's talk about the other side of the question: transparency. The transparency of blockchains is what makes the anonymity question tricky. But it *also* makes the verifiability question simple, which is way more important to far more people.

In fact, let's just talk about transparency and money in general.

Did you know that in Sweden the tax returns of everyone are public? It's very easy to find out how much someone earned in the prior year there. Pause here for a moment and ask yourself: How does that make you feel?

Imagine that it would be very simple for any of your friends, any of your neighbors, any of your coworkers to find out what you made.

Imagine you had had some windfall, perhaps an inheritance, and you bought something that didn't seem extravagant but did seem unusual. Now, how would it feel for you to know that others could see if you really had had some kind of bump that year?

It's different, right?

So on blockchains it isn't quite like that, *but it's close.*

Let's think about it a different way: What if there were a record of all the bank accounts in the world but all the names on the bank accounts were hidden by default?

Perhaps in such a world, *some people* (and some organizations) publicize their names. Most do not. But every time someone spent money, that would be shown on this giant balance sheet of every single bank account in the world.

Every time you or anyone spent anything, that would appear somewhere in public. People might not know it was you and they might not know what you got in exchange, but they would see the money move.

How does *that* make you feel?

That latter scenario is the blockchain world. Every transaction is in public. You usually can't see what people bought with their cryptocurrency (unless it was some other cryptocurrency), but you (me, the state, the FBI, anyone) can see all the flows of the funds themselves.

Imagine, for example, you had a boat that I wanted, and I had magic elf money that you wanted. The blockchain would log the fact that I sent you some magic elf money. It would not log the boat. The boat is invisible to the blockchain.

But, for now, not many boats are getting sold for magic elf money.

Mostly, people are trading one kind of cryptocurrency for another. Or playing weird financial games with it.

If, for example, I had magic elf money and you had magic dwarf money, we could trade. Both transactions would show on-chain. Someone might surmise that it had been an exchange.

So blockchains are places on the internet that keep track of all the digital money people spend, who has it, and where they send it.

Someone with enough determination and resources can *often* pin names to blockchain addresses, even if their owners try to hide their identities. This is why blockchains aren't perfectly anonymous. Some folks still manage to hide well, but the point is that all the transaction action happens in public.

Does that feel weird?

It is weird, but it helps us to get to a little bit of this story that we might not otherwise be able to get. Not many people inside Alameda or FTX are talking, but the blockchain is.

We are going to start with the token that enabled much of the success of Alameda and FTX, but also the token that also turned out to be their weakness: ftt (FTT), a token on Ethereum.

We've talked about tokens already, but let's look closely at one particular kind of token. It's one of the few kinds that we know really have a niche in the market. Those are exchange tokens (FTX even had an index devoted to exchange tokens).

These tokens are issued by cryptocurrency exchanges to lock customers in. They are the crypto version of a loyalty card at a coffee shop. Instead of giving the user free coffee, though, they *attempt* to share revenue.

They also get the user discounts on trading fees. If you have enough of an exchange's token in your account, you will pay less to trade. That can be really nice for people who trade a ton.

A lot of times, they also have funny little perks. Like maybe the exchange hooks token holders up with releases of new tokens from projects that want users (so-called airdrops)? Or maybe they make digital blockchain art that they only distribute to people with their tokens (NFTs)? Or maybe they have parties at conferences that only allow people with the token inside (tickets)?

Those are all benefits for the users. There's also a pretty huge benefit for the exchange because it keeps users coming back. But the big benefit of an exchange token to its creator is the same benefit that spinning up a token has for any crypto start-up: it allows them to spin money out of thin air.

And it can turn into real money. Take the exchange token for Binance, the largest crypto exchange in the world. Its token is bnb (BNB). It's now the fourth-largest cryptocurrency by market cap. According to CoinGecko, it hit the market at 10¢ in late 2017. Amid late 2022's bear market, it's trading around the $300 range.

Investors like to talk about making 3X returns, 10X returns, but that's STUPIDX returns, that's how much that is.

It should be noted that trading volumes are much thinner than they are on something like ether or bitcoin, but bnb is still a very big asset.

Really, exchanges and crypto start-ups don't use tokens that much to cover operational costs. Those free funds are better used as a way to accelerate growth. The question is this: Does the exchange founder use their exchange token like coffee or does he use them like cocaine?

FTX used its exchange token like cocaine.

So FTX's exchange token was called ftt. They created a total supply of 350 million of these tokens (hopefully that doesn't sound like a lot—the number of tokens just doesn't really matter on its own) and set aside 175 million of those for the company, according to the SEC's complaint against the firm.

The company tokens could not be sold all at once. It would unlock gradually over a three-year period (which ended in July 2022).

FTX sold a bit over 73 million of the tokens ahead of time, for anywhere from 10¢ to 60¢. Then the company had a bunch set aside for various purposes, like tokens for insuring users, tokens for attracting users, and tokens for funding projects that would be good for the value of ftt.

This is all very normal.

Once the token was live, people could buy it on FTX, and later it would appear on other exchanges too. For a power user of FTX, it paid to hold ftt because of the discounts on trading fees on the platforms. Every little part of a percentage point frequent traders can take off their margin was crucial.

Traders that committed to not sell ftt (this is called "staking") could get more perks, such as opportunities to buy new tokens (initial exchange offerings).

For people who really believed in FTX over time, though, it had another feature that it copied from the tokens of other exchanges (such as Binance). The ftt token offered a *sort of* revenue share with users. Every week, FTX took 33% of trading fees (and a couple other sources of revenue), bought ftt off the open market, and set it on fire.

That is, they would destroy the token. Doing so shrank the supply.

Dollar cost averaging

Dollar cost averaging is an investment strategy that undermines the temptation to attempt timing the market (that is, only buying at lows and selling at highs). A dollar cost averaging investor invests a fixed amount at regular intervals, ignoring price when they do so.

For example, they might buy $100 of bitcoin with each pay-check, every other week.

Crypto investors who have dollar cost averaged through any three- or four-year period have consistently done quite well.

The idea here, broadly, is that if demand stays fixed, burning ftt should drive up value for each token that remains. Before the collapse, it was buying and burning about $2 million of ftt a week.

The largest single burn ever, in ftt terms, was November 11, 2020, when they burned 434,000. But the biggest single week, in dollar terms, was in May 2021, when it burned $10.2 million in ftt.

If this all sounds like something that would have drawn scrutiny from the US SEC, yes, it would have. In fact, when the SEC updated its complaint against SBF on December 21, 2022, it specifically said ftt was a security, bringing it under its purview. But FTX's exchange token was not available to people in the US, technically. There were ways around that of course, but the company took measures to avoid offering it here.

US users got hold of the token, nevertheless.

Astute readers will note something else. FTX is centralized. In Chapter 9, I wrote that usually tokens were used to fund projects that ran themselves on a blockchain. FTX was very much not autonomous, though. It was a centralized company that operated more like Charles Schwab than any of these newfangled DeFi products.

Not every token was made for a decentralized product, and not every buyer even understood the difference.

We can have a debate about whether or not exchange tokens are really a good idea, but they are nearly standard practice in the industry at this point (though US-based Coinbase and Kraken don't have them).

That may not last forever. It's a young industry, but ftt is illustrative in the larger FTX story for another reason.

Here, as the SBF crew launched the ftt token, theoretically for FTX, they did it in a way that would stand forever as an immutable testimony on the blockchain. Their mistake would be an eternal testament to the fact that—while FTX and Alameda might have separate banking accounts and some distinct paperwork—they were, for all *practical* purposes, one operation. One Samglomerate.

Nansen is a company that provides tools for crypto investors to do analytics on-chain more easily. Mainly, people use it for watching the moves made by the richest people on the blockchain so that they can copy them.

The people at Nansen are good at very advanced blockchain analysis, though, and they like to do deep dives unpacking major events because that drives attention to the platform and shows off the fancy things it can do.

So naturally they published a deep dive on the FTX meltdown. They found something eyebrow-raising right at the start of the ftt story.

First of all, tokens get governed by a smart contract that runs on whatever blockchain hosts the token. In those days, everyone was launching tokens on the Ethereum blockchain, and that's where ftt lives as well.

A large portion of the total supply of ftt was not distributed at the beginning. According to Nansen's account and FTX's transparency page for the token, half the total supply, 175 million ftt tokens, would unlock over a three-year period. When that happened, the unlocked tokens would always go to the same wallet at first, one that was designated as an Alameda wallet, by Nansen.

So this looks strange. Why was it that it appears that all ftt were controlled by Alameda? Particularly if they are completely distinct companies that operate "at arm's length," as Alameda CEO Caroline Ellison put it in an interview with Bloomberg.

It's emblematic of how little barrier there was between the two companies. And this shows us a lot about the transparency of blockchains. Records are made there, and they stay there forever. Some event can get a timestamp on a blockchain, and people might think nothing of it at the time, but it will always be there when they want to look again.

But also it's in a flood of other information, so it might be hard to notice. Which also indicates something about anonymity. It's not impossible to find out who made each and every transaction, but it's not easy, either.

In many cases, no one ever does. But sometimes people do, and sometimes, once investigators can uncover the absent context missing from the simple record of transactions, blockchains have wild stories to tell.

Here's how SBF explained it when we spoke in December. "FTX never owned many ftt tokens, or any ftt tokens, in fact," SBF said. "Effectively, Alameda got ftt. [That] is the right way to think about it at the beginning of the day."

The relationship, he said, was less complicated when FTX first launched. "In mid-2019, neither Alameda nor FTX had any outside equity investors at all. And so at that point it was sort of irrelevant."

The funds raised in the early sale of ftt were going to Alameda. SBF said that this was basically paying Alameda back for turning over most of its senior executives to FTX for a while to get it launched.

"One way you can think of it is basically the right to sell that or issue that was given to Alameda in exchange for all of the work that Alameda did, setting up early FTX," he said.

I don't know about you, but that is not a way I would have ever thought to think about it.

Sources Referenced

FTX FTT page, archived, Nov. 10, 2022: https://archive.ph/R6Jtz.

"SEC v. Sam Bankman-Fried," US Securities and Exchange Commission complaint before the US Court of the Southern District of New York, Dec. 13, 2022.

"Crypto Quant Shop with Ties to FTX Powers Bankman-Fried's Empire," Massa, Annie, Anna Irrera, and Hannah Miller, Bloomberg, Sept. 14, 2022.

"FTX Has Made $34M in Trading Fees since Recent FTT Token Burn Despite Withdrawal Freeze," Knight, Oliver, CoinDesk, Nov. 10, 2022.

"Blockchain Analysis: The Collapse of Alameda and FTX," Khoo, Yong Li, et.al., Nansen, Nov. 17, 2022.

FTT burns, The Block: https://www.theblock.co/data/crypto-markets/exchange-tokens/ftt-burns.

Interview, Sam Bankman-Fried, phone call with spokesperson, Dec. 30, 2022.

Chapter 16

Uniswap and Decentralized Exchanges

In summer 2017, a certain category of person was getting very excited about cryptocurrency. A lot of them, who already had some, were excited because they were getting richer without doing anything.

Others believed that the ICO sales at that time would eventually make them even richer than the old bitcoin guys, if they got in soon enough.

However, there was one person who was not at all excited about cryptocurrency. Hayden Adams had been laid off from his job as a mechanical engineer at Siemens, and he wasn't sure what he was going to do. One thing he definitely didn't care about was crypto.

But with a little encouragement from a college friend, Adams would start to learn coding on Ethereum for want of something better to do. Eventually, his attitude would change and he would leap into crypto, a field he knew nothing about before he started learning to engineer it.

He would build an extremely basic version of what would eventually become the decentralized exchange, Uniswap.

Next, he would have a small piece of amazing luck: Adams would meet Vitalik Buterin, Ethereum's creator. Meeting Vitalik would eventually land Adams a small grant from the Ethereum Foundation to get Uniswap off the ground.

There are only two true mononyms in crypto: Satoshi and Vitalik, but Satoshi is gone. Vitalik remains, and while crypto is full of gurus and cult figures, Vitalik is bigger than any of them. He is now more prophet than guru.

As a decentralized exchange, or DEX, Uniswap was a robot on the internet that would trade any token it listed for any other token it listed. Unlike on an exchange like FTX, traders weren't trading with each other: they were trading with the DEX, a piece of software on the Ethereum blockchain that didn't need any day-to-day involvement by humans to operate.

A DEX where traders traded with the DEX itself was called "an automated market maker (AMM)" (more on this further down). Uniswap wasn't the first of its kind. That was an AMM called Bancor. Bancor had managed to raise over $150 million in crypto in a 2017 ICO. The ICO sold a new token called the Bancor network token (BNT), and Bancor required BNT to operate. Doing it that way turned off Ethereum users at the time. Uniswap built a DEX that drove demand for ether, which aligned it with Ethereum fans.

So Bancor got the early money. Uniswap got the early users. Bancor never got many users, but it got to keep the money.

The existence of a functional DEX would be key infrastructure for Ethereum's next mini-boom, because that made it possible to quickly move funds between different projects without leaving the Ethereum blockchain. In other words, users could control their own money, on-chain, and move their funds around between experiments start-ups were building *without* using an exchange like FTX at all (which would slow down their flow).

These sorts of users would simply buy cryptocurrency on centralized exchanges and then move it out as quickly as possible, to play around on-chain, without any need to trust anyone but themselves.

The way automated market makers work is strange, but it's worth explaining. It's exactly the kind of model that, crypto believers argue, could never blow up in the way FTX did.

Decentralization

Decentralization can really only be understood by using it; fortunately most people use it every day (they just don't think about it this way).

Email is decentralized. Anyone can deploy the email protocol on a server and send and receive email with any other email server.

Maybe you're someone who uses multiple messaging apps, like me. You have Telegram and WhatsApp and Facebook Messenger and WeChat, etc. These apps can't send messages between each other because they are all centralized architectures (whereas SMS, or "short message service"—texting—is much more decentralized).

We can also imagine decentralized data. For example, imagine if there were one big global database of TV listings that stations all over the world could use to post what's on.

Those stations could tap into the database to show their own schedules on their own website, but other companies could build apps for different purposes.

One app to help you see what's on when you travel around the world.

Another app to help you find specific kinds of niche television content.

TV creators might also build an app on top of the database to help them negotiate licensing deals between each other. In fact, one could imagine all kinds of applications of a decentralized dataset like this.

A hallmark of decentralization is this: strangers can come in and use it to build new applications that the original architects might not have thought of.

The degree to which others can publish to the dataset is another hallmark of decentralization. For example, you would only want TV stations to publish to the TV database, but you could still leave it open. Certain feeds could be vetted by known TV stations, and that would simply be a piece of the data. Non-vetted inputs would just be ignored.

> The blockchain industry is pushing to bust more data out of its lockboxes so creative developers can find ways to build multiple useful apps on top of each open dataset.

The point of a DEX is simple: users can always know funds are there because they can see the funds on-chain. Again: "Don't trust, verify."

In fact, a person doesn't need to put any of their own funds at risk just to make a trade. No deposits are needed for folks just swapping cryptocurrencies, unlike on an FTX, Coinbase, or Binance.

When you trade with an automated market maker, it's like you're trading with someone standing right in front of you, it's an internet robot that's always ready to make a deal. You hand over exactly what you want to trade, and it hands you exactly what you are trading it for. And it's done. The trade is over, with no counterparty risk.

DEXes have depositors, but the depositors are investors, not traders. The depositors do it because they earn a little bit on each trade the DEX makes.

So here's a way to think about how DEXes such as Uniswap and Bancor (and PancakeSwap and Pangolin and DODO and the many other imitators) work.

Let's imagine that everyone in crypto is a wizard.

Picture all these wizards walking around in a fantasy-like world, like *The Hobbit* or *Shrek*. In this world, the key to power is magic stones. Magic takes all kinds of magic stones that do all kinds of different things, and there are loads of magic stones all over the world. Some are more or less rare, more or less useful, but magic stones are all over the place.

Being a wizard is all about having lots of stones of lots of kinds, having the right stones at the right time, and knowing how to mix them together and use them. You can just go out and find magic stones, but if that's all you do, you'll never do any wizardry.

So most wizards trade stones more than they gather them, and therefore, there is *an economy* of magic stones.

Some wizards with magic stones to trade will go out among wizards they know and trade directly, but this is an inefficient way to trade. So a few business wizards set up magic stone stores and shops and exchanges.

Places where they facilitate the stone trading. But sometimes these wizards cheat. Or they get robbed. Or they run away with the stones.

But before long some enterprising wizard decides to use magic itself to solve the magic stone trading problem.

He finds a certain combination of magic stones to create a magic place for trading magic stones. He puts it in a big open field with a big pedestal in the center of it.

Once he decides it is ready, he invites a bunch of his wizard friends who have a lot of magic stones to come watch him demonstrate his new stone swapper.

On the appointed day, they all gather round and watch as he sets a bunch of his stone holdings on the pedestal, makes a gesture, and the stones start floating in the air above him.

Then he takes a stone out of his pocket (a blue one), sets it on the pedestal and touches a symbol for another stone that's been etched into the pedestal (a yellow one).

His blue stone floats up, and two yellow stones float down. He picks the two yellow stones up and pockets them.

Then he tells his friends that this is the new way to trade stones.

He also tells him that his cloud of stones in the sky works better the more stones it has. So he invites his friends to put their extra stones in the cloud too. The cloud takes just a little bit of stone out of every trade as fees.

All those fees are shared out among the people who put their stones inside, so, if they do it and they wait, they'll have a little more stones than what they put in when they come back to take their deposits out.

So wizards start joining in. They've all got more stones than they really need anyway. They go up to the pedestal and drop a bunch of stones in. When each one does it, the pedestal spins up a fresh new stone. That stone, the entrepreneurial wizard explains, is their deposit claim.

They could trade that, too, if they want.

One of the wizards asks how the cloud of stones and the pedestal know the right price to trade at.

The creator explains: the price is determined by the ratios of the stones inside. The pool he had just traded had twice as many yellow stones as it had blue stones, so the price was two yellow for one blue. Simple.

The cloud of magic stones floating above grows and grows as wizards catch on. Then they all start trading stones just for fun. Lots and lots of trades take place. Then one wizard goes to withdraw his deposit and, sure enough, he has just a little more.

And if a wizard ever wanted to check that his deposit was still there, he could just set his deposit token on the pedestal, and the cloud would show him all his tokens, plus whatever fees he'd gained. They could check as often as they liked. They could even check everyone else's deposits, to make sure it all added up, as it should.

And this new marketplace didn't need the wizard who made it to run. It would operate on its own, forever, autonomously, as long as it had stones to trade and interested traders. The cloud changed everything in the world of magic wizard stones.

And this is basically the story of the search for a decentralized exchange on Ethereum. DEXes were a direct challenge to exchange companies such as Binance, Huobi, and FTX.

That's why it's kind of weird that the first time Sam Bankman-Fried showed leadership in the larger cryptocurrency industry, he did so to save an AMM.

It wasn't Bancor he popped up to save, even though by then its defeat by Uniswap was almost complete. And it wasn't Uniswap he saved, either.

He popped up to save the DEX designed to take Uniswap out of the game.

Sources Referenced

"**Hayden Adams: King of the DeFi Degens**," Foxley, Will, CoinDesk, Dec. 8, 2020.

"**$150 Million: Tim Draper-Backed Bancor Completes Largest-Ever ICO**," Higgins, Stan, Alex Sunnarborg, and Pete Rizzo, CoinDesk, June 12, 2017.

"**Bancor Bounce Back? ICO Is Winning Adoption**," Dale, Brady, CoinDesk, Feb. 18, 2018.

"**A David vs. Goliath Battle Is Brewing in Ethereum Decentralized Exchange Race**," Dale, Brady, CoinDesk, Feb. 20, 2019.

Chapter 17

DeFi One Billion

In May 2018, the team behind the aspiring crypto lending company Dharma organized a party in San Francisco that might have been the progenitor of the term "DeFi" for "decentralized finance." At the time, Dharma was working on making a protocol that would provide loans on Ethereum.

They weren't alone in envisioning ways to bring traditional finance online. Other future stalwarts of the nascent industry would join them at that gathering, companies such as the Maker Foundation, Compound Labs, 0x, dYdX, and Wyre. These were the companies building the new robots on the internet I wrote about in Chapter 9.

Not our future AI overlords, but maybe our future AI savings and loans.

Brendan Forster, a cofounder of Dharma, told me once that these groups were starting to realize that they fit into a distinct portion of the blockchain industry. Crypto was becoming big enough that it wasn't one thing. It was breaking up into specialties, and DeFi was one.

But it took a while for others who didn't come to that shindig to see it.

A year after Dharma's party, in New York City, the founder of crypto data firm Messari, Ryan Selkis, was on stage at a conference called Ethereal, in Red Hook, Brooklyn, with Joe Lubin, founder of a weird crypto conglomerate called ConsenSys. Lubin was also one of the many founders of Ethereum. Folks in the know believe he's the largest holder of ether in the world.

Selkis pressed Lubin, asking him whether Ethereum wasn't trying to be too many things. Lubin's firm was well known for pursuing a vision where Ethereum would be used for decentralizing web applications such as social media and music fandom, but Selkis felt like DeFi alone had the potential to be a trillion-dollar market. So maybe, Selkis suggested, Lubin and his cohort should focus a bit?

"If you think about Ethereum as programmable money and decentralized finance applications, that's probably good enough," Selkis said in my report for CoinDesk on the encounter.

And the next year, in 2020, DeFi certainly would become the big crypto thing.

There are five key developments in the history of DeFi: the launch of bitcoin, The DAO, the initial coin offering boom, the realization of stablecoins, and—finally—liquidity mining.

Most people don't think of the first three parts as critical history of DeFi, but they are. The most basic function of finance is to create a medium of exchange that abstracts out all barter and debt. In other words, payments.

Bitcoin showed the world a path to payments using nothing but 'net.[1]

Then this thing called The DAO came along, and it attempted to create a hedge fund on Ethereum, run by a bunch of strangers. It was an interesting but poorly executed idea. People put in millions and millions in funds and got tokens that could vote on what The DAO should do with all of its money.

The DAO, famously, got hacked, though. Those millions were pilfered. There are three whole books out there already, largely about just that.

So Ethereum recovered the stolen money by returning to an old save point on the great video game of crypto. It was a hard fork. An

---

[1] Internet, that is. Bitcoin doesn't look like it will be a medium of payment, but it showed how it could be done.

unthinkable move, but they did it. And then The DAO was shut down. Don't worry: the hacker still made a lot of money. It was too late to stop that.

A year later, though, Ethereum would do The DAO again in a distributed fashion. There is very little difference between the ICO boom and The DAO when you think about it. ICOs were just The DAO exploded across the whole blockchain. The DAO asked everyone to buy in, get a token, and then decide what to invest in.

The ICO boom turned the whole of the Ethereum blockchain into a DAO. Holders of ether could turn it into other tokens that reflected bets on specific Ethereum applications, and they would get new tokens for each of those bets. If they didn't like any of the bets, they could just sit on their ether and bet that some of the applications would work and drive adoption of Ethereum itself.

And if later they decided they didn't like a particular bet, they could sell their tokens—no need for a silly governance vote in one big DAO. Everyone could just vote the way Adam Smith intended, with their feet (or their smart wallets).

ICOs succeeded where The DAO failed, with billions changing hands, lots of rug pulls, but no more hard forks. Sure, the ICO model would be found wanting, but developers would keep experimenting. The idea of using tokens for capital formation kept evolving even as ICOs fell out of favor.

The money market, EthLend, which would become Aave, had run an ICO. All of its LEND token would later be wiped out for the new AAVE token as it iterated further.

The synthetic assets exchange, Synthetix, had also run an ICO, but it also wasn't known as Synthetix then. It started as Havven, and it was trying to roll out a stablecoin, but it pivoted.

It's ironic that Havven became Synthetix, because the next key development for DeFi was the stablecoin bonanza that was just about to start in 2018 and has persisted to this day.

For a long time, people doubted stablecoins were even possible. Sure, there was iFinex's stablecoin tether, but tether was sketchy, and no one wanted to follow where it had led. However, in December 2017, as the rest of the market was going mad about bitcoin, MakerDAO quietly released the first version of dai (DAI).

Dai is a remarkable thing in DeFi. In its simplest form, it's a collateral-backed stablecoin designed to match the value of the US dollar, one-for-one. At a deeper level, dai enables lending.

A user deposits some asset on MakerDAO, and then they borrow dai. But the dai does not exist before the loan. The dai *is created* in that moment of the smart contract making the loan to the user.

If that sounds crazy, well . . . it didn't blow up, and that seemed to make others want to try their own stablecoins.

By the end of 2018, companies were launching them frenetically. Paxos, Gemini (the company founded by the Winkelevoss twins, the brothers famous for financing the founding of Facebook) and Circle/Coinbase would all launch their own stablecoins.

All of theirs were simpler than dai. They were all directly backed by dollars in a bank account, working like tether but bragging about their regulatory friendliness. Someone could deposit a dollar, and the company would issue them a token on Ethereum that represented that dollar.

If a user gave the stablecoin back, the company would return the dollar.

Those stablecoins have largely worked, and together the various flavors of stablecoin provided a retreat to value for traders on Ethereum. It also opened up a lot of new products for DeFi entrepreneurs.

Take Compound, which launched in late 2018. Compound kicked off as a lending application for people who were long some token. An investor could deposit that token in Compound, and it would earn a small amount of interest, like any bank deposit.

Of course, most people didn't stop there. Anyone who made a deposit had the right to borrow some other token that some other Compound user had deposited, because deposits doubled as collateral loans.

What did people usually borrow? They borrowed a stablecoin, because the borrower always knew what their debt would be that way. If the borrower borrowed a volatile coin, they risked it shooting up in value, either making their debt harder to repay or causing the protocol to take their collateral and exact a painful fee.

With applications like this, the pieces of DeFi were coming together to make a new kind of financial system. The insiders could see it. To outsiders, it just looked like crypto was reinventing finance all over again. And it *was*, but it was reinventing it with all the positions out in the open.

Sort of. Sure, all the data about it was there on-chain, but it was gob-bledygook to read. It was data, but it was illegible, so it wasn't really *information*.

Fortunately, one little group of DeFi enthusiasts had a helpful idea. They noticed that all these different DeFi protocols had something in common: they gave people a way to earn yield on their digital assets when such people entrusted their funds to these new internet robots.

The value of all those deposits could be measured at any moment and expressed in dollar terms. So they spun up a website called DeFi Pulse that showed the collective value of all the stuff locked in DeFi software at any given time. DeFi Pulse called that "total value locked."

Now, maybe it was because that week everyone was mad at partners at venture firm Andreessen Horowitz for banning handshakes in their offices amid concerns about COVID-19. It's hard to remember now, but when total value locked hit a billion dollars on February 7, 2020, hardly anyone who wasn't running a DeFi app seemed to notice or really care.

DeFi was a compelling idea, but even with these pieces in place, it wasn't *exciting* yet. One more innovation was needed.

Someone needed to invent a real version of what SBF called "the box" on that notorious *Odd Lots* episode.

Someone needed to invent liquidity mining.

Sources Referenced

"**One Billion, Two Billion, Three Billion, Four? DeFi's Knocking on TradFi's Door**," Dale, Brady, CoinDesk, Sept. 14, 2021.

"**The Big Question at Ethereal Summit NY: Is DeFi Enough for Ethereum?**," Dale, Brady, CoinDesk, May 10, 2019.

"**What was The DAO?**" Cryptopedia Staff, Cryptopedia, Powered by Gemini, Mar. 16, 2022.

"**What Is Synthetix? Ultimate Guide to SNX**," Makori, Josiah, CoinGecko, Sept. 12, 2022.

"**An overview of stablecoins**," Staff, Multicoin Capital, Jan. 17, 2018.

"**Silicon Valley VC firm Andreessen Horowitz is asking visitors to avoid hand-shakes due to the coronavirus outbreak**," Hartmans, Avery, Insider, Feb. 7, 2020.

"**Why DeFi's Billion-Dollar Milestone Matters**," Dale, Brady, CoinDesk, Feb. 7, 2020.

Chapter 18

Rationalist Line of Thinking

I f there's a simple way to describe just one thing that people in the Effective Altruist, rationalist, utilitarian, nerdy-about-probability culture that SBF came out of do that confuses people, it's this.

In any conversation or debate, they have this way of zooming out of the terms presented to them.

Imagine if they were talking about things such as:

- Should Austin create a light rail train system?
- Should height restrictions be removed on buildings in San Francisco?
- How much money should the United States spend on pandemic response?

People in SBF's world have this way of backing up from a question first before even considering it. This can be disorienting to those who aren't familiar with the move, but it's basically in the water for how such folks think and talk.

What they are doing is applying what can be thought of as "Bayesian reasoning," after Presbyterian minister Thomas Bayes (1701–1761), who described how to think about probability that has been latched onto (and often very lucratively applied) by a certain kind of geek.

Used less formally, it shifts how a person views the world and how they discuss it. A Bayesian approach, it is thought, helps them be a little more rational and a little less emotional. Practitioners can seem robotic at times, but it's a technique that tends to yield thoughtful outcomes.

To wildly, wildly oversimplify Bayesian reasoning as applied to day-to-day life, you can think of it this way: "Zoom out from any decision, and ask yourself what you might be missing, and then zoom in."

Said another way, don't let the framing of a question limit your answer. There could be a lot of useful information the question itself seems to be nudging you to ignore.

To put this in Bayesian terms, suppose someone presents you a question, and you make your first guess about your answer. This is your "prior." It's what you think before you do any work.

Then you gather evidence. Crucially, you don't go looking for evidence that supports your point. You go looking for evidence that tells you more about the question and allows you to make guesses about the outcome of different choices.

You might find that evidence shows you you had missed something. So then you update your guess about the best outcome. This is your "posterior."

In practice, people end up talking about "priors" a lot, but I've never heard anyone talk about a "posterior."

Just to give one example. Imagine I were debating building a light rail system in Austin. Most people would simply hear the proposition and ask themselves, "Do I want to ride a train, and how much will this cost me in taxes?" and that would be their whole analysis.

A Bayesian, even a selfish Bayesian, might first ask the question: "How many people don't have cars, how many of them live along the train route, and how many people might get rid of their cars if they had an alternative? Finally, what might the greater mobility of the former do for the local economy and what might the transition of the latter do for traffic?"

My *prior* might think, in fact, that everyone has cars in Austin, so there's no real reason for a train, because hardly anyone would use it. The only people who would use it would be folks who wanted to show their virtue by being a train rider, which isn't a good enough reason to build an expensive train.

But then they might do some research, and perhaps they find that Austin, which has about a million people, has about 50,000 working-age people who don't actually have personal vehicles (this is a made-up number). If the working-age population follows the national average, then that would be something like 8 percent of the potential Austin workforce.

He would have learned that it's not true that "everyone" has cars. His initial model has to change. They have to "update their priors," in the lingo.

But the important point is this: Bayesians don't decide what to believe about the world from evidence, but they do let evidence update what they believe.

Uncertainty will never be eliminated. At some point, people have to make a call. The rationalist view is, however, that you should try to update your basic beliefs as much as possible using evidence before making that call. Take as much gut feeling out of it as possible, and *then* go with your gut.

Crucially, try to articulate priors, and see if any of them create blind spots.

In the myth of SBF, he talks about the moment when he had quit working at the investing firm Jane Street and decided what to do with his life next. On the *80,000 Hours* podcast from April 2022, he talks about doing a bit of BOTEC (back-of-the-envelope calculation) about the likelihood that different options he might like to pursue could have a high impact on the world (his possible choices: journalist, political pro, EA movement fundraiser, entrepreneur, investment banker, or crypto trader with his own fund).

"I just got out a piece of paper and wrote down what are the 10 things that seem most compelling to me right now, and evaluate the expected value of each of them, just ballpark it," he said. That is, he put a dollar value for the impact he thought he might have.

Then he quickly realized that while a lot of the options he came up with looked pretty good, he only really had great information about one of them: going back to Jane Street and trading more.

For the rest, he asked himself how long it would take to get some idea of whether or not he was having impact. He realized that it could take a long time to find out if journalism or politics was doing any good. It could take years. Trading crypto on his own, however, he could assess that very quickly.

"This was one of these things where in a month I was going to be able to significantly investigate this, and figure out how good it was going to be. The reason is, you just try trading and see if that made money—and if it didn't, then that's that," he told Wiblin.

This is a good example of this kind of Bayesian thinking in practice. Faced with a series of choices that all have a high degree of uncertainty, make a choice on which one requires the least amount of time to investigate.

I'm not, in fact, convinced that this actually happened, but even if SBF didn't actually do the BOTEC, he did *think* that way.

In the world of SBF, no concept loomed larger than expected value. That is, the potential value of something discounted by the probability that the valuable outcome can actually be achieved.

Expected value can just as easily be flipped around to expected risk. They are no different. And managing risk, SBF believed, was his great skill.

After the fall, in his interview at the *New York Times* Dealbook summit, he would admit, "Clearly I was not nearly cautious enough from a downside perspective," he said, while adopting this sort of scared animal pose. "In my head I was looking at a 30 percent down move over a three-day period as an extreme tail case event" ("tail case" means unlikely).

In other words, he was saying that he bet his whole company on a world in which the value of crypto assets couldn't suddenly fall.

"When things get really bad," he admitted in retrospect, using the soft-spoken voice of a bookish teenager who found himself in the principal's office, "they get really bad for all the relevant correlated things at once in a very direct and correlated and quick way."

As I listened to this interview, I made a note to myself that I didn't believe him. I don't know quite what he was hiding, but I didn't think he was being honest about not foreseeing a hard turn in the market that would go against Alameda and FTX.

Perhaps it's not that he didn't know it could turn that hard. It's just that he didn't think the market would do it so soon.

Whether or not SBF told the *New York Times* the truth, we know SBF *had* seen enormous downturns before. He saw one in 2018. And he saw one briefly right after DeFi hit its billion-dollar milestone in 2020. Only a month later the blockchain markets would face a shock in the opposite direction, one of the worst days in crypto that believers had ever seen.

Of course the Samglomerate wouldn't need to learn any lessons in March 2020, because it still just didn't care which way crypto went. At that point, the team was still set up to make money whichever way the market moved, and that was a great position to be in.

The firm would be in a very different position today if it had just stayed that less lucrative but also less risky course, but it didn't.

Sources Referenced

"**Bayesian inference**," Wikipedia, last update, Nov. 14, 2022.
"**Sam Bankman-Fried Interviewed Live About the Collapse of FTX**," Sorkin, Andrew Ross, New York Times Events, YouTube, Nov. 30, 2022.

Chapter 19

Black Thursday

It's almost as if the blockchain gods gave everyone a warning that the next upswing would take a dark turn.

It was March 2020. The world had accepted the reality of a global pandemic, many people were coming down with COVID-19, hospitals hadn't learned to cope, and horrific imagery of straining health care systems was on the news every night, but people in the crypto world were facing the disease a bit more stoically than the rest of the populace of the US, partly because crypto's most notable had been sounding warnings about the disease since December.

They had been castigated in the press for being paranoid or worse, but they had doggedly masked up their Twitter profile pictures and stood their ground far earlier than the mainstream. So when March came and the general populace was rapidly moving from denial to acceptance of COVID-19, crypto people were a stage or two ahead. Instead, they were watching the global markets.

Blockchain types were in denial about something else, however. They were in denial about the broader economy dragging crypto assets down with it. That's something that people in the space tend not to be well prepared for. The notion that digital assets were uncorrelated with the rest of the market was breaking down.

Once when SBF went on Bloomberg's *Odd Lots* podcast, he told the hosts, "An interesting thing about crypto and the ecosystem. So one thing is: everyone is bullish in crypto, on crypto, and that has a massive impact on the ecosystem," he said. "Any way that people can find to get longer, they will."

Venture investor Haseeb Qureshi told me that SBF had said just this to him, as well, but more as a thing that baffled him, because no other market saw itself that way. And SBF never fully bought it, either.

And that dispassionate disposition would serve him and his firm, Alameda, well because the markets would break down in an especially bad way on March 12, 2020. That day is now known, especially to users of Ethereum, as Black Thursday.

We may never know exactly what happened on those days. Markets everywhere were destabilizing as a profound uncertainty was setting in. No doubt some of the big money that had come into crypto was getting out, and many retail traders were certainly following their lead.

Everyone was jittery.

Then it happened. From March 11 to March 12, the price of Ethereum's ether would fall from $198 to $102 in a matter of hours. Bitcoin would fall from around $7,900 to $4,700. Absolute chaos would break out within exchanges and on-chain as traders rushed to minimize losses and blockchains choked on the demand to push transactions through.

Unlike chaos in other markets where it's a word that anchors say on the news but just seems like an abstract concept to anyone listening, this was a sort of chaos that blockchain users could actually feel.

That's because blockchains are a finite resource. In particular, the number of transactions a chain can finalize per second is limited. This is one of the things that is hard to adjust to for newcomers, because we are so accustomed to an internet that seems to have infinite space for the data we want to shove into it—whatever it is, wherever we are.

For blockchains, though, every transaction has to be simultaneously copied everywhere in the world that's running that blockchain, so transactions have to be logged in a very deliberate way. This is the price blockchain users pay for a system that's totally open and completely public.

When there's an acute uptick in demand for access to the blockchain, it's often effectively impossible to get through. Users were trying to send bitcoin or ether to exchanges in order to sell for their local currency, but they *couldn't* send their deposits.

Transactions were just sitting for hours waiting their turn while piles more transactions came in behind them. There was no "block space" for them. It's the internet equivalent of 1,000 people at the door of a bank that only has three bank tellers.

Savvy blockchain users knew that you could skip the line by paying a high price for access to blocks, but even that method wasn't working as easily as it should. It was a traffic jam of ephemeral, invisible bits of code worth billions of dollars.

But for normal people, well: Have you ever been using a computer and you get that spinny wheel, and it just goes on and on, and you get that helpless feeling in your chest like you can't move? Except you can move. It's this disembodied untouchable thing inside the laptop screen that won't move. You feel paralyzed, but you don't need to move your body. You need data to move.

Well, imagine that exact same frustration but it has $1,000 or $1,000,000 tied to it? That was how thousands of folks felt on March 12, 2020.

One place where it was felt particularly acutely was on the grand old standard bearer of decentralized finance, MakerDAO. MakerDAO was what made the dai stablecoin that I described in Chapter 17. Dai was designed to hold its price steady, basically equal to $1.

It was thought of as the most decentralized, the most "crypto" of stablecoins, because it was run by a smart contract, and every aspect of its operation could be inspected on Ethereum at any time.

The important point here is that it made loans. The loans were collateralized. Under dai's rules, if there was too much debt and too little collateral, then the collateral would be sold before the collateral was worth less than the debt.

So when the price of crypto falls (especially ether), some loans go bad on MakerDAO. When that happens, some dai needs to disappear. Some debts need to be wiped. This happened just about every day. It was a normal part of the process.

But on March 12 it happened more than it had before.

To liquidate a loan backing some dai, a lot of digital hammers need to clang on various blockchain bells that yank on a series of cypherpunk ropes. It all needs to happen at once and in the right order, and at the end of it, a few people are poorer, a few people are richer and—most of the time—*the system comes out fine*.

It should hurt. But it shouldn't *fail*.

The trouble was, on March 12, everyone who'd ever given a few minutes' thought to Vitalik Buterin's brainychain was trying to use it that night, and nothing could get through.

So loans were going bad, but—and this is the key point—they weren't getting wiped.

Someone out there had been counting on this, waiting for this. Those opportunists had a plan ready to trick MakerDAO and make off with several million dollars' worth of crypto money, and their dastardly scheme worked. They had a script ready to close out bad loans with high gas fees but no actual bid to pay them back. How this all worked isn't worth going into here; all that needs to be said is that they had thought ahead about an edge case, a time when things weren't normal.

And so, by the time things settled down, MakerDAO was undercollateralized by $4.5 million.

That meant 4.5 million dai were *no good*. It had $4.5 million in bad debt on the books.

Which 4.5 million dai? Who could say? There were about 113 million dai in the world on March 13, which meant about 4% were no good.

This sounds bad, right? At the time, it looked that way. I saw it that way. I wrote about it that way at the time, but, looking back on it, this was really good. MakerDAO was in trouble here, but everyone knew instantly. It was all out in the open. No lies. No cover-ups. Just a problem to be solved.

This was DeFi's transparency put to the test, live, in real time.

Now, remember what we said about FTX's token, ftt, before. It was the magic token that SBF spun up to make his users like his exchange better. Its chief feature was the fact that the exchange burned some of it every week, making the supply just a little smaller and (in theory) the value of each one that remained a little greater.

Well MakerDAO had a similar setup. MakerDAO is governed by holders of its maker (MKR) token. Maker has a value like dai does, but maker's price is free floating. It reflects the value people place on the overall MakerDAO system.

If dai ever gets in trouble, like it did on March 12, maker holders come to the rescue by *printing more maker*. Dai is purchased with the maker printed, and the dai is burned. This gets the system back on track. In that way, it's just the opposite of ftt.[1]

Just as burning ftt increases the value of what remains, printing maker decreases the value of everyone who holds that token. So it hurts maker holders, but it's better than everyone losing faith in the MakerDAO system (because that would really hurt maker holders). This is the risk they accepted when they bought maker. This is one of their "jobs," to take that hit.

So MakerDAO printed $4.5 million worth of maker, bought the excess dai, and threw it in the trash. Problem solved. The token lost some scarcity, but the system remained solvent.

That's always how I think of Black Thursday: the day that MakerDAO had its most severe stress test to date, but other people remember it differently.

Former co-CEO of Alameda Research Sam Trabucco has fond memories of that day. "It was the best trading I have ever seen for the most part, but there were still a lot of scary moments," he said on the *FTX Podcast*.

The traffic jam of transactions got very severe, such that he describes how there were a lot of trades he wanted to make, but they just couldn't

---

[1] MakerDAO also has a worst-case-scenario solution that goes even further, which basically amounts to a hard reboot, but so far it has never had to use it.

get capital to where they needed it to be fast enough to make the buys they wanted.

"There were a ton of people who would have loved to buy bitcoin when it was $1,000 lower than everywhere else, and on its death march to zero, or whatever people thought was going to happen, us included," he said.

Normally Alameda made short-term trades, he said, but prices got so low at that point they took some long-term bets, at least as much as they could pick up in time.

In Trabucco's telling, "It was awesome."

So SBF's company had institutional memory that the crypto markets can turn very hard and very fast, but perhaps they didn't learn the lesson because instead of losing on Black Thursday, like so many had, inside Alameda it was just another day of wins that only served to make SBF and the firm that followed him cockier.

Sources Referenced

"**The Ex-Jane Street Trader Who's Building a Multi-Billion Crypto Empire**," *Odd Lots*, Bloomberg, Apr. 1, 2021.

Interview, Haseeb Qureshi, Mobile, Dec. 2, 2022.

"**Recent Market Activity and Next Steps**," MakerDAO blog, March 12, 2020.

"**The Market Collapse of March 12–13, 2020: How It Impacted MakerDAO**," MakerDAO blog, April 1, 2020.

"**DeFi Leader MakerDAO Weighs Emergency Shutdown Following ETH Price Drop**," Dale, Brady, and William Foxley, CoinDesk, Mar. 12, 2020.

"**Sam Trabucco on Trading 2018–2022**," The *FTX Podcast* #121, Sept. 16, 2022.

Chapter 20

Liquidity Mining

Very quietly, in February 2020, a guy named Andre Cronje—largely unknown at the time—published a Medium post about releasing iearn.finance, a set of smart contracts that were meant to be a simple way for him to start managing his stablecoins and earning a little more off them.

That iteration, iEarn, sought yield.

Basically, he had figured out that he could make more money investing in stablecoin dollars and sticking them inside various new DeFi projects than he could sticking fiat dollars in banks. Also, Cronje was the kind of guy who liked finding strategies for making extra money and, because he was a programmer, he liked to automate them.

So he wrote smart contracts that would move his stablecoins around as needed each day, chasing the best sources of yield. This was old-fashioned yield, just plain old interest on deposits or fees on trading.

With that Medium post, he invited other people to also deposit their stablecoins in iEarn and ride along on his strategies with him.

The post is a funny post, because he makes no effort to sing the praises of what he had built. Usually, a launch post in crypto (and tech in general) is so loaded in ebullient spin that it can be very hard to discern what the launched product actually does, but most of Cronje's first iEarn posts complain about how much he spent on gas fees to deploy his smart contracts—zero hype.

Nevertheless, and this was not at all evident yet, Cronje had built a yield-hunting robot that would turn into maybe the most influential community in all of DeFi—at least that year.

Meanwhile, Robert Leshner, the founder of Compound, a DeFi money market, was starting to talk about the next phase of his project. Now 18 months old, his smart contract lender had found decent product-market fit. Lots of money had been loaded up on Compound, and lots of money had been lent out. Despite that, all Compound Labs, the company behind it, knew about any of its users were their Ethereum wallet addresses.

Think of Compound this way:

> Imagine there was a guy who would make loans in dollars on the street of your town, but he was no loan shark. He only made loans on collateral, like a pawn broker. All you had to do was walk up to him and give him a piece of gold. He'd weigh it, stick it in his pocket, and give you two things: a ticket that would let you get your gold back when you repaid the loan and he gave you the cash you wanted to borrow, there and then. No further questions asked.
>
> He never even asked your name. You took your money, made your loan, handed you a ticket and walked away. In fact, you could give or sell that ticket to someone else and if they walked up to him and repaid the loan, he'd give them your gold.

That's basically how Compound works. So Compound (and Aave, a very similar project) might be thought of as an internet pawn broker.

In Spring of 2020, Leshner was saying he was ready to "decentralize" Compound, to share out the authority over how the product evolved. He announced that Compound was going to release a token, called comp (COMP).

Previously, I wrote that eventually tokens weren't sold. They were given away to users. This is the moment when that trend really got going.

Comp was a governance token. Its holders would have the power to make changes to the protocol that was Compound's smart contracts. They could add new assets. They could quit supporting assets. They could change the way the system decided yields paid on users' deposits.

It was a lot of *power*, but that was all comp was for. Comp only did governance. Holding it didn't get you a cut of the revenue on the platform. It didn't get you a special chair at Compound's parties or a seat on the board of Compound Labs.

There would be no NFTs.

The token only gave users the right to create rules for this blockchain pawn shop. If users wanted it to someday start shaving money out of the system and paying themselves, they'd have to write code and vote to do it.

Compound Labs, which had sole control of Compound at that point, announced a fixed supply of comp. Then it also announced that it would give away a large portion of it over four years to all of its users.

In fact, it would give comp both to people who made deposits *and* people who borrowed.

(Obviously, a lot of that comp was also set aside for Leshner, his investors, and his team—this was that new business model for start-ups in action.)

I wrote a story about Compound's plans to decentralize in February for CoinDesk, where I quoted Leshner as saying, "We're one of the few companies that are pioneering the idea of continuous and progressive decentralization."

This language echoed that of the former director of corporate finance at the US Securities and Exchange Commission, William Hinman. In 2018, he explained in a speech in San Francisco why he thought Bitcoin and Ethereum were "sufficiently decentralized," such that "applying the disclosure regime of the federal securities laws to current transactions in Ether would seem to add little value."[1]

This *seemed* like very good news. Crypto entrepreneurs started looking for ways that they could make their projects reflect Ethereum itself.

---

[1] This speech has become very fraught. It's worth googling "Hinman" and "Ripple." The SEC's antics around the speech since then and what the speech meant in terms of SEC policy really beg for comparisons to clown cars.

It didn't really work out that way. Even as I write this, there's not much in the way of clarity about which tokens are securities and which aren't. Nevertheless, the SEC pushing token project creators to do these mental calisthenics might have been the best thing to happen to many DeFi founders.

To be honest, when I broke the news that Compound was going to drop this token, I was a little ho-hum about it. Leshner's star was rising, so I took his word for it that comp was news. But I thought, Another token? So what?

Remember how I wrote that in 2017 the industry didn't get what tokens were for yet? I didn't either.

Here's how comp's distribution worked. The team had set aside over 4 million of their finite, fixed supply of comp to be distributed to all depositors and borrowers on its platform. Every block, it would distribute some of the token pro rata to everyone with deposits and loans on the platform, favoring the pools with the most demand. It still is.

Depositing on Compound is a kind of yield farming. Depositors get paid based on the borrowing people do. So that's yield. DeFi investors would trade and move assets around seeking the best yield deals.

Compound, however, was now also giving a new token to people who provided liquidity (and also people who used that liquidity), so it came to be called *liquidity mining* (because "mining" has become shorthand for any action that earns fresh new crypto).

Liquidity mining was a new wrinkle on yield farming. In fact, it ended up being the only kind of yield farming anyone would really seek out for the next year or more.

When Compound Labs actually released comp in June 2020, the market took to it aggressively, instantly. Soon I was writing stories about all the ways that demand for comp was causing weird bursts of activity elsewhere in DeFi, on protocols only tangentially related to Compound.

I had been wrong about comp, and I spent the next couple months writing stories showing just how badly I'd misjudged it—it was lots of fun. Since the downturn in 2018, crypto had been very nearly boring. Here, something was happening again. Lots of things were happening. It was like someone had shot a Mogwai with a firehose, and I was kind of hoping someone would feed the resulting little guys after midnight.

For example, Curve was a DEX/AMM (like Uniswap) that specialized in stablecoins. I hadn't paid much attention to Curve. Just as I hadn't understood comp, I also didn't understand what was so interesting about a DEX designed specifically for the most boring kinds of cryptocurrency: stablecoins.

Curve had one trading pair, tether and usd coin, that had skyrocketed in volume since comp launched. Curve's volume went from $3.5 million per day to $23.3 million in three days.

Users were borrowing tether on Compound and trading it for usd coin on Curve in order to deposit that and borrow more tether to do it again (because that maximized the amount of comp they could earn on both the borrow and lending side). In other words, people were *leveraging* deposits on comp just so they could earn more comp.

As soon as comp came out, its price started climbing far higher than I expected it would. Somehow the price in my head that made sense for comp was something like $40.

It quickly broke $100—*wrong again*.

In a few days, it would break $300, but not for long. It wouldn't go that high again until the New Year, but suffice it to say its price stayed well above $40. In fact, it's only fallen down that far again at the end of 2022.

Folks piled funds into Compound, borrowing as much as they could against those deposits, depositing what they had borrowed and borrowing again. Then a protocol called Instadapp released systems that would automate all these operations with smart contracts.

Here's when I knew that things had gotten really crazy with Compound: a person could borrow money on Compound and make money off the outstanding debt. That is, the comp earned in each block was *worth more* than the interest accruing on their debt.

Obviously, it all seemed a bit mad, but I came to think of it like this: imagine if a bank that ended up being huge one day had offered equity to its depositors early on. Wouldn't that early equity have outsize value? Of course it's hard to know which new bank will be bigger than another, but with Compound it was easier. There was hardly any competition yet.

It was amid the comp furor that I spoke to SBF for the first time. Up to that point, I barely knew of him. I had wanted to write about the shitcoin index on FTX, but I never got around to it.

Leshner had told me that FTX was about to list comp perpetuals. This meant that traders who wanted to bet that the price would rise or the price would fall had a way to do it with leverage.

When I spoke to SBF, he described FTX then as "primarily a derivatives exchange." He walked me through how futures worked and how perpetual futures are useful to traders who want to make educated guesses about what the right price for an asset is.

It struck me that he seemed happy to walk me through all this stuff. He seemed both excited and unhurried. I always feel like an idiot when I need to talk to someone about derivatives, and perpetual derivatives hurt my head.

In the story I wrote for CoinDesk, I quoted him talking about the horse race between different DeFi tokens, but that wasn't the part of the interview that stood out for me, personally.

At the end of our conversation I asked him how long it would be until the comp perpetuals market went live. He said, "About five hours."

These guys, I thought, move fast.

Meanwhile, iEarn creator Andre Cronje had been using Compound as one of his places to get a little extra interest on his stablecoins. He was yield farming, taking his tokens, and he was moving them between fields of yield, wherever it grew better from day to day. Compound was one of several spots his coins frequented. At that time, all he was growing, though, was more stablecoins from stablecoins. That is, if he planted dai, he got more dai.

Cronje had put out iEarn in the early part of the year and gotten a bit bored after a while. At a certain point, he had just let his protocol run and, in his telling, went back to playing World of Warcraft.

But Cronje hadn't anticipated how much more stimulating liquidity mining would make yield farming. Earning this fresh new token was a whole new source of yield, but also a whole new wrinkle. What should iEarn do with the comp his stablecoins earned?

Comp was a little soupçon for his liquidity, except it wasn't little at all. It was by far the biggest thing that happened in crypto in 2020. This was either a whole new kind of yield or the market was kidding itself.

So here's what Cronje decided: his machines would just farm the comp and dump it for more of whatever stablecoin his users had invested. That was his way, and his users were raking in a lot more stablecoins than they had before.

And of course, it didn't stop with Compound. Before long, every DeFi protocol of note and lots of complete nonsense, opportunistic and buggy thrown-together side projects, had some sort of liquidity mining program—tokens were spinning off lots of robots on the internet.

Before, yield farming had been a way crypto could beat sleepy returns in tradfi savings accounts and money markets. After liquidity mining, yield farming felt like a secret path, one people needed to do as big as they could as quickly as they could, before everyone else caught on.

"It was basically the only thing that mattered for most of the summer," SBF told me when we spoke in March 2021.

But former Alameda co-CEO Sam Trabucco put it a little more cinematically on the *FTX Podcast*. He said, "Alameda exists as a quant trading firm in crypto because that's where the money is, but then yield farming popped up, and that's where the money was."

SBF told me that the fact that Alameda moved into yield farming as fast and as hard as it did spoke to something fundamental about the company.

"There are not that many players that operate quite the way Alameda does," SBF said. When Alameda saw a good move to make, it didn't go into it gently, he said. "Actually the right level of big is pretty big," he said. When Alameda saw something that looked as lucrative as yield farming did, Alameda didn't ease in. It pivoted and did so hard because it knew the faster it moved, the larger its share of the take would be.

"I think that's maybe the thing that there might be the least competition for," he told me. "When there's conviction about a thing and you can manage the risk and being able to do it big."

This statement should shed some light on the events of 2022.

Everywhere anyone knew the difference between the basic attention token and rep, that Summer 2020 had become known as DeFi Summer. All the DeFi founders' machinations had finally begun to click with the Ethereum audience.

To be honest, "click" isn't really the word for the sound liquidity mining made in the market. It was more like: "Cha-ching!"

Sources Referenced

"**Things I wish I knew before building Ethereum #DeFi dapps**," Cronje, Andre, Medium.com, Feb. 4, 2020.

"**Compound Extends DeFi Ethos to Itself, Launches Governance Token**," Dale, Brady, CoinDesk, Feb, 26, 2020

"**Compound's Approach to DeFi Governance Starts with Giving Away COMP Tokens**," Dale, Brady, CoinDesk, May 28, 2020.

"**Expanding Compound Governance**," Leshner, Robert, Compound on Medium .com, May 27, 2020.

"**Digital Asset Transactions: When Howey Met Gary**," Hinman, William, Director of the Division of Corporate Finance, US Securities and Exchange Commission, June 14, 2018.

"**COMP's Sudden Growth Has Swamped a DEX Dealing Only in Stablecoins**," Dale, Brady, CoinDesk, June 16, 2020.

"**Some Numbers That Show Why Yield Farming COMP Is So Seductive**," Dale, Brady, CoinDesk, June 25, 2020.

"**FTX Releases COMP Derivatives to Keep Up with DeFi Frenzy**," Dale, Brady, CoinDesk, June 18, 2020.

"**Andre Cronje: DeFi Expressionist**," Dale, Brady, CoinDesk, Dec. 8, 2020.

"**The Erica Show EP4: Andre Cronje, Architect of Yearn**," KryptoSeoul, YouTube, Sept 30, 2020.

"**#121: Sam Trabucco on Trading 2018–2022**," Yver, Tristan, *FTX Podcast*, Sept. 16, 2022.

Interview, Sam Bankman-Fried, videoconference, Feb. 8, 2021.

Chapter 21

DAO Is the Way

Here's a weird idea that definitely wouldn't work in the real world but sort of does on blockchains.

Imagine having stock in a company, such as Pepsi. In this world, stockholders have one of two options. They can just sit on it and hope the company does well, like stockholders do now.

Or they can go to work at the company. If they do that (here's the kicker), their work would be remunerated not based on what they did but on the amount of equity they held in Pepsi.

In 2020, crypto people were starting to realize that tokens could be used that way—kind of. They could be treated as a sort of dual-use asset within a crypto project regulated by code, not by law.

In 2017, entrepreneurs thought tokens were like arcade tokens, keys to access cool tools online, but that approach never clicked.

By 2020, a new idea was taking hold: governance tokens. That's what comp was. Robert Leshner, the founder of Compound, has always been clear about this when I talked to him. He only wanted comp to control Compound. He didn't want it to do anything else.

If tokens were becoming a tool for governance, then something else was happening, too. A previously verboten idea was returning to polite crypto conversation: the idea of decentralized autonomous organizations, or DAOs. Tokens are the building blocks of DAOs.

DAOs may be one of the most idealistic concepts in crypto. The first DAO of any note also led to one of crypto's biggest disasters. The first important DAO was called "The DAO." It was an attempt at running a decentralized hedge fund before Ethereum was really ready (I mentioned it earlier). The DAO was founded by a company named Slock.it that aimed to build an internet-of-things system that worked with Ethereum, but they needed investors. After flopping with traditional venture capital investors firms, Slock. It's leadership decided to spin up their own pool of backers from thousands of strangers on the internet (in the hope they would choose to back Slock.it).

As I said before, The DAO was a disaster. It nearly wrecked Ethereum. Here's what I didn't say, though. Before the hack, The DAO assembled a pile of ETH (12.7 million, the equivalent of $150 million at the time, $15 billion today). For every ether anyone deposited, they would get 100 DAO tokens that they could use to vote on what the whole DAO would invest in.[1]

As people started to get their DAO tokens, they immediately started to have value. Pretty soon, 100 DAO tokens were worth more than 1 ETH, suggesting that the market saw that assemblage of money and expertise as worth more than what it had on deposit.

The human capital and the crypto capital were being considered together, and the market was trying to find a price for that collective. Writing about it was the first time I had really grappled with a notion of a token. The potential was alluring, but people also seemed a little too excited.

Full disclosure, I wrote a post at the time that aged more poorly more quickly than anything I've ever written about blockchains: "The DAO: How the Employeeless Company Has Already Made a Boatload of Money," published May 20, 2016, on Observer.com.

---

[1] DAO tokens could also be redeemed for ether at any time.

We've already covered the rest. It got hacked. It was a disaster. Nothing good. Though blockchains were meant to be immutable, Ethereum forked, and the DAO hack was wiped away—mostly. The old chain still runs as "Ethereum Classic." It has had a hard time since.

The DAO died. Slock.it disappeared in an acquisition by Blockchains, LLC.

Then, in July 2017 the SEC sat the entire blockchain industry down, gave it a thorough scolding, said it was disappointed, and asked it to promise not to do it again.

The DAO's creators never should have used the definite article. The Fates hate that.

So people in crypto eased off this concept for a while. No one talked about starting DAOs again for at least two years, but late in 2019 the lid started to come off.

See, crypto people had been hot for this idea of organizations that existed exclusively online and got business done with internet money since roughly 2013 when Dan Larimer described a "decentralized autonomous corporation" (a DAC) on the forum Let's Talk Bitcoin. Larimer is someone who seems able to see the future, but only ever part of it. Nothing he launches comes out quite right, though it often seems *directionally* astute, like a railroad that builds tracks between mountains without a plan for making tunnels that go through them.

Larimer's idea for a DAC was basically a robot on the internet that could perform some kind of function, much like the DeFi applications we see today. The DAC could pay for certain services it needed, such as validation or security. The only way it could pay, though, was by issuing more shares of its underlying crypto asset.

This is, in a way, how one can think about Bitcoin. There's only one thing Bitcoin needs, and that's for lots of people to attempt to validate its blocks. When someone succeeds in doing it under the rules of the Bitcoin system, Bitcoin pays them by issuing new bitcoin.

But this conceptualization is cold, robotic, and there are no people anywhere.

People on the Ethereum blockchain rejected the idea of a DAC. Ethereum people are very nice and friendly. They have a whole different character than bitcoiners. Ethereum adherents wanted coordinated *humans*; Ethereum wanted *organizations*.

DAOs were for people who used tokens and smart contracts to coordinate with each other. If you imagine that a DAO is like a nation, this is a world in which citizenship is tradeable. Anyone can be a citizen if they just control one of its tokens—of course, in this system, one person can be more of a citizen than another person, all they need is more tokens.

In theory, DAOs can be fairly leaderless, flat, and fluid, which is all very nice, but really the most important thing about DAOs is this: they have money, lots of money. When a DAO is created, the entrepreneurs behind it endow it with a native token, keep some for themselves, but usually leave a lot of it in the control of the DAO itself.

This is usually called the "development fund." The idea is that if the early work of the founders is any good, then they can drive a bunch of value to that token. By the time the community takes over, that fund will be worth real money. If that fund is worth real money, people will want to take over.

This just seemed like a hypothesis when DAOs started stretching their legs a couple years ago, but—to say the least about the most—it is very much a real thing now.

Lots of DAOs are going concerns. Are they "working"? That remains an open question.

But are they rich? Yes. So far. For now.

Sources Referenced

"**DAC Revisited**," Larimer, Dan, Let's Talk Bitcoin, Nov. 2, 2013.

"**What Was The DAO?**," Cryptopedia Staff, Cryptopedia by Gemini, March 16, 2022.

"**Report of Investigation Pursuant to Section 21(a) of the Securities Exchange Act of 1934: The DAO,**" US Securities and Exchange Commission, Release No. 81207, July 25, 2017.

"**The Startup Behind Ethereum's Infamous DAO Has Been Acquired,**" Kuhn, Daniel, CoinDesk, June 3, 2019.

"**Former Polychain Partner Ryan Zurrer Is Leaving Web3 to Start a DAO,**" Dale, Brady, CoinDesk, Aug. 5, 2019.

"**DAOs Prepare for the Next Crypto Winter with Treasury Diversification,**" Dale, Brady, CoinDesk, June 3, 2021.

Chapter 22

The Vampire and
the Unicorn

On August 23, 2020, a researcher who worked for The Block, a crypto news organization, posed a question on Twitter: What could the leading decentralized exchange, Uniswap, do if someone copied all of the code that ran it, made it a new website, and then gave a governance token to all its users?

The researcher's name was Larry Cermak. He concluded, "Sure it would be a shitty move, but a lot of people are pure profit driven."

Hasu, another crypto researcher (a pseudonymous one) with something of a cult-like following, replied, "This will absolutely happen."

Cermak tweeted back, "I think so too."

It did. *It was kind of a whole thing.* It also led to the first moment that SBF stepped into the role as a leader and problem solver in the larger crypto community, like I said he would at the end of Chapter 17.

Uniswap has already been described, but let me just emphasize one thing here: everyone who built the decentralized exchange could disappear tomorrow, and Uniswap would keep working as long as Ethereum kept running. It was a robot on the internet.

I cannot emphasize this point enough. We are all very accustomed to the idea of "companies," these legal entities that run on people doing work. On Ethereum, people build simple little companies that run themselves forever. They are financial robots that don't have physical gears that run out or maintenance that needs doing. They can work for all time. Uniswap is like that.

Despite Uniswap's autonomous nature, though, the company that made it and was working on its next version had been funded by some of the richest venture capital firms, and there was a growing mood on the Ethereum blockchain that the interests of VCs and the cryptoletariat did not align. This idea of an exchange owned entirely by its users had cultural appeal.

Either way, all the code that ran Uniswap at the time was public, free software, accessible to anyone on its GitHub page. Three days after Cermak's suggestion, on August 26, an anonymous developer going by the handle "Chef Nomi" announced on Twitter that he was going to fork Uniswap. He had a GitHub repository fired up for it and a timeline for rolling his new version out.

He called it SushiSwap. SushiSwap would be a straight copy of Uniswap.

So SushiSwap would work as Uniswap did; the only thing it would lack was Uniswap's liquidity providers.

To recap, the assets DEXes (decentralized exchanges) trade with are entrusted to it by people who want to earn trading fees. DEXes give everyone a chance to participate in decentralized market making.

The prices on a DEX are basically the ratio of the assets deposited on it. So the more money is deposited, the less the prices change when someone makes a purchase. That price change is called "slippage." Less slippage means a better experience. So more money makes them work better.

Uniswap had a lot of money already deposited, and that was its moat, that's what defended it against copycats. Sure, anyone could copy Uniswap's code, but what good would it do? Uniswap was much more than code. It was a big pile of crypto assets at work.

To compete with Uniswap, a competitor needed a similarly big pile of crypto. The code was easy. Getting the money that made the code worthwhile was hard.

Of course there was another option. A competitor could just take Uniswap's crypto.

That was Chef Nomi's plan. He wanted the money inside Uniswap, and there was about $290 million inside Uniswap when Cermak started this conversation.

So Chef Nomi explained how he would get it. He said SushiSwap would not only give depositors trading fees, they would also get emissions of a new governance token. Uniswap didn't have a token then, but SushiSwap would.

Chef Nomi would reward depositors with this new token. Not only that, but people who held that token would get a sliver of all the SushiSwap trading fees, whether they were depositors or not.

He wanted people to immediately commit to moving their money over when SushiSwap went live. To convince them to do so, he offered a one-time-only deal. He would offer the governance token right away, before SushiSwap even existed. If people turned over their keys to their Uniswap deposits ahead of time, he'd award those deposits 10X the amount of this new governance token that they would get for deposits after SushiSwap was live.

To be clear, these depositors wouldn't be giving Chef Nomi their money. They would only be giving him the right to move it to a different exchange. It would still be theirs. Plus they'd get this free token.

In other words, Chef Nomi has created a way to suck funds out of Uniswap. Nomi had invented a new kind of mining: vampire mining.

This was chaos magic on the blockchain. People had not seen a scheme like this before.

He called the new token behind this blockchain coup sushi (SUSHI). The crowd went wild.

★★★

Note that holders of sushi would get a tiny little piece of the trading fees on SushiSwap. Whereas, on Uniswap, depositors kept all of it.

So let's pause here for a second and peer inside the minds of a crypto denizen. To me, at first, this arrangement sounded like a chump deal for liquidity providers. They'd move their assets over to SushiSwap and for what? So they wouldn't even get to keep all the trading fees on the liquidity pools they supported?

But I hadn't thought quite deviously enough. The first sushi holders *would be* the liquidity providers. And the liquidity providers who got in first would end up having the most sushi, so over time they could actually earn more from their LP position than they would on Uniswap.

By getting there first, early entrants would get a privileged position in sushi, so they'd always earn more than LPs that came later.

That was because an early hoard of sushi, thanks to the 10X promotional deal, would be larger, stealing from the liquidity providers who arrived later. In other words, SushiSwap might be a less appealing deal in the future, but, from the jump, it was great. And in crypto, everyone is always thinking about returns next month, next week, right now.

Chef Nomi's initial smart contract was set up in such a way that, when SushiSwap went live, it would redeem all the liquidity provider tokens deposited with it for their underlying tokens on Uniswap. Then it would move those tokens over to SushiSwap and send the Uniswap depositors brand-new LP tokens for SushiSwap.

In a way, Uniswap LPs had very little to lose in Chef Nomi's scheme. They were not earning a token on Uniswap. Their LP tokens would still stack up fees while waiting for the SushiSwap launch.

In fact, if an LP wanted, they could deposit their tokens in SushiSwap before the migration, earn some sushi, and then withdraw just before it started. There was risk, of course. There might be something in Chef Nomi's contract that everyone was missing, something that would make it fail or something that would allow him to steal everyone's deposits.

But, overall, loyalty to the top DEX was really looking like the loser move.

OK, but where was this all headed? Sure, sure, this was a nice little free money play, but would SushiSwap actually become *a thing*?

By giving away this governance token, sushi, from the start, Chef Nomi was theoretically signaling that he wanted SushiSwap to operate as a fully decentralized autonomous organization, as a DAO, as quickly as possible.

Up to this point, when entrepreneurs founded DAOs that ran a protocol, like in the SushiSwap case, they would spin up some magic space money for it early on, but they probably sat on it for a while. When the time came that they felt ready to "decentralize," they would then have something to entice others to join and take part.

In other words, they would run it autocratically until they felt users were ready.

SushiSwap did this totally differently. though. Chef Nomi started giving away the power over his DEX from the very beginning. Actually, he did it before it even started. He started giving away the power while he was still coding up the product.

Unlike the ICO era, though, he wasn't *selling* sushi. He was giving it to people signaling their intention to be part of it. As the kids say: that hit different.

$MEME and $FEW

In the far distant future of the next month, something else weird would happen because of Twitter. Jordan Lyall, a designer at ConsenSys, would make a fake user interface for spinning up a new token. It depicted options to choose a basic token contract from a few successful projects and an emoji to name the token after. Once picked, it suggested it would deploy a smart contract and launch the token.

He called it The Degenerator.

It was just a graphic. There was no website. But it inspired something. Pretty soon, someone spun up a smart contract for a token called meme (MEME) and gave it away to folks talking about it on Telegram. Faster than anyone suspected, meme had a $3 million market cap.

Before long, they were minting bespoke non-fungible tokens for people staking 500 or more meme.

While eventually it would devolve into a normal company, for a moment meme was a special, organic enterprise that just sort of appeared and brought creative people together.

Shortly thereafter a cabal of crypto influencers with large followings tried to recreate the magic with a token called few (FEW). They were exposed on Telegram, and it looked to everyone as an attempt to lever easy money out of the cryptoletariat. Everyone whose name showed up in the chat suffered a reputational hit.

The first was special. The second would have been a con.

While a lot of people were playing the SushiSwap trade just to rake in sushi and dump it for tether, not everyone was like that. Some people saw an opportunity to be part of something. And that's the funny thing about DAOs.

For example, there was this fellow 0xMaki who now has a pretty high standing in the Ethereum and DeFi world. He rose to prominence through SushiSwap. He had felt that he had missed out on a lot of other projects and got excited when SushiSwap started, so he joined its Discord server (basically, a message board) as soon as it opened and became very active, welcoming newcomers, answering questions, and fostering a positive community.

That's sometimes what happens when a token gets passed out: a community forms. Some people find they have a genuine affinity for certain endeavors.

SushiSwap had some additional help here in that its creation had sparked a certain David v. Goliath kind of drama that was driving lots of conversation and media coverage. That seems to have given a sense of camaraderie.

Some people find they really gel with the people talking about a project in the Discord servers and they stick around. They find work for themselves to do. Before long those people start getting paid and become pillars of their completely disembodied, legally non-existent company.

Remember how in Chapter 6 I wrote that community is the real security layer? This is what I was talking about.

SushiSwap was very informal from day one. Folks found niches and took on leadership roles. Chef Nomi didn't seem to be paying a lot of attention.

That turned out to be fortunate.

Sources Referenced

Larry Cermak, @lawmaster, Twitter, Aug. 23, 2020: https://twitter.com/lawmaster/status/1297480268341796870.
DeFiLlama: https://defillama.com/protocol/uniswap-v2.

"**The SushiSwap Project 🍱 🍱 🍱**," Chef Nomi, SushiSwap on Medium, Aug 26, 2020, The Internet Archive: https://web.archive.org/web/20200903050615/https://medium.com/sushiswap/the-sushiswap-project-c4049ea9941e.

"**The Cointelegraph Top 100: 0xMaki #59**," CoinTelegraph: https://cointelegraph.com/top-people-in-crypto-and-blockchain-2021/0xmaki.

"**Yearn, YAM and the Rise of Crypto's 'Weird DeFi' Moment**," Dale, Brady, CoinDesk, Aug. 31, 2020.

Chapter 23

The Fuckup and
the Savior

On September 1 2020, Uniswap had $1.5 billion worth of liquidity, quintuple what it had when Cermak had tweeted out the idea. That made it, for the first time, the largest app in DeFi.

This rapid growth was great for Uniswap. Every little bit that its pools grew made it that much better to trade on. Bigger pools had less slippage, which was the equivalent of tighter spreads on centralized exchanges. Less slippage encouraged bigger trades, which brought in more money for liquidity providers, which in turn made more people want to put in liquidity. Which made more people want to trade.

Traders follow liquidity. It was a virtuous cycle.

But the people behind Uniswap knew that most of the people putting this new money into it were doing it mainly to earn sushi emissions for the new exchange that was out there trying to destroy it.

Since more than a billion dollars had come piling into Uniswap ahead of SushiSwap's plan to migrate all that liquidity back out, one would think that Uniswap's bonanza was only a blip, that all that new liquidity would gush back out when Chef Nomi was done with his

147

work and the migration happened, leaving Uniswap on the other side as a distant number two.

That's not quite what happened, though.

Meanwhile, 1000 sushi were coming out per block ahead of the SushiSwap liquidity migration. It was very much like manna from heaven for those in the know enough to be in the right place to collect it.

And as with biblical manna, people became covetous. They realized that they would always be well ahead of any latecomer to come along after them, and they wanted to preserve their lead.

The early converts wanted SushiSwap to launch so that sushi emissions would plummet to 100 sushi per block, where it would stay thereafter. It wasn't how much sushi a person had, but how much larger their pile was relative to everyone else's.

Hearing the community's hunger to go live, Chef Nomi put out a vote asking committed SushiSwap migrants if they wanted him to launch SushiSwap as soon as he could. The poll was "Liquidity Migration™ Proposal."

It would run one sushi, one vote.

Sushi holders voted to move up the timeline. Of course they did. If sushi started generating yield from SushiSwap's swapping, the token would likely go up in value, and the people with the most sushi would benefit the most.

So Chef Nomi said he was going to be able to run the migration on September 7 or September 8.

Now, like most DAOs or token projects, SushiSwap had a dev fund, like the ones we discussed before. It was made up, primarily, of sushi tokens.

Like SushiSwap itself, the dev fund was created at the suggestion of Larry Cermak, The Block's influential researcher. Basically, it sliced off a little tiny bit of each block's fresh sushi into a wallet that Chef Nomi controlled.

Most protocols view their dev fund as sacrosanct, something to be stewarded thoughtfully. For SushiSwap, it would be the only source of income for the protocol itself, the only way to pay developers and others working to keep SushiSwap competitive post-launch.

Until the future DAO needed it, the dev fund was supporting sushi price on the open market. Chef Nomi was driving all the new sushi into a sushi-ether trading pool that he had set up *on Uniswap* (of all places).[1]

---

[1] Since Uniswap is decentralized and permissionless, there was nothing the team that built Uniswap could do about the fact that their own tool was being used to distribute the token created to destroy it.

This gave people who just wanted to buy sushi a way to do so. To community members, this shaved-off portion belonged to all of them, but they supported it because they felt the funds would be needed to support future SushiSwap development.

Chef Nomi apparently saw the dev fund differently.

On September 5, he announced that the smart contract audits were done. He said that he had everything set up to move control of all the contracts and its assets to a multi-signature wallet (think, board of directors, but blockchain style). But then he announced something else.

He announced that he had taken the $13 million worth of assets in the Uniswap pool and sold it all for ether, moving it to a private wallet in his control.

That is, he'd taken the dev fund.

As people began to react, he attempted to tweet out explanations, saying that the tokens in Uniswap had been losing value and that he did it for the community. He invoked crypto's favorite phrase for dismissing critique, FUD ("fear, uncertainty, and doubt"), but his followers were unmoved.

The price of sushi cratered on the announcement, falling from $4.63 to $1.20 (it would recover the next day and hover around $3 through the eventual launch).

Chef Nomi's protests assuaged no one. SushiSwap's future liquidity providers saw the dev fund as the future treasury of a forthcoming SushiSwap organization. A consensus quickly formed on Twitter that Chef Nomi was doing a rug pull.

A rug pull is something crypto denizens are hyper-scared of because it has happened so many times. In a rug pull, a con man describes a project that sounds plausible and asks people to invest in exchange for some kind of token or the promise of a future token. He does whatever it takes to make it all seem legit.

Unsuspecting users buy up a lot of the new token with ether or dai or something, looking forward to launch, hoping that it's a good project that will build something people want and realize lots of gains for the token later on. Then, instead of building whatever he promised, the con man pulls the rug out from under investors by walking away with their investment money and building nothing.

The money investors turned over is worth something, sure. The token he gave them, though? Nothing.

That's a basic rug pull.

Because everyone knows that rug pulls are an endemic threat in the scammer-rich world of crypto, it hurts to be rug-pulled two ways: first, it hurts to lose money, but, second, it hurts even worse to feel stupid.

But if what Chef Nomi did was a rug pull, it was a rug pull in a much less direct way. No one had paid Chef Nomi money for sushi. He hadn't sold sushi. People *earned* it. Everyone's liquidity deposits were still there in the smart contracts, and they could still withdraw them. He'd only taken some of the token he'd invented.

If he was pulling a rug on anything, it was on their trust, time, and attention—not their investment. Still, those things are valuable too.

Rug pull or not, it was a bad move that destroyed his credibility.[2]

Technically, no one knows who Chef Nomi is. He had worked pseudonymously. That said, if you sit major players in the DeFi space down and ask them, more often than not they will all give you the same answer: most believe it was a member of the team at BAND. BAND is a company building a platform that reliably feeds information to Ethereum's robots on the internet. It's an "oracle" company.

The BAND token, band, was one of the 14 tokens SushiSwap would trade at launch. Its market cap at the time was $266 million. That made it the seventh largest token on the list. Smaller than lend (LEND) (the since-deprecated token of the money market now known as Aave) but still larger than the six-week-old yfi (YFI) token for Andre Cronje's Yearn Finance, at the time.

The person rumored to have been Chef Nomi has already denied it on Twitter. I've asked folks from BAND about this since then, and they also denied it. They answered it like they were sick of hearing about it.

Another source, Joseph DeLong, told me he was confident about who had been behind SushiSwap. DeLong would serve as SushiSwap's

---

[2] If you read Chef Nomi's messages at the time carefully, it sounds like perhaps what he was trying to say was that he was just taking the funds out of Uniswap because he wanted to protect the nominal value for their future DAO. But that's a generous read. I think I am probably the only person who saw that potential interpretation at the time. Everyone else was just outraged, and he lost the SushiSwap community.

CTO for a time after it launched. The biggest tell, to him, was the fact that he'd found that the user interface for SushiSwap was running on the same server as BAND's website. Others noted this on Twitter as well.

Then Hayden Adams, founder of Uniswap, revealed on Twitter on November 17 that a BAND staffer had asked him a bunch of questions about Uniswap a couple weeks before SushiSwap launched.

As it happens, though, Adams also said SBF had hit him up with a bunch of similar questions, including about whether or not Uniswap would launch a token. That said, it's well established that SBF was already thinking about DEXes at this point, irrespective of SushiSwap, because of another project I'll explain soon.

In order to save SushiSwap from Chef Nomi's mistake, SBF stepped into public view and became a leader in crypto above and beyond FTX. On September 5, amid all the fury, SBF started tweeting. He wrote, "First of all, Chef Nomi sucks."

Then he went on about his thoughts with regard to SushiSwap moving forward. He said that Chef Nomi had to go, and he said he'd be happy to run the migration plan. He also offered to pay out millions of dollars' worth of sushi from his own supply to people who stuck around through the migration (he had plenty of sushi because Alameda had been farming the hell out of it).

Shortly thereafter Chef Nomi wrote in the SushiSwap Discord server that he was game to turn the keys over to SBF.

It should be noted here that SBF was not Chef Nomi's first choice. The founder had asked Andre Cronje, the creator of the aforementioned iEarn, which had become Yearn Finance. Cronje confirmed this to me over Telegram, but he didn't want to do it.

As an investment opportunity, SushiSwap had grabbed SBF's attention immediately. He told me, "Some people found what they claimed to be Alameda's farming wallet and claimed it was big. And they were right," he told me. He agreed, it was really big. That, he said, was the right way to approach an opportunity like SushiSwap. He was, at that point, very much invested in its success.

Maybe he wouldn't be for long, of course, but in Fall 2020 he was all about SushiSwap.

He confirmed to me that Alameda had been ploughing wild amounts of funds into yield farming sushi.

The Box, revisited

Pause here for a moment and note these sorts of things were what liquidity mining really is. It was meant to support a real blockchain tool. They were borrow-lend boxes, trading boxes, index-making boxes. They were neutral robots on the internet that ran familiar financial instruments with rules that were open for anyone to inspect and *verify* that they always followed those rules. Here he was taking a lot of risk to benefit from the launch of one such robot. A new exchange. If there's one thing it was absolutely clear that people really liked to do in DeFi, it was trade.

By the time SushiSwap was announced, Uniswap's liquidity providers had already collectively earned well over $2 billion in trading fees, according to TokenTerminal. It had an actual business model.

These were not boxes doing nothing, and SBF knew that when he described The Box on *Odd Lots*.

Once Nomi gave Sam the keys, SBF canceled the original migration and put his developer resources toward re-checking the migration of Uniswap assets over to SushiSwap. Then he laid out a plan for electing a multisig (the equivalent of a board on the blockchain) to steward SushiSwap into its new era.

Meanwhile, in the background, another leader was working to hold SushiSwap together: 0xMaki. He was trying to keep its early team committed despite Chef Nomi's perceived betrayal.

So here the project was at the most critical moment in its launch process, and its leader had been shoved out by a furious community, the value of the token was plummeting, and no one knew whether or not SushiSwap would ever go live.

Around $1.3 billion in crypto had been committed to SushiSwap, but the actual assets weren't controlled by SushiSwap's smart contracts yet. Those funds were still sitting on Uniswap, but, with the LP tokens users had given it, SushiSwap could withdraw funds from a bunch of Uniswap's different LP pools and deposit them into SushiSwap.

The next few days were a blur of Twitter threads from SBF as his team canceled the migration, de-bugged the Chef's code, and created a new plan.

While there was a lot of uncertainty in the community from the moment SBF took control until when the migration started, once it began everyone felt relief.

On September 9, under SBF's stewardship, $830 million dollars' worth of crypto assets gallivanted safely across the Ethereum blockchain, from Uniswap's coffers to SushiSwap's. SBF live-tweeted pool after pool as they went through. Once he finished, he declared himself done with his reign as chief of SushiSwap.

You could be very sure, too, that every cybercriminal with a trick to try was looking for an angle to snag some of those tokens as they moved. But nothing was lost. Everything worked. SBF looked competent and generous.

From that moment on, he was happy for the project to be run by community votes and the newly elected multisig that had power over the SushiSwap contracts.

Meanwhile, every reasonable person saw the creation of SushiSwap as an attack on Uniswap. Obviously, it was. It was a scheme to convince people to migrate from one service to another. It *paid* them to do so.

However, the day after SushiSwap's attack, there was $650 million in deposits on Uniswap, double what it held before Cermak's fateful suggestion. By then, SushiSwap would be up to $1.4 billion, according to a report from The Defiant at the time.

Then the multisig was elected. The project was officially in the hands of multiple people.

On top of all that, on September 11, Chef Nomi would pop up one last time before he was never heard from again. He returned all the ether he had taken from SushiSwap believers.

"To everyone. I fucked up. And I am sorry," he tweeted in his final thread. His last message ever said, "It has a lot of potential, don't let my action alone fuck it up."

DeLong told me that, as he was coming on to SushiSwap, he got the impression from talking to 0xMaki that SBF had been around for longer and involved more deeply than he had let on. 0xMaki never said it flat out, DeLong said, but he hinted that he and Chef Nomi had had talks with a big-money guy in the space from early on, and DeLong always believed that had been SBF.

SBF denied this when we spoke in December. "I was not involved at all when it was launched. I was not involved at all when it was designed," he said. Somewhat before he took on a public leadership role, he said he'd had a conversation with 0xMaki about improvements he'd like to see and a potential deployment on Solana, but that was it.

SBF also put a surprise twist on the question of Chef Nomi's identity. He said he never knew for sure, either, but that he had looked into it. He found evidence for and against that conclusion.

"My best guess was that Nomi was an account run by two people or run by multiple people, and that one of them was the BAND guy, and that there was at least one other person in that account, and that it was likely the other person who had actually taken the funds," he said.

Whomever started it, SushiSwap was a disruption in the nascent market, but the prevailing order would be restored. While it was behind in the moment, Uniswap would grow from there, never again holding as little as it did the day after SushiSwap's attack was executed (which was still vastly more than it held before SushiSwap began).

Today, Uniswap is much bigger than its rival and has been for a long time, but that's not really what makes this story so interesting.

Setting aside FTX and SBF for a moment, this is a story in which one protocol tried to destroy another, and both came out bigger and stronger at the end of the confrontation than either could have reasonably expected.

It was one of those outcomes that shows how the cocktail of business shenanigans tastes differently when magic space money is one of the ingredients in the shaker. But in the grand scheme of an envisioned decentralized future, not everyone liked this outcome.

For example, software consultant Ben DeFrancesco had tweeted on September 9, "If Sushi succeeds in vampire attacking Uniswap, after the latter's founders spent years doing the actual hard work, you'll never see a project launched w/o a useless token in this ecosystem again. The incentives for builders trying to do the right thing are shitty enough as it is."

But SushiSwap had succeeded. The vampire's bite was in.

Sources Referenced

"Uniswap Rises to Top of DeFi Charts Thanks to Rival Looking to Unseat It," Dale, Brady, CoinDesk, Sept. 1, 2020.

"Liquidity Migration™ Proposal," Chef Nomi, Sept 3, 2020, on Snapshot: https:// snapshot.org/#/sushigov.eth/proposal/QmXm9T791myT62Jj3iokarQYuUF2X KMBUXmqUKh5fKpK1L.

Interview, Sam Bankman-Fried, video chat and mobile, Feb. 8, 2021.

Uniswap, Token Terminal, https://tokenterminal.com/terminal/projects/uniswap.

"Fishy Business: What Happened to $1.2B DeFi Protocol SushiSwap Over the Weekend," Foxley, Will, CoinDesk, Sept. 6, 2020.

"SushiSwap Will Withdraw Up to $830M from Uniswap Today: Why It Matters for DeFi," Dale, Brady, CoinDesk, Sept. 9, 2020.

Interview, Sam Bankman-Fried, phone call with spokesperson, Dec. 30, 2022.

"'I F*cked Up. And I am Sorry:' Chef Nomi Returns $14M of ETH to SushiSwap," Russo, Camila, The Defiant, Sept. 11, 2020.

Ben DiFrancesco, @bendifrancesco, Twitter, September 9, 2020, 9:42 AM: https:// twitter.com/BenDiFrancesco/status/1303690152871686146.

Chapter 24

DeFi Summer

Governance tokens were like acne in 2020, and DeFi was like a teenage boy who would only drink Dr. Pepper.

A little while after the comp mania kicked in, Balancer, a protocol for making indexes of tokens, started luring users with its own token, balancer (BAL). In July, RARI, a platform for selling crypto art and collectibles (non-fungible tokens), released a new token to everyone who had ever owned an NFT, rari (RARI).

They started yield farming too, rewarding rari to anyone who traded on their platform, pushing up volumes. Liquidity mining was expanding beyond finance.

As I mentioned before, another automated market maker blew up in the summer of comp, and it was called Curve. Curve had a very special niche in the decentralized exchange business. It specialized in swaps between tokens that tended to have the same value, such as between stablecoins that followed the price of the dollar. Curve was also big on bitcoin derivatives running on Ethereum.

Weirdly, this turned out to be an enormous use case. It was like a used car lot where no one bought or sold anything, but people showed up to exchange Camrys for Sonatas and Sonatas for Altimas and Altimas for Camrys again. And they just did it all day, every day. Why so much excitement over the most boring stuff? But this was and remains super-hot on Ethereum, and Curve was king in the-like-for-like, hella-boring-for-hella-boring game.

As it happened, the founder of Curve, Michael Egorov, had been working on the smart contract for Curve's governance token. I asked him to let me break the story when the token came out. Egorov had said noncommittally that he probably would let me break it, but then (while I was on vacation one week) someone found the token's code in Curve's smart contracts ready to go. The stranger did the blockchain equivalent of flipping a switch, and Curve started distributing its new token, crv (CRV).

The whole story was a little suspect, but anyway, Egorov just let it go. No scoop for me.

Today crv is probably the single most sought-after token in all of DeFi. Curve has become the engine at the heart of many a yield strategy since, but that wouldn't be evident for a few months.

While there were a lot of these discrete events where new tokens were rolling out, driving blockchain denizens to chase the next hot new source of value, really there were four big milestones to DeFi Summer.

The first, obviously, was the launch of Compound's comp token in June. That's how it all began.

The second was the upgrade of iEarn to Yearn and the release of its yfi (YFI) token in July, the most exciting token of the era. The big idea in yfi's release was this: no tokens were set aside for the project's creator, Andre Cronje (he would later say he regretted doing it this way, though). They called it a "fair launch." Its release spontaneously created a DAO that persists to this day, without any official existence in the nations of the world's books.

Third, the launch and subsequent implosion of Yam Finance in August, a wacky experiment in aggressive yield farming that showed Ethereum that magic space money is only *just so* magical. Yam was DeFi-as-game, basically. It was an experiment in running a stablecoin powered by a bunch of degenerate blockchain gamblers hustling to maximize gains. It didn't work! Lessons were learned!

Fourth and finally, September's vampire attack by SushiSwap on Uniswap, which ultimately resolved into Uniswap releasing its own token, uni (UNI) on September 16, 2020. That marked the end of DeFi summer 2020. Sure, there would always be more tokens, but the chapter closed on a high note, a pink new coin from the venture-backed team.

By the end of the summer, comp's price would sink back below $100. People hadn't abandoned yield farming, but a lot of the fervor was gone. It still worked (sort of). It still brought people in (sort of). But it was less urgent. It was more like business.

After the battle over SushiSwap, ConsenSys alum Joseph DeLong joined the team at SushiSwap. From the outside looking in, he seemed to be basically the other CEO, alongside 0xMaki, who took the spot at the helm. DeLong eventually left in frustration. Now he's doing a project called Astaria, which aims to unlock value in non-fungible tokens.

He told me in an interview that he came in very excited about the possibilities for non-hierarchical organizations and DAOs, but his experience at SushiSwap disabused him of all of that. He also doesn't feel great about many of the growth hacks used then. "Farming was cool. Unfortunately, I think it doesn't work. That's the sad part. We just didn't know yet," he says now.

Which isn't to say that at the end of 2020 it was over. It wasn't. It just became a little less game and a little more grind.

But there's money to be made in a grind, too.

"I think people's financial sophistication now is much higher than it was at the beginning," DeLong said. "As we went along and made these mistakes like farming and airdrops and retroactive airdrops, we started to learn that there's a reason companies don't give you Coca-Cola stock just because you buy a Coca-Cola."

Sources Referenced

"**Yield Farming Expands from Finance to Digital Collectibles**," Dale, Brady, CoinDesk, July 15, 2020.

"**DeFi's 'Agricultural Revolution' Has Ethereum Users Turning to Decentralized Exchanges**," Dale, Brady, CoinDesk, June 30, 2020.

"**Yield Farming Expands from Finance to Digital Collectibles**," Dale, Brady, CoinDesk, July 15, 2020.

"**Following COMP's Surge, DeFi Platform Balancer Begins Distribution of BAL Tokens**," Dale, Brady, CoinDesk, June 23, 2020.

"**Troll Token? Why DeFi Yield Farmers Are Now All About YFI**," Dale, Brady, CoinDesk, July 20, 2020.

"**Mergers Position Yearn Finance as the Amazon of DeFi**," Dale, Brady, CoinDesk, Dec. 14, 2020.

"**Newest DAO Project Was Thrown a Curve, but the Team Is Rolling with It Anyway**," Harper, Colin, CoinDesk, Aug. 14, 2020.

"**Deposits in 'Monetary Experiment' Meme Token YAM Break $460M**," Foxley, William, CoinDesk, Aug. 12, 2020.

"**DeFi Meme Coin YAM Succumbs to Fatal 'Rebase' Bug, Makes Plans for 'YAM 2.0**,'" Foxley, Will and Paddy Baker, CoinDesk, Aug. 13, 2020.

"**Uniswap's Distribution Is Built on Something That Can't Be Forked: Actual Users**," Dale, Brady, CoinDesk, Sept. 17, 2020.

"**With COMP Below $100, a Look Back at the 'DeFi Summer' It Sparked**," Dale, Brady, CoinDesk, Oct. 20, 2020.

Chapter 25

CREAM Finance

It was around this time, a little over a year after FTX launched, that the company finally had its own bank accounts, according to the CFTC.

This meant customers could wire it dollars or other currencies directly, but some continued to use the old Alameda account anyway.

"Consistently from the launch of FTX and throughout the Relevant Period, Alameda accessed and used FTX customer funds for Alameda's own operations and activities, including to fund its trading, investment, and borrowing/lending activities," the agency's complaint alleges.

SBF would later describe this practice of using an Alameda account for FTX customers' deposits as an "accounting artifact." According to the government, that artifact would cause a multi-billion-dollar hole.

But we're getting ahead of ourselves.

I promise, pretty soon we're going to get back into the world of famous people, physical buildings, and sports teams that made FTX and SBF famous on the global stage, but we need to cover a bit more pure blockchain, in part because this next story encapsulates what's to come at the end too perfectly to skip.

Despite his Summer 2020 rescue of SushiSwap, it didn't take long for the cryptoletariat to start giving SBF side-eye.

Yes, he had come out of that crisis as something of a hero, but no one in DeFi had ever really heard of him. He ran a centralized exchange. He'd cynically spun out a token that had no power. He seemed like a rich guy who would be happy to play them.

Crypto people are always looking for someone who is going to make big promises and then steal their money.

Even more than not wanting to lose money, people in crypto want to feel like they aren't suckers. The whole idea is that you're investing in blockchain ideas because you are savvy enough to see a future the normal people can't (they call them "normies"). It feels good to feel smart, but the trouble is that so many hustlers in the space are looking for ways to make you feel stupid. Actually, they don't care how you feel. They just want your money.

So SBF and Alameda took to DeFi pretty fast in 2020, but DeFi was not in their DNA. Their whole business had been about working on trades between exchanges, working some angles off stablecoins, and finding ways to source liquidity and fill in gaps around the world.

Then in 2019 they started their exchange, FTX.

This was a company that was basically the Millennial version of crypto grump and Doctor Doom economist Nouriel Roubini. Roubini's stance: *Centralization is great, what's the problem?*

Alameda's version: Centralization is great, but we'll play the DeFi casino if we think we can take money from all the rubes.

And it moved fast. Alameda started looking for all the yield farming trades that it could get, and people started to notice there was something of a theme to the projects it got involved with.

The first one the world heard about was SushiSwap, of course. SushiSwap was a fork of Uniswap, as we have discussed.

Then SBF would accept an offer to join the multisig for Swerve, which was a fork of the aforementioned Curve.

Swerve was basically a copy of SushiSwap. Take an existing decentralized exchange, argue that the people who use it should really own it, create a token, and see if people hop on. Swerve never energized the masses like SushiSwap did (the sequel rarely matches the original), but it got some traction for a minute.

The third one did work, because it was a copy, but it was a copy that was different in an important way. That one was CREAM (it's always written as caps because it's a reference to the Wu-Tang track "C.R.E.A.M."—"Cash Rules Everything Around Me." The DeFi app's founder was actually a pioneer in Taiwanese hip-hop, from the 1990s).

CREAM was a fork of Compound, but CREAM was also different from Compound. Compound was rigorous about security. CREAM was not. That made CREAM more fun.

To recap, Compound let people deposit tokens (which earned interest), and then they could use that deposit as collateral to borrow some other token. Compound was extremely careful about the tokens it chose. It commissioned complex risk analyses and did everything it could to maintain a status as DeFi blue-chip project.

Lots of tokens got listed on CREAM. Its approach was YOLO!

CREAM has been hacked enough times at this point that it's not even worth adding up, but that appetite for risk is the niche it fills.

So it may not be a huge surprise that the Alameda crowd found CREAM, and it turned out to be useful for them. It should be no surprise, either, to find out that Alameda persuaded CREAM to accept ftt as a collateral for loans.

A flap broke out in October 2020 when Ethereum users found on-chain evidence that Alameda had loaded CREAM up with its ftt token and then borrowed a bunch of Uniswap's token, uni, and Yearn Finance's yfi.

The market jumped to the conclusion that Alameda had borrowed these tokens to short them. This was viewed with distrust by CREAM users because it looked as if the founder of a big, centralized project was attempting to undermine the value of DeFi projects.

It looked as if Alameda was borrowing these well-liked DeFi coins to send them to exchanges, sell them, and then profit when the price fell.

And to be clear: this is in no small part what apps such as CREAM *are for*. Shorting is a key function. When Robert Leshner launched Compound, that was the use case he used to explain it to journalists. It's not so much the use that made people mad but the fact that a rich guy who was heavily invested in centralization was doing it, all while presenting himself as DeFi's friend.

For his part, SBF went on Twitter and said Alameda had only done a little shorting, also asking, "What exactly is the point of a borrow/lending protocol, if borrowing coins is evil?"

On a YouTube interview later, he said Alameda had done a small hedge against the fact that most of the market was so long DeFi projects in general.

But it was an investor in the space who drilled down a level deeper to what was really at stake. Spencer Noon, then of DLT Capital, now a part of Variant Fund, wrote on Twitter on October 8, 2020:

> 40% of all $CREAM collateral is a single centralized exchange token. 25% of the entire $FTT float is in $CREAM too. This is straight up reckless from a risk perspective, and the people who are going to get hurt the most are $CREAM holders.

For what it's worth, the reporters at Rekt, a crypto news site, would also find that 96 percent of all ftt deposits on CREAM were from Alameda.

Just in case this isn't obvious, let me spell this out.

Noon was saying that CREAM users were permitting a small group to borrow a significant portion of their deposits based on a token (FTX's ftt) that *barely trades*. When a token barely trades, it has a *price*, but that price isn't stable. It has a market price, but not a fair price. That market price can easily collapse.

If that were to happen, Alameda would have more valuable assets (such as uni and yfi), and they can just walk away from their worthless ftt if it comes to that. CREAM depositors would be the ones screwed.

Noon took it further in a subsequent tweet:

Looking to print millions of $$$ out of thin air?

Step 1: Create a CEX token, huge supply

Step 2: Keep the float low, huge mcap [market cap]. You could never sell all of those tokens anyways

Step 3: Get a lending protocol to add your token as collateral

Step 4: Deposit

Step 5: Withdraw $

Does this sound familiar? Hint: see Chapter 2, the one about FTX collapsing because of Alameda's debts collateralized by ftt.

On October 10, SBF went on Twitter with a mini-tirade about how it was very unlikely that ftt would collapse and if CREAM users booted it entirely over that fear, the whole project would lose a lot of its total value locked.

He was urging a community of strangers to trust him and his exchange's token.

In November, CREAM users would vote to put a cap on the total collateral ftt could represent on the app. In other words, this scrappy DeFi app run by a bunch of anons whose core idea was fundamentally about letting users throw the dice decided it made sense to do some risk mitigation around ftt's potential volatility as collateral.

Two years later, FTX still hadn't followed the lead of a DAO that catered to degenerates.

And here we are.

Sources Referenced

"**CFTC Charges Sam Bankman-Fried, FTX Trading and Alameda with Fraud and Material Misrepresentations**," Press release and complaint before the US Southern District of New York, Commodity Futures Trading Commission, Dec. 13, 2022.

"**Ethereum Co-Founder Battles 'Dr Doom' Roubini to Crypto Debate Draw**," Dale, Brady, CoinDesk, May 10, 2018.

"**Swerve Forks from 'Unfair' DeFi Exchange Curve**," Behrens, Alexander, Decrypt, Sept. 4, 2020.

"**Swerve Finance's total value locked hits 40% of Curve's deposits within four days of its launch**," Khatri, Yogita, The Block, Sept. 8, 2020.

"**Whale Hunt—SBF and Blue Kirby**," Anonymous, Rekt, Oct. 9, 2020.

"**Whale Hunt—Sam Bankman Fried (SBF) & Julien Bouteloup**," *rekt news*, YouTube, Oct. 21, 2020.

Spencer Noon, @spencernoon, Twitter, Oct. 8, 2020: https://twitter.com/spencer-noon/status/1314185884288376833.

"**What Does Sam Bankman-Fried Have to Say for Himself?**," Wieczner, Jen, *New York Magazine*, Dec. 1, 2022.

"**Decrease the Collateral Factor for FTT**," Snapshot, Nov. 3, 2020: https://snapshot.org/#/cream-finance.eth/proposal/QmXcXLufGxH1mAjf1De4dttTs9qExFt FaQb7UhdrnHyEK9.

Chapter 26

Solana

Race Capital's Chris McCann tells a fun story about how the FTX team got sold on the Solana blockchain. It was an experiment that one of the FTX developers did with an app on the Solana testnet.

Solana is a superfast blockchain created by Anatoly Yakovenko, an alum of the mobile computing teams at QUALCOMM, and others. McCann invested in it in 2018, which was very early. His fund, Race Capital, also got in ahead of almost everyone else.

McCann would find FTX later and connect it to Solana. The team building this new blockchain was working out of the 500 Startups offices in San Francisco, and they had spun up an app for people to play with. It was very simple.

Testnets are versions of blockchain running without real value at stake. Usually new blockchains run a testnet for a while and invite others to try it out and look for bugs before they fire up the real one.

As McCann told it, Yakovenko had built a testing app called Break in 2020 as FTX was looking into either starting its own blockchain or building on someone else's. Break was simple. It just let a user type on a keyboard, and they could see their keystrokes get logged on the blockchain as fast as they typed.

It was a way to see that the blockchain really did run at the speed of thought.

According to a test by some fairly unbiased investors and researchers in March 2022, Solana could do 273 trades per second. Meanwhile, Ethereum, the dominant blockchain that Solana was challenging, could do maybe 18, and, to be fair, Ethereum was even slower back in 2020.

So one of FTX's lead engineers decided to test Break, McCann said. He tried autoclicking keys into the blockchain. He tried writing scripts to make clicks for him. Whether he ever managed to overwhelm it or not, McCann doesn't say, but Solana did well enough that it impressed him. That was its thing: being fast.

And that's what sold SBF and his team. I asked SBF when we spoke in early 2021 why he was so into Solana. He told me that "if you imagine DeFi was going to be big," and noted that he wasn't sure it was, but if that was the bet you wanted to make, "most people are just not close to right."

His problem with most blockchain developers' thinking is that they worry about all sorts of factors when looking at blockchains. Things such as decentralization, security, and censorship resistance. These developers care about getting lots of users, what crypto people call "scaling," but SBF objected to where it was prioritized. Scaling, he said, "is treated like *a* factor."

He put it in his distinctly SBFian way, with a sentence that had a math equation somewhere in its DNA: "It's closer to being the only factor that matters," he told me.

SBF had this vision of a blockchain that could scale up to do the kind of things we do on the current, centralized internet. He wanted finance apps. He wanted social media. He wanted ten thousand people dogpiling on Elon Musk at once because he had posted something crazy.

But there's a point one has to ask: Well, if speed is *that important*, then why even mess about with blockchains?

A blockchain is just a database, and it's kind of a crappy and difficult and buggy database, but it does one thing really well: it stymies abuse. It's designed so that you don't have to trust anyone that's running it, so you can trust the whole thing to operate fairly all the time.

This was put really well in something written by Adam Ludwin, an early founder in the crypto space who built a company called Chain. In 2017, he wrote an open letter that can only be found now if you dig around on the Internet Archive, but it's a great letter. If they ever make a cryptocurrency portable reader anthology, that letter is a sure bet. The letter was addressed to the CEO of JPMorgan Chase, Jamie Dimon. Dimon has always been a deep crypto skeptic.

In that letter, Ludwin wrote [emphasis is his]:

> Centralized applications beat the pants off decentralized applications on virtually every dimension.
> **EXCEPT FOR ONE DIMENSION.**
> And not only are decentralized applications better at this one thing, they are the only way we can achieve it.
> What am I referring to?
> **Censorship resistance.**
> This is where we come to the elusive signal in the noise.
> Censorship resistance means that access to decentralized applications is open and unfettered. Transactions on these services are unstoppable.

But in blockchain years it's been a long time since Ludwin wrote that. A lot of people have moved on. Even Ludwin has moved on.

The newcomers care more about other matters now. They want the crypto ecosystem to be easy and look more like the tech world people are familiar with.

They want lots and lots of users. They want this world to get really big. And that's what Solana is built for: connecting lots of people on a blockchain all at once. As one investor said to me, it's the blockchain that thinks everything can be done on a blockchain. Ethereum, on the other hand, thinks only the crucial things should be done on a blockchain.

And it's not like the two blockchains couldn't coexist.

"It's important for people to stop thinking about this as one layer-one vs another one. I feel like Ethereum is a proof-of-work network[1] where tokens are issued and settled," Yakovenko told me in an interview

---

[1] Ethereum is actually no longer a proof-of-work network, but that change only happened in late 2022. It's now "proof-of-stake," which is not something we need to go into here. But it's less pricey in terms of energy than its old approach. Proof-of-stake is how most newer blockchains run.

Hostesses in bear costumes, to play up the notion of a coming bear market. FTX/
Multicoin party, Solana Breakpoint, Nov. 6, 2022, at Suspenso Lisboa, Lisbon,
Portugal. (Photographer's name withheld, used by permission.)

in October 2020, as we discussed his new bridge he was building to
Ethereum. "We're not trying to fight Ethereum. There's now this awesome execution engine that is fast enough to run a central limit order
book that's impossible on Ethereum."

But Solana did have a security issue. No one's funds got stolen, or
anything like that, but it proved that it was more censorable than a network like Ethereum.

Solana, because it was designed for speed, didn't launch with a notion
of *paying* for usage. On Ethereum, if you want it to do something, you
have to pay a little bit for it (and you have to pay *more* if more people
want to do something at the same time). It's an anti-spam measure. It
makes sure no one is trying to post transactions maliciously. For example,

imagine if it cost one penny to send 100 emails. That's not very much, but spammers would be more circumspect.

Solana didn't have that. So guess what? People spammed it.

They didn't do that for a while, not until it got to be big enough. What's the fun of vandalizing a place if no one is there to see it? But eventually, it happened, and it caused the blockchain to become unusable again and again.

Solana had 14 days with some kind of downtime in 2022. Three days in 2021. It *has* gotten a lot better. Staff there have told me that there are all kinds of improvements on the way to make it harder to spam.

And Bitcoin and Ethereum also had early hiccups, it's true. Solana hasn't had to completely reboot its chain because an early application fell to pieces and people lost $60 million or so (like Ethereum had to after The DAO).

That said, a Solana app had a screwup this year so bad that it cost $320 million in crypto. Its bridge to Ethereum (called Wormhole) got exploited by cybercriminals. But the blockchain was seen as so valuable to one major player, Jump, the high-frequency trading firm, that it just covered the stolen funds for victims.

Before Jump found Solana, though, the Samglomerate did. Before SBF set his sights on the blockchain, it was this very fast blockchain that hadn't yet given people a reason to use it.

A blockchain is nothing without use cases. Without those, it's just a very quirky database that hobbyists run and sends them some pointless digital assets periodically for engaging with their strange hobby.

For its first several months of operation, developers weren't showing much interest in building anything on Solana, according to McCann. It used a different programming language than Ethereum, but all the blockchain developers had already learned Ethereum's. And Ethereum wasn't even maxed out at the time anyway. What was the point?

But then SBF and FTX decided that Solana was the digital byway along which they wanted to set up their first superstore, a new decentralized exchange called Serum.

And that's what did it for Yakovenko's chain. As McCann told the podcast's hosts, "Solana did not have its first big break until Serum."

Sources Referenced

"**Race Capital, Crypto Investing, and FTX + Solana's Early Days**," Gilbert, Ben, and David Rosenthal, *Acquired*, Jan. 26, 2022.

"**The AMM Test: A No BS Look at L1 Performance**," GM and Haseeb Qureshi, Dragonfly Research, Medium, Mar. 1, 2022.

"**A Letter to Jamie Dimon**," Ludwin, Adam, Chain blog, Medium, Oct. 16, 2017: https://web.archive.org/web/20171101233841/https://blog.chain.com/a-letter-to-jamie-dimon-de89d417cb80.

"**More than $320 million stolen in latest apparent crypto hack**," Sigalos, MacKenzie, CNBC, Feb. 3, 2022.

"**Trading Powerhouse's $320 Million Save Suggests It's Crypto-Rich**," Baker, Nick, Yueqi Yang, and Olga Kharif, Bloomberg, Feb. 3, 2022.

Chapter 27

Market Cap

S erum brings us to the serum (SRM) token. Tokens mean prices, and prices mean market caps. Market caps are key to understanding what went so horribly wrong with SBF.

So here's a fun fact for you: market caps are nonsense. They aren't *complete* nonsense, but they are *mostly* nonsense.

From Apple stock all the way down to garlicoin: a market cap is less a fixed number and more a bit of wishful thinking.

Market caps are much like the gross domestic product (GDP) of nations: both are terrible ways of measuring what each is attempting to measure (the value of a company or the health of a nation's economy), *except for all the other ways.*

Market caps are simple: take the spot price of a token (or a company's equity, for that matter) and multiply it by supply. So if there's a thousand tokens and they are selling for $1 each, it has a market cap of $1,000.

Spot prices (market prices) are real for you and me, but they are not real for someone like SBF. He knows this. He made a business out of this.

But for you and me, if we have 10 or 100 or 1000, *say*, sol tokens and the websites are saying they are selling for $10, we can probably get $10 each for our whole portfolio. That's because, well, we just don't *have much*. To the market, our trades just don't *really matter*.

But try to sell a million? That's going to fetch a lower price. No one is paying full price for a giant pile.

This is why, big picture, market caps are perhaps more misleading than helpful. Here's how they are helpful: on a day-to-day basis, market caps help you easily compare different tokens' *relative* presence in the public's collective consciousness.

So a $1.00 with a supply of a billion has a larger footprint in the market (probably) than a $10,000 token that only has a supply of 1000 (a billion-dollar market cap versus a ten-million-dollar one).

Make sense?

But the market cap doesn't reflect the "value" of the enterprise. The total fair value of any token is much lower. There's just no good way to know quite how much lower. It's *more true* the more often a token trades, the more liquidity it has, but it's tough to know just how much more.

This matters for SBF because he made ftt for FTX. Plus, in 2021 and 2022, he helped spin up several "independent" projects that each had their own tokens. More on these in the next chapter. In each case, the teams only actually released a small amount, and then they drove a lot of hype around them.

So there were tiny, new tokens that hardly anyone was using, but they each had a price, although it was an inflated price. There was just no way to know how inflated.

For smaller tokens, the "price" is just the last price someone paid for it. It gets more complicated with a really important, constantly traded token such as bitcoin or ether, but for minor tokens, sites are just reporting the last numbers that came in. If no one trades it for a while, it just sort of stays where it is.

But smaller tokens can also warp prices another way: Imagine you have a token that is launched with a supply of 1 billion, right? But only, say, 300 million initially get distributed (that's 30%). It is often done this way.

One hundred million gets sold onto the open market to fund operations, 100 million gets put into various DEXes so newcomers have a place to buy them, and 100 million gets airdropped out to early support-ers, community members, and investors.

Let's say the market (hypothetically) quickly settles on a price of a penny each for all the tokens out there. The other 700 million are all locked up in various ways, not moving any time soon. So really you only have a float[1] of 30 percent of your supply, right?

But the convention here is that you apply the value to the whole supply. So the market cap of a billion tokens valued at a penny each is $10 million, the "fully diluted market cap." This despite the fact that 70% aren't on the market at all.

There's growing pushback on this. For example, CoinGecko, the chief competitor to CoinMarketCap (the leader in tracking crypto's horse race), tends to favor a market cap based on circulating supply. It's not monolithic.

But neither of those sites get to weigh in when a founder goes on Bloomberg TV confirming: Yes, I am for sure a billionaire.

The float can be driven even lower, even if some tokens are on the market. Projects give users some incentive to take their tokens off the market temporarily. For example, lots of projects promise new tokens to anyone who locks what they have up on a DEX of some kind.

This has the double impact of making the liquidity of a token appear to be better, but most tokens inside a DEX are basically idle. So the more that goes in, the better the price discovery and the lower the slippage for traders, but the real upshot is you have a giant supply of tokens in a sav-ings account.

All of this conspires to restrict supply. If supply is restricted and demand stays the same, price goes up.

*Now. Let's imagine—just bear with me here—*that a really rich crypto entrepreneur is trying to inflate the wealth of a company as fast as possible.

Maybe? Maybe it would make sense to spin up a bunch of new tokens, generate buzz around them, work with some *well-known market maker* to make sure they had liquidity on some exchanges, and then set aside a big sack of this new magic space money.

---

[1] A "float" is the supply that's actually live and trading on the market. There might be 1,000 of some rare baseball card in the world, but if only 50 are for sale online or in card shops around the world, it has a supply of 1000 but a float of 5%.

So then all of a sudden the company has all these "assets" on its balance sheet that it can use to claim that the company is worth even more than it already is worth.

It's not like the company's value is based on *quite nothing*. It would be unfair to go that far. But it's a slender reed.

Could something like that really happen?

Sources Referenced

"Why Market Cap Is a Meaningless & Dangerous Valuation Metric in Crypto Markets," Back, Anthony, Blockchain Review, Medium, Dec. 27, 2018.

"ApeCoin & the death of staking," Cobie, Cobie's substack, April 21, 2022.

Chapter 28

Sam Coins

SBF had a busy run of launching tokens in 2020 and 2021, and it paid off.

Until it didn't.

I came into crypto covering new tokens, but after a while I became cynical about launches. It's suspicious that folks are so eager to talk when something is beginning. I found that often I'd write something and then never hear about the project again. Eventually, it felt more responsible to pass until something has come of the project and its token.

Of course, at that point, it might be going so well that the leaders don't feel a need to talk to you any longer.

Ignoring new stuff was basically my approach in 2020. Take the launch of the new token comp, from Compound. It was coming out on top of a project I first learned about in 2018. Two years may not sound that long, but crypto moves fast. Two years later, Compound was basically a Knight of the Table Round, as far as proven DeFi projects went.

So I was happy to cover comp, but if some other project wanted to launch with a token from day one and expected me to be just as interested, my attitude was, "No, thank you" (usually, though circumstances could create exceptions—see: SushiSwap).

Even as I started to realize that SBF and the FTX empire had become uniquely powerful, my attitude through 2020 and early 2021 was that his new projects on Solana sounded fine, but I wanted to wait and see.

There are, by my reckoning, four big Sam tokens (five if you count Solana's sol—and many would).

A note: Through most of this book I've preferred to use a token's name rather than its ticker symbol (ether vs. ETH), but for these I'm going to go with tickers, because they all basically share a name with the app they were built for.

The four tokens are: Serum's SRM, Maps.me's MAPS, Oxygen's OXY, and Bonfida's FIDA.

The first to move was Serum. FTX investor Chris McCann said on the *Acquired* podcast that it was the idea for Serum that led SBF to start looking at blockchains besides Ethereum and Bitcoin. He wanted to build a decentralized exchange, but he didn't want it to be designed like Uniswap or SushiSwap. He wanted a centralized exchange that worked like his exchange, as a central limit order book.

"I think the bar is extremely high to get people to move from Ethereum to anything else," he admitted to me when we spoke in February 2021.

Which doesn't mean he thought that Ethereum's builders were doing what they should. When we spoke the next month, he said, "The back story is do everything you can to kind of get DeFi to the most ambitious thing it can be . . . I don't think the current DeFi ecosystem is trying."

So Serum was this way to give traders a trading experience like they could find on FTX, one that was faster, more flexible, and more capital efficient.

Going back to our discussion of AMMs, or automated market makers, at this point in the story, they always had one price for any trader. It's true the price would change if a user wanted to buy or sell a lot (slippage), but the automatic market maker model gave a trader one price.

He couldn't go on an AMM and say, "Well, I'd like to pay $5 less" and wait until someone took it. If that's what he wanted, he'd have to set up a bot and wait for it to hit that price. On an order book model, though, that kind of thing is easy to do.

The reason central limit order books (CLOBs) hadn't worked on Ethereum so far was because people could easily steal good trades. Each Ethereum block took about 17 seconds. A trader had to post a transaction and wait for miners to pick it up and verify it before it was real. Bots could watch the posted transactions, and if the bots saw a money-making trade, they could steal it by posting the same trade with a better fee for miners so they would post the bot's trade first—stealing the trade (that fee to miners is colloquially referred to as "gas" because it pays the Ethereum machine to grind its gears).

Solana was thought to be fast enough to avoid this problem while also supporting lots more users. That was the whole concept for Serum. That way a person could just post an offer below the market price and maybe the mere fact that the offer was there in the order book would incline someone to take it.

Next was Maps.me, which was a travel app that apparently is popular with the globe-hopping set of young European travelers (I hadn't heard of it). It was owned by the Russian conglomerate Mail.ru until November 2020, when it was spun out. Then in January 2021, Alameda Research led a $50 million funding round for Maps.me.

Alex Grebnev, the cofounder of Maps.me, told Cointelegraph at the time, "The industry is waiting for a catalyst for the mass adoption of DeFi tools," and that they planned "to give our users the ability to trade a wide range of assets that are not limited by geographical boundaries or transaction size."

When we spoke, SBF told me that Maps.me was "bigger than almost any product you've heard of in the world. It's bigger than any fintech app maybe."

He said travelers were using the app and hacking together all kinds of weird payment solutions to use money in different parts of the world as they moved. SBF's vision was to give them an app that worked everywhere. Under the hood, shifts in value could be made using Serum, but travelers would have a seamless user experience in the app. Payments on the road might eventually be as easy as posting travel selfies to Instagram.

On Twitter, he wrote, "Paypal is likely the product with the largest userbase in crypto, at around 300m. Soon, the second largest will probably be MAPS."[1]

Then Oxygen billed itself as a prime brokerage for DeFi, but really, to start, it was copying Compound and Aave, providing basic borrowing and lending services in a decentralized fashion.

Oxygen was founded by the same team that ran Maps.me, and SBF was an advisor. Alameda put in $40 million behind their token too.

Then finally there was Bonfida, a bit of a catch-all project. It aimed to do all the things that would make Serum easy to use and fun. It was going to create bots, a market for non-fungible tokens, and a wallet app. It was aiming to make all the graphical user interfaces.

There was a Bonfida wallet for a while, but then the Phantom wallet came along and the Bonfida team got behind that.

So those are the tokens that are most associated with SBF's vision for DeFi. SRM's public token sale was August 2020. FIDA had its public sale in December 2020. The MAPS token sale was January 2021. OXY sold in March 2021. Eight months to get them all out.

There are some common themes to their token launches.

In every case except FIDA, the supply was 10 billion tokens. Also with the exception of FIDA, they each aimed to raise about $600,000 in initial sales on exchanges (called "initial exchange offerings," or IEOs).

They all generally released about 30 percent of the total supply onto the market (low float). And if it helps to illuminate just how powerful this low float effect could be when supply and demand meet, how about this: when SRM was listed on Binance, the world's largest exchange, in August 2020, its price leapt 1000 percent.

That's the kind of effect that could be attained when there was this limited supply. Of course we can't know for sure, but it stands to reason that Alameda was standing ready to meet that demand as SRM hit and was able to recoup much of what it invested in building Serum on that day alone.

And just in case these tokens didn't have long-term potential, FTX was able to use them to drive perks for holders of ftt. People who had 500 ftt or more on the exchange were eligible to retrieve token giveaways (airdrops, in cryptospeak) when FTX had tokens to give away.

---

[1] Reader: it was not.

It had plenty in late 2020 and early 2021.

When Alameda and FTX fell apart in November 2022, a lot of crypto assets on their balance sheet would turn out to be these "Sam coins," and there might be a simple logic to that.

From the very start, SBF's exchange, FTX, featured cross-collateralization. Basically, a trader could use all the tokens in their portfolio as collateral in making margin trades (that is, borrowing from the exchange to win bigger when trades went right, also known as leveraging trades).

On other exchanges, a trader that only had $500 in bitcoin and $500 in ether was out of luck if they wanted to do a margin trade for $1,000. They could do two different trades at $500 each but not one loan for $1,000.

On FTX, they could. This made collateralizing margin somewhat more convenient and less math-heavy for traders, but it had another upshot too. It meant that Alameda, which had all kinds of tokens coming in as it made investments in lots of projects, had lots of random little tokens it could use as collateral too.

Which meant it could make bigger bets, *which is always what Alameda preferred to do*.

And honestly the benefit of successfully trading off the fresh launches of the Sam coins might have been less important for the Samglomerate than the larger effect they had on the Solana blockchain itself.

Very little of 2021 would pass before people started to see that Solana looked to be the winner for the year. The token hit a sort of escape velocity. It started the year at $2.16, but would rise as high as $259 by November.

Other comparable chains to Solana also had their moments of glory in 2021, but Solana was by far the largest. Its market cap pushed $80 billion at one point. Avalanche's pushed $30 billion. NEAR topped out around $12 billion. (As noted in the previous chapter, this sort of comparison is the one way market cap it useful.)

Several people I spoke with said something along the lines of Nick White, who was working for the team behind the Harmony blockchain in 2021. Harmony was also competing in the Ethereum-but-faster game with Solana and others.

"I remember very distinctly a phase change. Him choosing Solana was like a kingmaker move," White told me. "It all of a sudden made the

Solana ecosystem sort of the chosen L1 ecosystem." Harmony's market cap peaked late, breaking $4 billion in January 2022.

All of these chains are way down from their highs, but that king-maker move looks different now. Solana is down the furthest.

One of the chief virtues of cryptocurrencies is thought to be decentralization. In other words, any crypto system is not meant to depend so much on one company or group or person that it can't survive without them.

But the SEC remarked on Alameda's positions in Sam coins (without calling them that) in its December complaint:

> The collateral that Alameda had on deposit, consisting largely of enormous positions in illiquid crypto assets issued by FTX and Bankman-Fried (including the "FTT" token, the native crypto asset of FTX), compounded the undisclosed risk to FTX's investors. Bankman-Fried and FTX's system valued this collateral at trading prices, but the collateral deposited by Alameda was not worth the value assigned to it.

As soon as the FTX empire started to crumble the value of all these tokens crumbled. It turns out all the Sam coins had a central point of failure: Sam.

Sources Referenced

Interview, Sam Bankman-Fried, via video chat and mobile, Feb. 8, 2021.
"**Mail.ru Group Sells MAPS.ME**," VK.company, *Investor News*, Nov. 2, 2020.
"**SBF leads $50M funding round to bring DeFi to Maps.me's 140M users**," Haig, Samuel, Cointelegraph, Jan. 18, 2021.
"**Alameda Research doubles down on Maps.me, invests $40 million in Oxygen**," Thurman, Andrew, Cointelegraph, Feb. 24, 2021.
Interview, Nick White, mobile, Dec. 13, 2022.
Sam Bankman-Fried, @SBF_FTX, Twitter, Dec. 6, 2020: https://twitter.com/SBF_FTX/status/1335531934269591556.
CoinGecko.com, for coin prices and market caps.
"**SEC v. Sam Bankman-Fried**," US Securities and Exchange Commission complaint before the US Court of the Southern District of New York, Dec. 13, 2022.

Chapter 29

Effective Altruism

I've been debating about what I want to say here, and I have come to a decision. I'm going to give you a personal account of my own experience with Effective Altruism, the social movement that SBF credited with moving him to go big in crypto.

If you've read anything about SBF already, you know he's an adherent of this philosophy espoused by Princeton's Peter Singer and Oxford's Will MacAskill, among others.

Quick summary: a dherents find a way to do the most good they can with their lives, and their decisions about what to do are driven by data. A subset of such people can do the most good by doing good things, but, for most people, the good they can do comes from making money and giving away as much as they can afford to good organizations.

This spins out into all kinds of philosophical directions, but that starts the spin.

SBF opted to make lots of money. Sam was also a utilitarian. Utilitarianism and EA have a lot in common. Utilitarians just try to boil questions down into good and bad, pleasure and pain, and be really frank about trade-offs. Add up the good side, subtract the bad side, and then make a decision.

An example: in Politico, they quoted SBF talking about his shift to veganism in a very utilitarian way. He said, "Quantitatively, you enjoy eating a nice meal for 30 minutes and there's five weeks of torture that went into producing that."

It's also worth noting that EAs are strongly related to another strain of philosophical thinking found online, that of rationalism. Rationalists aren't all EAs, but most EAs are at least somewhat rationalist. In short: rationalists like to base decisions on facts and data. Their most famous website is called LessWrong. In other words, one can become "less wrong" through accumulating evidence, but you'll probably never be "right."

This reflects the Bayesian reasoning from Chapter 18.

So what I could do here is go through some of the famous EA talks and cite some of its seminal texts, give you highlights, break it down. But I'm not going to do that, because that's the crux of every other EA account you're going to read from a reporter like me. I can give you something else, and I think it's better: I can tell you about my experience with the movement.

In 2019, I found the New York EAs. I like to talk about public policy. I'm avidly green, and I've given to a decent number of organizations. I had recently learned about the (weirdly controversial) EA-leaning blog Slate Star Codex, and I liked it (it's fine; the *New York Times* needs to relax).[1] All this makes me an ideal candidate for hanging out in this scene—and it is very much a scene.

So for about maybe six months to a year there, starting in 2019 and ending a little before the pandemic, I went to EA meetups often. I hung out with a few in small groups as well. I went to a handful of EA-adjacent parties. I probably never would have done shrooms if I hadn't found that crew.

Ultimately, I decided that their world wasn't for me. My problem was mainly that I couldn't commit to it. Before becoming a journalist, I spent about a decade working in very grassroots organizations dedicated to

---

[1] The *Times*' Cade Metz did a pearl-clutching profile of the blog in 2021, but that post isn't the story. The larger story is what happened as he pursued the story and how the blogs' readers reacted.

different left-leaning social causes, making way less money than all my other friends. So, to a certain degree, I already had given up a lot trying to do good the best way I knew how, and I'd come to mostly regret that time.

So I felt like a phony sticking around.

But I will tell you this: I came away glad they exist.

There's a lot of folks online having panic attacks about EAs, but that's silly. Everyone: breathe.

EAs are, overwhelmingly, a bunch of very nice, extremely earnest men and women. And by the way, as someone who has lurked in a few weird subcultures, one of the things that leaps out about EAs is its gender balance. A lot of women and men are into it.

EAs are open and welcoming, though they do have their own weird language that can take a while to pick up on, but it is not a dangerous mind virus attempting to justify the excesses of the tech industry. Stop.

To my eyes: they are the first really good example I have personally found of a modern, secular answer to churches.

Not the institution of the Church or the concept of the small-c catholic church, but churches, local places where people feel a non-familial kinship with other members, a nurturing network that mixes people across classes and ages. We do not have much in the way of such places to speak of now in the secular West.

As religion has faded, that non-family local-level support system has been lost. EAs are the most fun and friendly answer to them I've seen. Yes, you definitely have to learn some weird norms, like with any group, but EAs are very into web-forums, so there's a lot of material to help you from home.

Being an EA, as far as I can tell, largely means going to meetups and talking about policy and philosophy and philanthropy in intense, energetic detail for a while and then hanging out afterward and drinking and bullshitting. Hopefully, eventually people who join start giving some money as well, but in my experience no one grills newcomers about that.

I found it nice, and it felt positive. It made me want to be a bit better, and I did start taking giving seriously again even as I quit showing up at the meetups. I just didn't give as much or as fastidiously as an EA might.

And the other nice thing about EAs (and this is something you won't learn about from just about any profile of the movement I've seen) is that it's like having a global network of *actual friends* whom you just haven't met yet.

An EA can go visit a new city, find the local EA Facebook group, and ask if anyone wants to hang out one night. Odds are, at least three or four people will come out. Maybe more.

And they will spend the night hoisting beers and talking about—I don't know—the relative merits of transit systems in different major cities or whether it's more pressing to reduce disease or poverty or the merits of a political push for nuclear power in the states.

That's really most of what EA is. I wish there were more networks like that, scratching other itches, because people need each other, but they also need a reason to be together like that. An ethos helps make such networks stick. In a secular world, there's a lot fewer reasons to stick with people.

EAs found one reason.

But on the other hand, nice groups of people who share a common set of ideals and earn status points by showing each other their commitment are always vulnerable to charismatic leaders who see a means to an end in their ideals.

I think that was probably Sam. EA was his means to glory, and the movement got him far.

"I totally looked up to this guy, this motherfucker who I hate now," a former New York EA leader turned crypto hedge fund cofounder told *New York Mag.* "I'm still licking my wounds and I'm sheepish and embarrassed." The fund is down 80 percent after much of its assets got stuck on FTX.

Even EAs with no direct stake in FTX are now reeling. As it happens with EAs, much of their discontent is playing out in discussions on their online forums.

The staff of its charitable arm, the FTX Future Fund, quit as a group before bankruptcy was declared, on November 10. They wrote on EffectiveAltruism.org:

We don't yet have a full picture of what went wrong, and we are following the news online as it unfolds. But to the extent that the leadership of
FTX may have engaged in deception or dishonesty, we condemn that
behavior in the strongest possible terms. We believe that being a good
actor in the world means striving to act with honesty and integrity.

The CEO, Nick Beckstead, lead author of the post, never got back
to me about discussing it more after I messaged him on LinkedIn.

On the day it declared bankruptcy, MacAskill wrote:

> I want to make it utterly clear: if those involved deceived others and en-
> gaged in fraud (whether illegal or not) that may cost many thousands of
> people their savings, they entirely abandoned the principles of the effec-
> tive altruism community.
>
> If this is what happened, then I cannot in words convey how strongly
> I condemn what they did. I had put my trust in Sam, and if he lied and
> misused customer funds he betrayed me."

A number of EAs have also been reflecting on whether or not they
should have known, but Haseeb Qureshi is both an EA and a crypto VC
with Dragonfly Capital (which passed on investing in FTX). Qureshi
argued that EAs should stop wringing their hands over whether or not
they could have foreseen this. The funds that did back FTX could have
looked more closely than they did, however.

"I think the real failure here with FTX had much more to do with
the VCs than it had to do with the public, than it had to do with a fucking social movement. These people are not responsible nor are they
equipped for understanding the veracity of somebody making business
claims. The only people who are equipped to do that are the investors,"
he told me in an interview.

SBF's alleged fraud should not reflect on everyone else in the EA
movement, just as ransomware shouldn't reflect on bitcoin. I write that
knowing that these two statements are both logically sound and cogni-
tively balderdash. And yet, I stand by them. Someday, most may agree;
probably not right now. Fair enough.

EA has gotten big enough that it's going to have a complicated relationship with the rest of the world, and SBF created the moment that made it weird. But it was going to get weird one way or another.

That's just what happens when a thing in the world becomes big enough to matter.

Sources Referenced

"**How the newest megadonor wants to change Washington**," Schneider, Elena, Politico, Aug. 4, 2022.

"**Silicon Valley's Safe Space**," Metz, Cade, the *New York Times*, Feb. 22, 2021.

"**Still Alive**," Alexander, Scott, Astral Codex Ten, Jan. 21, 2021.

"**Is Effective Altruism now defective?**," Van Zuylen-Wood, Simon, New York, Nov. 21–Dec. 4, 2022.

"**The FTX Future Fund team has resigned**," Beckstead, Nick, Leopold Aschenbrenner, Avital Balwit, Ketan Ramakrishnan, and Will MacAskill, EffectiveAltruism.org, Nov. 10, 2022.

"**A personal statement on FTX**," MacAskill, Will, EffectiveAltruism.org, Nov. 12, 2022.

Interview, Haseeb Qureshi, Mobile, Dec. 2, 2022.

Chapter 30

Reef Finance

"If only people knew how balls long crypto Alameda has been."

—SBF

On Twitter, March 17, 2021.

In March 2021, Alameda Research approached Reef Finance, a DeFi project that has a token called reef (REEF). When a dispute broke out between the two companies, according to Reef, Alameda threatened it with getting its token delisted.

It would be seven more months until SBF officially stepped down from his role as CEO of Alameda.

Reef is a stand-alone blockchain (running using technology from the Polkadot blockchain) that's designed to be faster and cheaper than Ethereum, the category leader. Reef was made specifically with DeFi in mind.

Reef was a new project when its flap with Alameda broke out. It had only raised its seed round the previous September.

According to all accounts, Alameda did a deal for $20 million worth of reef tokens in March 2021, or 675 million reef, at a 20 percent discount. They had an agreement to sell another $60 million right afterward.

Then the Reef team watched as the same tokens immediately moved onto Binance, the biggest crypto exchange in the world. Soon, 50 million tokens left Binance and moved to FTX.

Sam Trabucco, then a trader with Alameda, told The Block that they hadn't sold even close to all that they had bought. It's possible that this is true. As market makers, they might have largely kept most of the reef in place on Binance for future trading. However, Trabucco would not answer The Block's question about how many tokens it sold.

What no one can dispute, however, was that reef prices briefly fell 30 percent across the market, though they largely recovered shortly thereafter.

Reef CEO Denko Mancheski told CoinDesk that his team had understood the round to be a strategic, long-term investment. That said, their perhaps hastily written blog post describes the situation as follows: "The Alameda team had refused to offer a legal contract for the transaction and had asked to operate on based on 'trust.'"

So, feeling betrayed, Reef reneged on the deal to sell another $60 million worth of reef to Alameda.

"We agreed to an OTC trade with REEF; they immediately went to the press to brag," Trabucco wrote on Twitter. "We obviously do not recommend anyone do business with REEF in any way."

The part of the Reef blog post that stands out, though, is this one. The team wrote:

> After seeing that the additional tranche would not go through, Alameda began threatening to delist the Reef token from FTX and said that they would try to get Reef delisted from other top exchanges as an act of retribution if we did not give them the $60M tranche.

In response, Alameda published excerpts from their chat log. "These are all verbatim excerpts from the conversation; we believe this accurately represents what happened," the team wrote.

That said, it doesn't seem like all of it is there. Mancheski did not get back to me about revisiting this incident. Alameda is gone, and Trabucco had already resigned anyway.

In Alameda's version, there's an agreement to sell an overall investment of $80 million, 2,702,702,703 reef for basically 3¢ each. After the first 20 percent was delivered, Reef tried to get an agreement for some kind of clearly stated vesting schedule (that is, a rate at which Alameda would sell, rather than dumping all at once).

In Alameda's account, Reef wrote on March 13: "Discussing with the team, some resistance due to the no lockup."

So Alameda countered, offering a three-month linear lockup (meaning they get a little to sell each day), but they wrote: "Only if we get custody of all up front; we obviously don't trust you to deliver."

It's hard to see which side is on the right in this one, but the part that jumps out is this claim that Alameda threatened to delist the token on FTX. That's not reflected in Alameda's account, just in Reef's.

However, Reef CEO Denko Mancheski posted a screenshot of the threat. In it, Ryan Salame, CEO of FTX Digital Markets, says that the firm is "likely to" delist reef and ask Binance to do the same, unless Reef proceeds with selling the other $60 million in tokens.

The claim of the threat to delist is further supported by a tweet that Reef showed as a screenshot in their post. In it, the FTX account wrote: "Should FTX delist coins that have rug pulled (e.g. DMG, REEF), or keep them?" The tweet is from a CoinDesk report, which also noted that the tweet had been deleted.

Even if Reef had reneged on a deal with Alameda under false pretenses, that wouldn't be a rug pull. Tweets responding to the allegation of a rug pull at the time point out the same.

As @testinprodcap put it at the time, "I don't think $reef is innocent. Just don't think ftx should be alameda's enforcement arm because of a deal gone bad."

For what it's worth, SBF didn't push back on this interpretation of events. He told me, "I think it was a moment for us to revisit practices and to basically . . . feel like we needed, internally, to clarify that separation as well."

According to CoinGecko, On March 12, ftt was trading at $37.14 and reef was trading at $0.046. In mid-December 2022, ftt is at $1.52

and reef is at $0.0031. They are each down so much it barely matters that reef is doing slightly better than ftt.

But Reef Finance is not in the middle of an epic bankruptcy that has left the whole world agog, either.

★★★

Sam Kazemian is the founder of Frax Finance, a stablecoin project that tries to be mostly a fiat-backed stablecoin but also a little bit an algorithmic YOLO machine. Frax has its own loyal following, and it has built up its own treasury. In order to keep growing that treasury, Kazemian has been involved with yield farming a number of DeFi projects.

Kazemian told me he has found himself on the other side of Alameda's farming and dumping multiple times. For example, in 2022, he watched as Alameda played much the same game on a project called Magic Internet Money as it had played on CREAM, loading it up with ftt so it could print out a stablecoin to trade.

He long ago came to the conclusion that Alameda was not a company he wanted to collaborate with. "You didn't have a smoking gun to point to, you would just be like: This does not look like anyone who is actually good for the industry, in any way," he said.

Sources Referenced

Sam Bankman-Fried, @SBF_FTX, Twitter, March 17, 2021, 2:18 p.m.: https://twitter.com/SBF_FTX/status/1372250887222030337.

"Our Official Response to Recent Events Regarding Alameda," Reef blog on Medium, March 15, 2021.

"REEF updates," Alameda Research blog on Medium, March 15, 2021.

"Token deal drama between Alameda, Reef Finance breaks into public view," Khatri, Yogita, The Block, March 15, 2021.

"$80M Deal Gone Wrong: Alameda Research, Reef Finance Spar Over Unloaded Tokens," Foxley, William, CoinDesk, March 16, 2021.

Denko Mancheski, @denkomacheski, Twitter, March 15 7:10 p.m.: https://twitter.com/denkomancheski/status/1371599781835984899.

"Alameda Research Pumps $20M into Cross-Chain DeFi Platform Reef Finance," Akhtar, Tanzeel, CoinDesk, March 12, 2021.

Sam Trabucco on Twitter, @Alameda Trabucco, Twitter, March 15, 2021, 7:55 a.m.: https://twitter.com/AlamedaTrabucco/status/1371429927698886657.

Tipc, @testinprodcap, Twitter, March 15, 2021, 8:46 a.m.: https://twitter.com/testin-prodcap/status/1371442646841954304.

Interview, Sam Kazemian, Nov. 19, 2022.

Interview, Sam Bankman-Fried, phone call with spokesperson, Dec. 30, 2022.

PART II

STAR POWER

Chapter 31

Celebrity

Between July and October 2021, FTX raised over $1 billion across two separate rounds (the first led by longstanding venture firm Sequoia Capital, the second including Ontario Teachers' Pension Plan Board among others). It was also able to buy Binance out of its stake in the company from its early days (which is how the rival exchange would get its hands on its fateful bag of ftt).

And so SBF had a giant pile of money.

In other words, in 2021 FTX moved to a new level on the global stage, and anyone following the crypto market could feel it.

So this next part will be constructed a little bit differently. The story has been basically chronological. But by mid-2021, there is simply too much going on to go straight through. So for Part II, I'm going to break the story into three separate threads: SBF's celebrity, his bailouts, and his political efforts.

Up first: FTX's aggressive acquisition of attention in the United States.

Michael Arrington, an investor and the founder of the news site Techcrunch, has a famous selfie he took in January 2019 at a crypto party in Singapore. It shows him with Tron's Justin Sun, Binance's CZ, and SBF, among others. It was a portrait of some of the industry's most notorious. Arrington tells me that SBF had been lurking nearby and then basically photobombed the shot.

According to Frankel, the crypto OGs that she was friends with found Sam off-putting at first. He was viewed with suspicion for a long time. But even if everyone didn't immediately take to SBF, "There's this magical effect when you make people money. It makes people like you," Frankel said.

In February 2022 SBF appeared on an episode of CoinDesk's YouTube show *The Hash*, the morning after Superbowl LXI, the TV broadcast of which featured FTX's inadvertently prescient Larry David spot. He made a comment on that show that helps to set the table for this part of the conversation.

One of the four hosts of *The Hash* asked him what he thought about the various meme coins, led by the king of meme coins, dogecoin.

"I think the popular answer to give here is they hurt the industry," SBF replied. "I think on net they have almost certainly helped the industry."

Dogecoin has brought a great deal of attention to cryptocurrency but what it didn't do was illuminate anything for the masses. It takes a long time deep inside the crypto culture to *get dogecoin*, and even then, not everyone agrees it has actual value.

Like Bitcoin and Ethereum (and not many other blockchains), Dogecoin has a core idea. Dogecoin's idea is that ideas alone have value that increases as they grow. In fact, SBF would tell Tyler Cowen that thinking about Dogecoin made him question how he thought about the value of *everything*.

But in that moment, on that episode of *The Hash*, SBF seemed less philosophical and more opportunistic. He seemed to be saying that any attention is good, and a lot of attention is great. Once people know your little subculture exists, it's inevitably going to grow. The costs of misunderstandings or frustration are less than the benefit of growing.

To that end, he slapped his company's name on Miami's pro basketball arena in Miami, in a $135 million, 19-year deal announced in March 2021.

If anyone wants a benchmark for a tech bubble: when fairly new companies put their names on sports arenas, that indicates that folks have become long on money, short on plans.

"Sam posted in Slack saying, 'I feel very strongly we should do a stadium deal,'" Zane Tackett, FTX's former head of institutional sales, told me.

He said FTX had done well with institutional clients because Alameda had a lot of relationships through its over-the-counter trading offerings. "Right from the beginning we had pretty good pickup from large trading firms. The issue is we needed the softer retail flow, as well. Because institutions want to trade where there's retail, because otherwise the flow's more toxic. And so we needed something to get a bit more of that retail adoption."

"Toxic" here means smart money, entities trading so well it's hard to make a profit as their counterparty. Retail is slow and uninformed. There's money to be made trading against amateurs.

On the *Unchained* podcast around that time, SBF said, "As one of the latest entrants to the game on the exchange side we're definitely lagging in terms of raw user numbers," he said.

In SBF's mind, doing something that connected the firm to something people knew and cared about, like a sports team, was additive for FTX's brand, whereas a lot of advertising is dilutive, meaning you see a brand more and more, but it makes you care less.

"That's the sense we're trying to avoid, completely commercial, completely bland, completely replaceable," he said on the show.

Sports deals might cost more up front, he seemed to be saying, but the truth is cheap advertising does nothing for a brand. It might even diminish it.

It got Miami's basketball arena because the city found itself pressed to find somebody to take the sponsorship as American Airlines had decided to let the spot go. That gave FTX a chance to get a stadium deal at a better price than the company might have if its staff hadn't decided to go shopping for one as a pandemic was winding down.

This is a key point. Many big companies had done badly through 2020 (such as airlines), but crypto companies had generally done very well. Lots of people were sitting at home learning how to trade coins.

In other words, FTX was buying in during a mini-boom (it was not a true bull market quite yet). I asked Tackett about the fact that stadium deals have a history of backfiring for companies, and I used the word "curse," which was a mistake. Tackett said no one really talked about a curse, but he called the concept "stupid."

"Are we going to start checking astrology about what we want to do next?" Tackett asked.

The Heat deal, he argued, as a proportion of FTX's profits, was cheap. It's easy to focus on that first number: $135 million, but the next number really changes it: over 19 years.

And he's right. Put that way, it was a steal. But the attention seeking didn't stop there. In May, FTX would commit to spending a million dollars every year in carbon offsets, in part to confront cryptocurrency's negative association with climate change.

But that decision might have also been informed by talks the company was having with the quarterback, Tom Brady, and his wife, the model, Gisele Bündchen. The latter, in particular, was always portrayed as more interested in SBF's philanthropic work than she was in crypto.

SBF said on *Unchained* that the company had been talking to the couple for a while, so crypto's carbon impact might have been a sticking point to get the deal done.

Whatever the back story there, in June 2021, word came out that the famous pair would be serving as brand ambassadors for FTX. Around that same time, FTX also inked a deal with a big e-sports team (young guys who play video games while lots and lots of people watch—it really is huge) that was pricier than the stadium deal.

At that point. FTX was inking deals like a Gatorade salesman at the end of a foot race in the Mojave.

FTX would become the official cryptocurrency exchange for Major League Baseball, because. . . some of the hot dog vendors prefer getting paid in litecoin, maybe? Why baseball needed a crypto exchange is a bit fuzzy, but it got the FTX name on patches umpires wore.

Not to ignore the fact that many sports fans prefer the college game, in August it got its name on the stadium at the University of California at Berkeley.

And to be fair: some of these deals really do seem to have been bargains. Watching a few minutes of a Miami Heat game, the FTX branding is everywhere. If all a company wanted was visibility, like SBF said about dogecoin, it seems like a no-brainer.

Plus that first year of play turned out to be great. The Heat made it to the last game of the conference finals against the Boston Celtics, at the end of May 2022. Both the Heat and the exchange sponsoring their stadium appeared to be destined for greatness.

But in September, FTX ratcheted it up once more, with an ad that went on national television, and, of course, this being the era that it is, exploded across social media.

In the ad, Bündchen and Brady decide that they are "in" on FTX and start calling around to their friends about getting in as well. Everyone says to them, "I'm in."

The ad ends on a joke about the fact that Brady abandoned the Patriots for the Buccaneers that works even if you don't *really* know which teams the guy played for (like me). It was a good ad.

Shortly thereafter, SBF scored a *Forbes* cover.

One source with knowledge of FTX tells me that its efforts in 2021 weren't even really so much calls to action as they were building brand awareness. When the company really wanted to try to get people to sign up, it wanted them to know the name. That's it.

In that discussion with CoinDesk the following February's Superbowl spot, SBF says that the company looked at 200 concepts for a Superbowl ad before settling on the one with Larry David (the actor and writer known lately for his roles in creating *Seinfeld* and *Curb Your Enthusiasm*).

How well did the spot do? Looking at several clickbait roundups of best ads after the game, it made a few lists. Not all. Zendaya's SquareSpace ad seems to have won the vibes for tech sector ads, but FTX's might have been the only crypto ad that had any mainstream appeal.

The top US exchange, Coinbase, did a weird ad with a QR code that bounced around the screen. When I heard about it, I thought: *Well, that does accurately reflect the janky user experience of crypto in 2022. . .*

But the Superbowl ad wasn't the only thing that happened in February. Katy Perry showed up—again.

Back in January 2018, Katy Perry had posted an Instagram photo where she showed her hand with fingers curled in, freshly manicured with the logos of various cryptocurrencies: ethers, lumens, monero, etc. At the time, the pop star had the 18th most followed Instagram account, according to Insider.com. Slate wrote about the post with the headline, "Katy Perry's Bitcoin Manicure May Foretell the Coming Crypto Collapse."

Nicely played, Slate, because the good times of 2017 had about a month left when Perry posted her paintjob.

Perry, it should be noted, hadn't completely sat out cryptocurrency since then, but she hadn't been especially vocal, either. She had also fallen four spots to #22 on Facebook's mobile photo app, according to Wikipedia.

Then, on February 12, 2022, just before the big game, she posted a few portraits to Instagram, with the caption: "im quitting music and becoming an intern for @ftx_official ok 🫰."

On Twitter, FTX eagerly shared her post, writing "FTX intern candidates have some competition!"

And for a certain somewhat superstitious cadre of longtime crypto denizens, it engendered dread. Much like her last appearance, she had shown up after bitcoin had hit its high mark but when it still felt like maybe everyone could muddle along for a while without really suffering.

Her second cameo appearance in this land of countercultural contrarians, with a very similar mood prevailing across the subculture made longtime investors worry: Is it about to happen again?

Reader, It was.

Sources Referenced

"Crypto Exchange FTX Secures Naming Rights for Miami Heat Arena for $135M," Crawley, Jamie, CoinDesk, March 24, 2021.

Michael Arrington, @arrington, Twitter, January 20, 2020: https://twitter.com/arrington/status/1219736350196301825.

Interview, Tamara Frankel, mobile, Dec. 13, 2022.

"Sam Bankman-Fried on Arbitrage and Altruism (Ep. 145)," Cowen, Tyler, Conversations with Tyler, March 9, 2022.

Interview, Zane Tackett, videoconference, Dec. 5, 2022.

FTX, @FTX_Official, Twitter, May 20, 2021: https://twitter.com/FTX_Official/status/1395510416298577928

"TSM Esports Signs $210 Million Sponsorship with FTX Crypto Exchange," Cohen, Andrew, SportTechie, *Sports Business Journal*, June 7, 2021.

"Tom Brady and Gisele Bündchen Take Equity Stake in Crypto Firm FTX," Hajric, Vildana, Bloomberg, June 29, 2021.

"FTX Becomes Official Cryptocurrency Exchange Brand of MLB," Kelly, Liam, Decrypt, June 23, 2021.

"FTX Crypto Exchange Buys Naming Rights for Cal's Football Field," Cohen, Andrew, SportTechie, *Sports Business Journal*, Aug. 24, 2021.

"Tom Brady And Gisele Bundchen Build a Crypto Trading Posse in First Ads for FTX," Jardine, Alexandra, AdAge, Sept. 9, 2021.

"Crypto Exchange FTX Buys Super Bowl Ad, Deepening Sports Push," Greifeld, Katherine, Bloomberg, Oct. 26, 2021.

"FTX's Sam Bankman-Fried Gives the Tom Brady/Gisele Bundchen Backstory," Shin, Laura, Unchained Podcast, July 2, 2021.

"FTX CEO Sam Bankman-Fried Talks Super Bowl, Future Plans, Crypto Regulation," The Hash, CoinDesk, YouTube, Feb. 14, 2022.

"Katy Perry's Bitcoin Manicure May Foretell the Coming Crypto Collapse," Schwedel, Heather, Slate, Jan. 25, 2018.

"The 50 most followed Instagram accounts in 2018," Hartmans, Avery, Insider, Dec. 31, 2018.

"List of most-followed Instagram accounts," Wikipedia, revision Dec. 29, 2022: https://en.wikipedia.org/w/index.php?title=List_of_most-followed_Instagram_accounts&oldid=1130356130.

Katy Perry, @katyperry, Instagram, Feb. 12, 2022: https://www.instagram.com/p/CZ5Qw2-vVoW/.

FTX, @FTX_Official, Twitter, Feb. 12, 2022: https://twitter.com/FTX_Official/status/1492658009151057922.

Chapter 32

Crypto Bahamas

I wasn't there, so my account of FTX's last big event, Crypto Bahamas, is going to be rendered through a glass darkly, but I have one thing going for mine: it has hindsight on its side. No one writing then knew that FTX would be a crater made out of legal filings inside a Delaware bankruptcy court filing cabinet by the end of the year.

The problem with conference reports is that they focus so much on what happens on stage, but the truth is, people don't go to crypto conferences to see what's on stage. They go to *be* on stage. Failing that, they go to network outside the auditorium. The agenda isn't actually about something to watch so much as a signal to potential ticket buyers whether or not the organizers can put on an event that will attract the kind of people other people want to kiss up to in person.

To signal that, organizers have to spend money, and if there's one thing FTX knew how to do, it was how to spend money. FTX, and its partner SALT, spent a lot of money on the guest list at this event, that's why the agenda included folks like Tony Blair, Bill Clinton, Brady,

The crowd watches former President Bill Clinton speaking at Crypto Bahamas via the jumbotron, April 28, 2022. (Photo by Lucinda Shen.)

Bündchen, and Perry. Based on social media, Perry even canoodled a bit off stage with eager fanboys.

In short, Crypto Bahamas was the pinnacle of FTX's starfucking story arc.

Crypto Bahamas ran from April 26 to 29 in Nassau, Bahamas. It was a joint venture of FTX and Anthony Scaramucci's SALT (an organization that does events for thinkfluencers at nice places led by a former Trump administration official who is informally known as "The Mooch").

Proprietary trading firm Dexterity Capital's Michael Safai went. He said that he appreciated that the event had a carefully curated attendee list, with lots of blockchain companies. It had more CEOs than random business development guys, so it felt like time better spent.

As the conference opened, the prime minister of the Bahamas took to the stage and said, "The arrival and presence of FTX underscore the

SBF looks on at NFL Quarterback Tom Brady. (Photo by Danny Nelson.)

readiness of The Bahamas to be a home for global leaders in the crypto space."

He described how his government had put out a whitepaper on digital assets, saying, "This paper sets out our vision and the supporting framework to transform The Bahamas into the leading digital assets hub in the Caribbean and a global leader in the progressive regulation of businesses in this profoundly innovative space."

The web page where the paper was posted now shows an error message.

The *Financial Times*' account made much of the fact that attendees had to walk through a casino. The writer found that symbolism note-worthy enough to ask other attendees about it but was somewhat non-plussed that they didn't seem to make much of it. Maybe they had attended the Consumer Electronics Show? The largest tech conference in the world has had its attractions interspersed between slot machines for many years.

SBF sits between former FTX staff member Lauren Remington Platt and fashion model Gisele Bündchen, as they announce the company's editorial campaign. (Photo by Danny Nelson.)

Usually the formula for a crypto conference dispatch is: (1) find some theme that seemed to be echoed across multiple conversations, (2) say something about the most famous person who spoke, and (3) specifically for crypto events, include a scene from a too expensive-looking party.

Safai said the culminating party did look very expensive, complete with a celebrity-laden VIP section that everyone could see into but hardly any mere mortal besides SBF could get into.

But the crucial stuff is always the side conversations that might not have happened elsewhere, like when a small gang decides to do something absurd like forking bitcoin, sending the entire industry into a years-long flamewar.[1]

---

[1] In 2017, at CoinDesk's Consensus conference, the so-called New York Agreement attempted to change how many transactions could fit in each Bitcoin block, and it led to the hostile launch of Bitcoin Cash. For more, see *The Blocksize War: The battle over who controls Bitcoin's protocol rules*, Jonathan Bier (2021).

None of that stuff shows up in the day-after reportage.

Instead, if you're lucky, you get a few pithy quotes from on stage, like on the Prosek blog where the writer paraphrased Scaramucci as saying, "Millionaires wear suits; billionaires wear shorts."

There was a little falling action ahead: FTX had already purchased advertising real estate in *Vogue*. They ended up splitting their print real estate equally between Bündchen and SBF—because, obviously, they each appealed to the *Vogue* audience roughly equally.

Makes sense.

That magazine spread showed there was more to Scaramucci's haberdashery take than might be readily apparent. There's a divide in crypto that takes time to pick up on. Both sides intermingle a lot, but they aren't the same and they aren't even really aligned. One group is the actual crypto native. They yearn for crypto to succeed in shifting how humans coordinate with each other, and they want to see how far they can push it.

It would be an overstatement but not quite a useless illustration to say that this group is generally (though not completely) unlikely to be seen in Oxford shirts or pants from Bonobos. There's a lot of denim and sweatshirts in the disruptive camp, but there's definitely no uniform.

Even Brian Armstrong, Coinbase's CEO, has taken to making a point of favoring t-shirts. And his rhetoric (at least) clearly puts him on the side of disruption, even if his company can be timid.

The second group can best be described as TradFi-who-see-a-crypto-play. These are the ones who believe *there is money to be made* in blockchains, but don't believe in its promise particularly. They just want boat money.

Many of these types may be the sort who learned just enough in traditional finance to be a little more sophisticated than the average crypto trader about some tricks of the trade but couldn't quite cut it on Wall Street.

It's a lot like the difference between actual rock stars and the bands on Christian Rock labels. One was able to win by playing by the same rules as everyone, and the other needed to market themselves to a group that wanted a taste of the forbidden but with safety rails and parental approval.

Both TradFi-crypto and Christian Rock are easier paths to more limited success.

Looking at the conversation at Crypto Bahamas, it definitely seems like it leaned toward the TradFi take. Crypto but *just enough*. It's the same language at the end of the day that SBF primarily speaks.

And this brings me to SBF's shorts. Alameda's former chief operating officer Andy Croghan told the *New York Times* that he wore the shorts all the time to affect a mystique. It was about being the kind of guy who wouldn't touch long pants, who couldn't be bothered for anything shy of Congress (see Chapter 37).

The stark relief of this insistence created a contrast as sharp as a lit up neon sign in the center of a forest when he wore the getup on stage with Tony Blair and President Bill Clinton. His schlubby shorts and t-shirt actually managed to appear to be trying *too hard* in that context.

It was even worse when he sat between one of the more fashionable members of his staff and Bündchen, who appeared in a demure business casual dress. In videos and photos from that panel, SBF seems to be slouching down more than usual, as if he's realized just how far he'd taken this affectation.

Former United Kingdom Prime Minister Tony Blair and former U.S. President, Bill Clinton, with SBF at Crypto Bahamas. (Photo by Danny Nelson.)

Next to her and former world leaders, his sartorial flex made him look like a prisoner of his own bit.

But SBF doesn't accept that characterization. "So it's a weird look, but what I will say is that, like, it was just legitimately the case that I was way more comfortable," he told me. "Basically I overheat really easily."

In November, on the *Bloomberg Crypto* podcast, *Odd Lots'* Joe Weisenthal would say that one way he found SBF refreshing was that he never saw him trying to pitch ways that crypto would change the world. Crypto seemed to just be the way he made money.

Yet his looks and some of his public moves (SushiSwap, pushing Solana, pushing Serum) had brought a contingent of crypto natives around to SBF. He was seen as something of a leader, something of a hero. To me, the costume helped.

But in retrospect SBF seems more like a member of the second crypto contingent, the TradFi-who-see-a-crypto-play sort. He just didn't dress for that particular part.

In the next few months, his former fans would start to see through the look, even before his company fell.

Sources Referenced

Interview, Michael Safai, Dexterity Capital, video conference, Dec. 14, 2022.

"**Crypto's strange new respectability**," Schreckinger, Ben, Politico, April 29, 2022.

"**Crypto Is a Lifestyle, Not Just a Currency**," Prosek, Jen, Prosek.com, May 3, 2022.

"**Gisele Bündchen Stars in FTX Trading's Print Campaign**," Lockwood, Lisa, *Women's Wear Daily*, April 28, 2022.

"**Crypto bros on the beach feel a cold wind at their necks**," Oliver, Joshua, *Financial Times*, May 3, 2022.

"**Wall Street Goes Crypto in the Bahamas**," Wang, Tracy, CoinDesk, May 4, 2022.

"**A Crypto Emperor's Vision: No Pants, His Rules**," Yaffe-Bellany, David, the *New York Times*, May 14, 2022.

"**How did FTX end up at the Met Gala**," Schneier, Matthew, New York, Nov. 21–Dec. 4, 2022.

Bankman-Fried, Sam, interview, phone call with spokesperson, Dec. 30, 2022.

"**Revisiting the 'Magic Money Box' After the FTX Collapse**," Ishmael, Stacy-Marie, *Bloomberg Crypto*, Bloomberg, Nov. 23, 2022.

Chapter 33

Cult of Sam

One of my sources (who didn't want to be named) told me a story about arriving to work on the FTX campus in the Bahamas to work on one of the venture-backed teams. The source told me about going on a walk with one of the higher-ups. The executive explained that my source was now hanging out in a cult of Sam.

The new arrival took it as a joke and laughed, but they later realized it had never been meant as a joke. People at FTX were committed 100 percent to do whatever it took for FTX to succeed, and part of that was hewing close to the vision of its wonder boy founder.

Part of it was money, of course. "They were printing," I was told. "The bonuses were good."

As to other motivations, the source couldn't really say, but people behaved as if they were extraordinarily driven by something. He also noted that they didn't have a lot in the way of distractions. While it might sound glamorous to work from The Bahamas, the truth was that their office park in Nassau was a really boring place. It was a parking lot with some buildings—nothing like the vibrant life the team had left behind in Hong Kong.

But who had time for life outside of work, anyway?

Tackett, who supported FTX's power users, didn't seem to be personally moved by SBF's charisma, but something drove him. When he described how much work he was doing, it seemed unsustainable. No one told him to work that much, he said, it was just that there was so much to do.

Tackett wasn't motivated by saving the world. He was motivated by a business that could be huge and paid him well for helping it get bigger. Regardless, if he exaggerated his hours, he was working like a zealot even if the amount he claimed was discounted by 20 or 30 percent.

But this cult of Sam thing also fits with something another source told me: if you disagreed with SBF, if you questioned him, you had a way of getting shut out.

Which is worth mentioning because SBF presented himself as open to and eager to hear critiques.

There's an organization in the Effective Altruist (EA) world called 80,000 hours (the idea being that you have about 80,000 hours of work in you to do something good with your life), which also has a podcast by the same name. SBF's episode came out in 2022. It's a mostly fawning treatment of someone who was early in the movement and became one of its success stories.

The conversation SBF has with host Robert Wiblin has a very EA tone, with that probabilistic language that marks out members of the tribe. It also takes a particularly EA turn when Wiblin points out that SBF has recently become one of the biggest givers in the EA world.

This is a controversial point to make much of here, by the way.

Most of the time, here, after the debacle, when everyone talks about SBF's giving, it's always crucial that there be some kind of bent to that coverage. You can't just say he gave a lot of money; it has to be characterized, preferably suspiciously.

On the same day that I am writing this, crypto people are expressing outrage on Twitter about a story from the *New York Times* that goes to some lengths to characterize much of SBF's charitable and political work as a snow job aimed at burnishing his public image.

It opened with a story of a donation SBF promised that never came through and accompanying public relations efforts to get him credit for the donation with authoritative people. In other words, it kicks off with a story about a lie.

That wasn't good enough, though.

Crypto commentators are mad because it didn't use the word "fraud" in the headline. Because the post didn't lead with a reminder that he had lost customer funds after risking them in an undisclosed way.

Emotions are running high on the guy as I write these words, but we do know that he gave a fair amount of money and he was giving consistently well before he was truly rich. In fact, from where Wiblin sat, it sounded as though his giving had come to fairly dominate contributions within the EA network of organizations, and this was a group that had already come to marshal over a billion dollars even before SBF showed up (mainly by way of Cari Tuna and Dustin Moskovitz, whose wealth came from early days at Facebook and the productivity firm Asana).

So Wiblin calls SBF on this, suggesting that he might want to start taking steps to ensure that his own perspective doesn't dominate. Wiblin says, "You might even want to go out of your way to fund some things that you personally don't think are good, just because other people think they're good."

This probably doesn't immediately make sense. It's also not—I can tell you from past professional experience—how other grantmakers operate. But here is what Wiblin is saying: he's suggesting that Sam give at least some of his money to causes he doesn't think are important precisely because he doesn't think they are important (as long as other people he respects do). This would be a way of hedging against his own blind spots.

Funders would probably pay lip service to this sort of approach on a panel at a conference, but in the normal foundation world, *yeah*, my experience as a former grant seeker tells me that this isn't a thing people even *sort of* consider. Funders have some pretty ridiculous ideas about what's important, and organizations do back-bends to meet their expectations.

But Wiblin takes it just a little bit further. He says, "That could even be good by your own lights because of the risk that you could make a mistake."

In other words, Wiblin is saying that you should take out a philanthropic *hedge*, a bet that runs counter to your main bets.

Say, for example, your investment portfolio is full of solar power companies, but 5 percent of it is in Chevron and Exxon. That's your hedge. Just in case.

A lot of crypto people strongly, strongly favor either bitcoin or ethereum. They don't all like to admit it, but most of them have a little bit of the one they aren't crazy about, because there's no reason to completely let gains pass them by if they are wrong. I know one investor who took out a limited partner position in a fund she thinks is ridiculous just to guard against her own prejudices.

Hedging is something very familiar to investors, but a philanthropic hedge is something else entirely. SBF, however, does not dismiss it.

"Very explicitly," SBF replies, "we are excited to fund people to tell us how we might be wrong. I think that that's something that we've already written down as being on the stack of things that we're going to express potential excitement to fund."

The last area of interest listed on the FTX Future Fund website is/was: "Research that can help us improve," and it highlights a few pretty esoteric areas of EA thinking that the fund has largely ignored so far but invites outsiders to convince the organization why they should consider them in their funding.

Then on the very last line, it says: "We'd be excited and grateful to see rigorous criticisms of our priorities and concerns."

So his philanthropic org invited disagreement, but it didn't last long enough for us to learn if that plank was serious or rhetorical. If it really funded research that ran counter to SBF's philanthropic priorities, that would be a good counternarrative to this story of SBF, the conflict-averse control freak.

At this point, it's a data point, but it doesn't give much information.

More telling, on that podcast, was when SBF clearly articulated how he thought about risk.

Wiblin says, "You were often doing things that created some risk of going bust but offered the potential of making manyfold more money. That was kind of your modus operandi."

SBF replied, "Yeah. I think the way I saw it was like, 'Let's maximize EV: whatever is the highest net expected value thing is what we should do.' As opposed to some super-sublinear utility function, which is like, make sure that you continue on a moderately good path above all else, and then anything beyond that is gravy."

In other words: playing it safe and doing okay would be no way to reach outsized impact.

SBF said, "I do think those are probably the right choices, but they were scary."

Sources Referenced

Interview, unnamed source, Telegram chat, Nov. 19, 2022.

Interview, Zane Tackett, video conference, Dec. 5, 2022.

Interview, unnamed source, phone call, Dec. 19, 2022.

"Sam Bankman-Fried on taking a high-risk approach to crypto and doing good," Wiblin, Robert, and Keiran Harris, *80,000 Hours* podcast, April 14, 2022.

"Inside Sam Bankman-Fried's Quest to Win Friends and Influence People," Voge, Kenneth, Emily Flitter, and David Yaffe-Bellany, the *New York Times*, Nov. 22, 2022.

"Areas of interest," FTX Future Fund, Internet Archive, August 20, 2022 capture: https://web.archive.org/web/20220820163919/https://ftxfuturefund.org/area-of-interest/effective-altruism/.

Chapter 34

Looks Fucking Good

Su Zhu, the cofounder of the hedge fund Three Arrows Capital, had become a bull market guru in the crypto space. He had made a bold prediction and said he was trading based on it.

His prediction was this: the price of bitcoin would not fall dramatically again. His thesis was that this cycle was different. Real institutional money had finally come into the industry, and it would be enough to maintain a new base level into perpetuity.

Historically, bitcoin loses anywhere from 80 to 90 percent of its value from the peak of each bull run. Longtime bitcoin fans don't mind this because the floor keeps getting higher. This means they can take profits in the bull runs and then they can buy cheap again once it's over, while their overall portfolio grows in value—so long as they think in years, not weeks.

Rinse and repeat. Just another day in Satoshi's office in the sky.

People have gotten rich operating as if this is a *fait accompli*.

But Zhu argued through 2021 that those traders would be disappointed this time. Bitcoin wouldn't crash that hard again. We had found a new normal. He called it "the super-cycle." This created urgency for people who heard him make his case. It made people feel like they should get in or be forever left behind.

There's nothing wrong with being wrong. Making a bold trade is what makes investors. Your LPs can afford to take a hit.

The problem is that Zhu didn't stop when it looked very likely that he'd been wrong. Instead, he appears to have doubled down. And all the centralized lenders in the space doubled down with him, because he was a guru. The stage was getting set for the downturn to get worse. As of December 2022, it's still getting worse.

Here's what we actually learned about institutional money in 2021 and 2022: it was fickle.

Whenever bitcoin took a decisive turn south, the big money got out fast. Those who hadn't dealt with the big money players before learned the term "risk off" quickly.

The upshot: it turned out that institutional money didn't relieve volatility. In fact, it seems to have accentuated it. At least for now. This probably won't be true forever. If some portion of those old money funds are willing to ride the waves a bit, the sea should calm down some. But the crypto market is not there yet.

Bitcoin started 2022 $20,000 below its all-time high from November, at around $47,000. By mid-April, $40,000 was looking more like the real level.

In other words, the super-cycle looked like a bad thesis. An 80 percent fall from the top was starting to look like something that could happen again; $40,000 had been established as a sort of psychological line for the market, and folks were there.

Going into 2022, SBF told me in December, "My reading now, given what I now know, which is still not everything, is that basically there's some number of black swans that would be necessary to blow out Alameda. And like that number was slowly decreased over the course of the year."

Meanwhile, in February, a cadre of investors had bought heavily into the project that would be at the center of the industry's first big shock of 2022. Su Zhu's Three Arrows Capital would join Jump Crypto (a subsidiary of one of the world's best-known algorithmic trading firms), DeFiance Capital and others to buy a billion dollars' worth of luna tokens.

The funds would be put into the care of an organization called the Luna Foundation Guard, or LFG. LFG would turn around and use the money to buy a billion dollars' worth of bitcoin.

LFG was a familiar acronym for "looks fucking good" or "let's fucking go." It's something bitcoiners started posting as the run-up began, and it became a shorthand for good news.

LFG was there so that the luna token didn't have to do all the work if terra usd looked weak.

The luna token was the governance token and a defense mechanism of the algorithmic stablecoin terra usd (UST). There was more than $10 billion worth of terra usd (UST) on the market at the time. Both terra usd and luna were powered by the Terra blockchain, created by South Korea's Terraform Labs.

This was a stablecoin secured by code. To massively oversimplify it, it would release new terra usd into the market if the price was going above the $1 peg. If the price was falling below, it had incentives for people to destroy terra usd by redeeming it for new luna tokens, thereby shrinking the supply and getting the price back in line with the market.

The reason the ecosystem wanted to buy a bunch of bitcoin was because it wanted a strong, reliable source of value to backstop the value of terra usd ahead of luna.

Even insiders knew this whole project was either a flex by the blockchain world or a terrible mistake. UST was a way for engineers to demonstrate that they could take a wildly complex thing (a free market running at the speed of the internet) and make the price of a pure commodity behave.

This is roughly like corralling a group of eight-year-old boys to build a toothpick sculpture of the RMS *Lusitania* with nothing but verbal instructions.

"The world seemed to be a fully testosterone-driven MMO.[1] Everyone has to show maximum confidence," Frankel, the investor and crypto veteran, told me.

---

[1] MMO stands for "massively multiplayer online." Basically, anything lots of people can do at once, together, on the web. Usually it's a game. There are MMO college courses and social spaces as well, however.

Do Kwon, the CEO of the company behind the Terra blockchain and the person in charge of LFG, had a penchant for flexing. For example, in March 2022, he made a $10 million bet with Twitter personality @GiganticRebirth that terra usd would still be worth a dollar in a year.

The year's not technically up as of this writing, but it would take some kind of miracle for Kwon to win it. The money's already committed, though, so that's one thing he doesn't have to worry about.

On the other hand, when Kwon appeared on Anthony Pompliano's podcast to talk about his purchase of bitcoin, he was frank about the risk.

Terra needed bitcoin as an extra defense, he explained.

If terra usd was trading at 97¢, you could get $1 in luna for burning the stablecoin. That's all well and good as long as the problem isn't bad. If burning a few million terra usd led to getting the peg back on, no worries.

But what if it was worse than that?

Every time one new luna popped out, every preexisting luna was worth just a little bit less (remember when we talked about how maker was printed to save dai). If lots and lots of luna were getting printed, luna could start appreciably losing value.

If that happened, people could start to lose confidence in the whole system, and then, people would start selling even more terra usd, which would make the value plummet. If the value plummeted, more people would try redeeming for luna, minting an infinite supply and driving the value of luna toward zero and wrecking the stablecoin too.

That was the "death spiral" that everyone knew was the chief risk in a design like Terra's, and Kwon explained it to Pompliano without any spin. He just said it.

So LFG bought a bunch of bitcoin. The idea was that if terra usd depegged from the dollar, it could always buy and burn terra usd with bitcoin, and then it wouldn't impact the value of luna. It was a backstop for the backstop.

Let's review the facts of the case:

Zhu, the guru-level investor in the space, had spent the year saying crypto prices were at a new normal high. Yet, in the midst of a market where bitcoin, basically the Vanguard S&P 500 index of the whole industry, had lost 30 percent of its value, he decided to join a billion-dollar bet on the industry's most brazen experiment, the economic equivalent of lassoing a hurricane.

In the background, it was plain to see on-chain that most of the demand for terra usd was coming from a savings project called Anchor that *was very clearly* not making enough money through lending to justify its 20 percent interest rate for savers.

On top of that, a project whose name was, no joke, Magic Internet Money, had rigged up a loop such that users could leverage deposits into Anchor so they could borrow against their deposits and deposit even more.

How's all that sound?

It was then that these investors thought it was the right time to long terra usd and put crypto's stalwart, bitcoin, at its back.

It didn't work. At all. Not even a little. It was roughly pointless. When Terra lost control of its market in early May, that bitcoin stash evaporated like the ethical principles of a newly elected member of Congress when leadership starts passing around cigars and committee assignments. It looked bad.

There's a lot we could say about that period. There's conspiracy theory atop conspiracy theory about what *really* happened as Terra started losing it.

Obviously, many people have suggested that forces from within the Samglomerate, particularly Alameda, might have been behind attacking terra usd in order to profit off a big short against it or luna. It seems like the kind of thing the company would do. In fact, there have been reports of an investigation by US prosecutors into the question, but there exist reasons why this case doesn't look that compelling.

It looks more like events followed their inevitable course as the irrational exuberance of 2021 eased, but rich people with highly leveraged bets didn't let their egos go in time.

Indeed, it can be easy to forget that crypto is not inside a bubble. It's part of a bigger world, and something bigger than Terra or Three Arrows Capital or bad loans made to overextended founders was happening.

As 2022 began, it was becoming clear that the Fed was going to end the era of low interest rates that had prevailed since the Great Recession of 2008.

This was really important. It closed the chapter in which crypto had begun, with the launch of bitcoin. For the first time, cryptocurrency was going to face a massive shift in global macroeconomic conditions.

For as long as bitcoin has existed, money had been cheap. When the economy had some excess energy, crypto had been a nice place for people with disposable income to stick their play money. For those who timed it right, they could make a lot.

Most don't time it right, which makes it *even better* for those who do.

With money getting expensive, it was going to be tougher for the casual man-on-the-street investor or playful hedge fund to justify some discretionary bitcoin-and-adjacent-asset gambling. For that reason, it wasn't just that an ill-advised stablecoin had created a scandal; *people were going to leave anyway*.

Terra was that moment at the dinner party when the hostess flips off the record player and turns the overhead light on.

"Everyone focuses on the Terra crash as, like, *the thing*. But if you look, there were really like a very long string of things that happened over the course of 2022," SBF told me.

Above and beyond Terra and macroeconomic forces, there was just the simple fact that volumes were down. Even without a shock like Terra, volumes dropping is bad news for any market maker. "By 2022, you know, sizes were shrinking. Competition had gotten tougher. And, you know, in 2022, I think Alameda's trading profits were quite a bit smaller than they had been in 2021," he told me.

And yet he acknowledged, if only tacitly, that Alameda's problem at that point wasn't so much Terra as the fact that its portfolio was still long the market as the market began to shrink.

In this way, he argues that it's clear that Alameda wasn't so much the aggressive dumper of new tokens. It probably was not, in Sam's take, trying hard to crush Terra. Nor, he said, was it trying hard to pump-and-dump the little new token projects it did market making for.

"It did not in general try to really aggressively sell out of those tokens. Like as evidenced by what ended up happening. Alameda did end up substantially long the market, and this is, you know, one of the ways that it did," he said.

★★★

The contagion after Terra was easy to track because Zhu's Three Arrows Capital had borrowed billions from companies such as Voyager Digital, Celsius, Genesis Trading, and BlockFi. Their various hiccups would cause every single one of these companies to suspend withdrawals for customers.

As of this writing, all of them have gone into bankruptcy, except Genesis (but it looks shaky in December 2022). These firms made many mistakes but 3AC, one way or another, seemed to be the mistake they had in common.

At the time, Three Arrows Capital's fall looked like Samson defeated, but once FTX crumbled in November, 3AC looked like a different metaphor: the canary in the coalmine.

Sources Referenced

"**Terraform Labs CEO Do Kwon seals $10 million bet over LUNA price**," Copeland, Tim, The Block, March 15, 2022.

"**#880 The $10 Billion Stablecoin Bet on the Bitcoin Standard w/ Do Kwon**," *Pomp* podcast, March 24, 2022.

"**FTX Founder Sam Bankman-Fried Is Said to Face Market Manipulation Inquiry**," Flitter, Emily, David Yaffe-Bellany, and Matthew Goldstein, the *New York Times*, Dec. 7, 2022.

"**Three Arrows Capital, a cyberpunk Icarus story**," Dale, Brady, Axios, June 30, 2022.

"**On-Chain Forensics: Demystifying Terra USD De-peg**," Barthere, Aurelie, et.-al., Nansen.ai, May 27, 2022.

Interview, Sam Bankman-Fried, phone call with spokesperson, Dec. 30, 2022.

"**Genesis crypto lending unit halts services, adding to FTX contagion**," Kim, Crystal, and Brady Dale, Axios.com, Nov. 16, 2022.

Chapter 35

Savior Complex

At the beginning of June 2022, SBF would announce that he had signed The Giving Pledge, an initiative led by Warren Buffett, Bill Gates, and Melinda Gates, by which very wealthy people promise to give their wealth away. CoinDesk quoted his pledge later as saying:

> A while ago I became convinced that our duty was to do the most we could for the long run aggregate utility of the world.

Then, on June 22, bitcoin proponent Pierre Rochard would make a forecast on Twitter:

> Easiest prediction I'll ever make:
>   Fiatbrained bozos try fractional reserve banking with #BTC and get rekt
>   SBF fancies himself to be a savvy JPM, bails out the bozos (u r here)
>   Which only encourages more bad risk-taking
>   SBF needs a bail out, but can't print #BTC 💀

He could have been more civil about it, but you can't fault his accuracy.

To translate Rochard's point: one of the chief services that firms such as Voyager and BlockFi offered was the ability to make deposits of bitcoin and other cryptocurrencies, earn interest for doing so, and also, for those that wanted to, borrow against it as collateral.

The theory, like in any such arrangement, was that it could broker enough deals between lenders and borrowers to make it profitable for everyone. And, like any lender, the hope was to lend out most of what was deposited.

That's what Rochard means by "fractional-reserve." Modern banking keeps a fraction of its assets on reserve, in hopes that its customers won't want more withdrawals at once than it's keeping in cash on hand. Mostly, it works out.

Fiat

It's easy to read Rochard's tweet as "flatbrained," but it's "fiat-brained." That is, "fiat-brained."

"Fiat" is bitcoiners' preferred word for government-issued money, like dollars, pesos, and yen, though the term comes from economics.

In normal conversation, we don't usually make a distinction. Government money is just "money" today. Unless you're in the blockchain-powered economy.

Fiat means "a decree" or "arbitrary order." In other words, government money is only money because an authority says it is. Which is true! Though it's a bit of a simplification. The strongest fiat currencies have years of history and trust built into them, much as nations emerged organically from long historical processes that eventually resulted in grand abstractions such as borders, monarchies, legislatures, and departments of motor vehicles.

But neither were just spun up one day on the whim of some king, either.

That said, it's also not wrong. Dollars, euros, renminbi—these are payment instruments that governments will into being.

To be very clear: if your bank faced the kind of demand to exit that FTX faced, it would be doomed as well. On the other hand, you know your bank is a bank. The whole point of a bank is to lend out customer deposits.

FTX customers thought their deposits were on an exchange. The point of an exchange is to let deposits sit while users trade them.

An exchange shouldn't ever have a problem with withdrawals, because (as Chapter 11 illustrated) *all of the deposits should always be there.*

After Terra spun out into a nightmare chain, timestamping little more than immutable regrets, SBF was able to manufacture a heroic perception in the public imagination, but Rochard didn't buy it.

See, Terra engendered fear across the whole market. It was more a catalyst than a cause. People were already getting antsy due to rising interest rates anyway, and they started to get out.

But at that point, SBF told me, he did not believe that his firms were in a scary position. "Through the Terra crash basically, yeah: Things got a bit more leveraged. The leverage was still not super-high."

The first sign of trouble looked like a positive development. Babel Finance, a lender in Hong Kong, announced it had attained a $2 billion valuation in late May on a new $80 million funding round, as the shocks of Terra worked their way through the system.

Then, a month into the crisis, Celsius, a centralized lender, announced that it had to freeze withdrawals, though it would fight declaring bankruptcy over the weeks to come.

It was hard to guess what this suggested about the rest of the industry because Celsius had a less than stellar reputation. Funded initially by an ICO during the last bull market, it wasn't, in fact, decentralized at all. The Celsius token, cel, worked much more like FTX's ftt, in fact, than aforementioned tokens such as maker or comp.

Like ftt, cel didn't really have any power. It only had benefits.

Then Coinbase announced it was cutting 18 percent of its workforce, this not long after announcing tons of new hires. This was easier to read. If careful Coinbase was cutting, things looked to be bad for a while.

A few days later, freshly funded Babel would announce that it had to freeze withdrawals, suggesting that the prior fundraise had been more a liquidity bandage than a vote of confidence. As far as I can tell, it hasn't reopened withdrawals as of mid-December. A request for an update hasn't been answered yet.

At this point, SBF—as the kids say—entered the chat.

Then BlockFi, New Jersey–based crypto lender, started having trouble. BlockFi had made a lot of money off a discrepancy in the market created by the Grayscale Bitcoin Trust. The Trust gave investors a sort of backward way to invest in bitcoin through their brokerage accounts. For a long time, bitcoin at the trust traded at a premium to bitcoin.

An investor could buy bitcoin, give it to the trust and sell its instrument at a profit. It was very easy money, until the premium started shrinking and turned into a discount. Three Arrows Capital had been one of the bigger players in this trade. If you had a little patience and a lot of capital, it worked great. That is, until it didn't.

So BlockFi faltered, and SBF stepped in. His first big save. BlockFi announced a $250 million credit facility with FTX.

Nevertheless, BlockFi would announce withdrawal limitations shortly thereafter.

At the end of the month, reports would come out that SBF had looked at Celsius for a rescue but looked away. That said, it also extended its credit line with BlockFi, winning various options to buy the firm, based on the health of the company.

Not quite everyone thought that SBF was a hero here. Binance's CEO actually wrote a post on the Binance blog in June 2022 about bailouts. He wrote: "Don't perpetuate bad companies. Let them fail. Let other better projects take their place, and they will."

He hadn't named names, but his intent was easy to read.

It was at roughly this time that a crazy headline appeared in *Forbes* with a photo of SBF looking like he knew a secret. He warned that many exchanges were secretly insolvent. The intimation *felt weird* at the time because which exchange could he really have deep knowledge of but his own?

Then, another centralized lender, Voyager Digital, would file for bankruptcy in early July. This time FTX would put out a press release basically offering to move all Voyager's customers to its platform, refilling their accounts in the process.

Voyager made public its distaste for the FTX offer, but FTX would ultimately win the auction to acquire the lender through the old-fashioned process anyway, in September. That deal is shot now.

It didn't really matter. By this time, the narrative had been locked in. Reporters were saying SBF was the JP Morgan of this particular era of crypto disaster. He somehow seemed to be the one entrepreneur who had done so unbelievably well that he had infinite money to rescue good businesses stuck in the wrong time period.

"I do feel like we have a responsibility to seriously consider stepping in, even if it is at a loss to ourselves, to stem contagion," SBF told NPR in June. "I want to do what can help it grow and thrive."

How had SBF's companies come out of 2021 mega-rich while all the other big guns were bleeding? It didn't seem possible. Never mind the companies that were in serious pain. What about companies such as Binance and Coinbase? They were bruised by the downturn but far from beaten. Yet they also weren't on acquisition sprees.

Why would the Samglomerate be the bailout king, but they couldn't? I think other reporters were like me. The fact that he just seemed to have no end of money was definitely the story. It wasn't what he said he was going to do with his money in the future. It was how much he seemed to have in this moment when no one else did.

Later, it would prove that, in a certain way, Alameda Research did in fact have no end of money. In one way, in a fictional way. It's just that that way mattered little in light of all the other ways it actually didn't.

The litany of turmoil goes on: August would bring a withdrawal freeze at Singapore-based Hodlnaut (again, a centralized crypto lender). It's under a "judicial manager" now, which is a sort of state-managed customer protection system there. The firm had the double hit of losing almost $200 million in the Terra meltdown and then getting $13 million stuck on FTX.

Much of the blame for all of this financial pain would be pinned on Su Zhu and Kyle Davies's venture, Three Arrows Capital (3AC). By mid-July, the formerly avid social media users had gone silent. Reporters were saying they were on the lam. It really seemed as if they owed basically everyone massive amounts of money.

Genesis Trading, for example, which had a lending business, would file a $1.2 billion claim against 3AC. Backed by the deep-pocketed Digital Currency Group, Genesis would make it to November before freezing withdrawals itself, but the lending group's chief would get the boot before then.

FTX should not have fallen the way it did, but the companies that fell first were less surprising.

The problem for them was that they *were* like banks. They were lenders. They let people deposit crypto assets and borrow against them. Companies that lend what others deposit are always prone to bank run– like risks.

As things got dire, centralized lenders started freezing withdrawals. We can presume they did this in hopes that borrowers would make payments or meet margin calls, and then it would have more assets on hand to honor withdrawals once it reopened.

But their clients weren't borrowing crypto to build cash-generating factories or grocery stores. They were—one would presume—most likely traders who were making bets on the crypto market. As we've explained before, in crypto, people tend to go long. Traders that went long in early 2022 weren't going to be making their loan payments.

By July, it seemed as though most of the contagion had worked itself out. The trifecta of crypto's crash was: Do Kwon, of Terraform Labs, the creator of the Terra blockchain, the man who had conned the masses; Su Zhu, of 3AC, the man who had come up short for the money men; and SBF, the academic-class kid turned mega-financier who calmed the terror in the nascent industry.

And that's how it looked till November.

Rochard was not the only one to perceive problems with the Samglomerate's summer vanity acquisitions, but unlike most, he said it. He came as close as anyone could to forecasting just how the rest would go down.

Sources Referenced

"**FTX Founder Sam Bankman-Fried Signs Billionaires' Giving Pledge**," Wang, Tracy, CoinDesk, June 1, 2022.

Pierre Rochard, @BitcoinIsSaving, Twitter, June 22, 2022: https://twitter.com/ BitcoinIsSaving/status/1539605346469253120.

"**Crypto's last man standing**," Buttonwood, the *Economist*, July 5, 2022.

"**Crypto lender Babel Finance valued at $2 billion after latest fundraising**," Saini, Manya, and Sohini Podder, Reuters, May 25, 2022.

"**VOIP Pioneer Says New Startup Is Paying Users Interest on Millions in Crypto**," Cuen, Leign, CoinDesk, Oct. 5, 2018.

Celsius (Finance), ICO Drops, https://icodrops.com/celsius/.

"Crypto lender Celsius pauses withdrawals due to 'extreme market conditions,'" Browne, Ryan, and Arjun Kharpal, CNBC, June 13, 2022.

"A message from Coinbase CEO and Cofounder, Brian Armstrong," Armstrong, Brian, Coinbase blog, June 14, 2022.

Interview, Sam Bankman-Fried, phone call with spokesperson, Dec. 30, 2022.

"BlockFi Receives $250M Credit Facility From FTX," Mishra, Parikshit, and Sam Kessler, CoinDesk, June 21, 2022.

"BlockFi Raises Deposit Rates, Eliminates Free Withdrawals," Kessler, Sam, CoinDesk, June 24, 2022.

"FTX walked away from a deal with Celsius after seeing state of its finances: sources," Khatri, Yogita, The Block, June 30, 2022.

"A Note on Bailouts and Crypto Leverage," Zhao, Changpeng, Binance Blog, June 23, 2022.

"Sam Bankman Fried: Some Crypto Exchanges Are Already Secretly Insolvent," *Forbes*, June 28, 2022.

"FTX signs a deal giving it the option to buy crypto lender BlockFi," Rooney, Kate, CNBC, July 1, 2022.

"Crypto lender Voyager Digital files for bankruptcy," Patel, Shivam, Sinead Cruise, and Tom Wilson, Reuters, July 6, 2022.

"FTX Proposes Joint Plan to Offer Early Liquidity to Voyager Digital's Customers in Bankruptcy Proceeding," FTX Trading press release, Cision, July 22, 2022.

"Sam Bankman-Fried's FTX Aims to Become the 'Everything App,'" PYMTS, May 19, 2022.

"Bankrupt Voyager Digital Calls FTX's Bailout a 'Low-Ball Bid'," Key, Alys, Decrypt, July 25, 2022.

"Crypto exchange FTX to acquire bankrupt Voyager's assets," Babu, Juby, et. al, Reuters, Sept 27, 2022.

"Troubled Crypto Lender Hodlnaut Had $13M on FTX Before Withdrawal Freeze," Kinght, Oliver, CoinDesk, Nov. 10, 2022.

"Crypto billionaire says Fed is driving current downturn," Gura, David, NPR, June 19, 2022.

"How Three Arrows Capital Blew Up and Set Off a Crypto Contagion," Lee, Justina, Muyao Shen, and Ben Bartenstein, Bloomberg, July 12, 2022.

"Genesis Files $1.2B Claim Against Three Arrows Capital," Knight, Oliver, CoinDesk, July 18, 2022.

"Genesis CEO Steps Down as Crypto Broker Slashes Its Workforce," Yang, Yueqi, and Vildana Hajric, Bloomberg, Aug. 17, 2022.

"Sam Bankman-Fried Has a Savior Complex—And Maybe You Should Too,"
Fisher, Adam, Sequoia, Sept. 22, 2022, Internet Archive: https://web.archive.org/web/20221027180943/https://www.sequoiacap.com/article/sam-bankman-fried-spotlight/.

"Crypto lender BlockFi files for bankruptcy," Lawler, Ryan, Axios, Nov. 28, 2022.

"Genesis crypto lending unit halts services, adding to FTX contagion," Kim, Crystal, and Brady Dale, Axios, Nov. 16, 2022.

"Silence from Digital Currency Group's Genesis spooks crypto," Kim, Crystal, Axios, Nov. 21, 2022.

Chapter 36

Politics

Has there ever been a more unflattering photo of a billionaire than the one *New York Magazine* chose for its mini-profile of SBF in February 2021?

The publication wanted to highlight the role he played in electing Joe Biden as President of the United States. They depicted him lying down on one of his bean bags, pasty legs sticking out from his unfortunate khaki shorts. He had his New Balance sneakers off, a fleece blanket clumped on one side, and his arms tucked behind his head in such a way that he has about four chins, because—in fairness—no one's face looks good from that position.

Why had he agreed to the pose? How was there no one to stop him?

His style has always been bad, but it was as if he went out of his way to make it worse. Yet, from that unfortunately illustrated dispatch forward, he wasn't just one of the biggest spenders in the crypto biz, somehow he had become a power broker too.

I remember seeing that story and thinking something like: Now this? It seemed too much to be possible. How could one person become this big this fast?

Even then, though, we didn't know everything. After his fall, SBF would tell Tiffany Fong, an internet personality, during a phone call that she later shared (excerpted) online, that he'd given just as much to Republicans as Democrats. He'd just given to the Republicans in dark money. "The reason was not for regulatory reasons; it's because reporters freak the fuck out if you donate to Republicans. They're all super-liberal, and I didn't want to have that fight," he told her.

So what did SBF want?

There's a natural inclination with a story like this to put one goal on a person, to make them singularly focused. But who is truly singularly focused? And who can really know? The person might not even really know. A human being can tell themselves a lie about what they are doing.

So when any person says why they are doing something, are they really lying if they believe it?

Here's what we know. SBF spent about $40 million that was reported in the 2022 election cycle. If he really did spend roughly as much on Republicans, then let's call it $75 million, with that second half dark. Whatever.

The goal he said he had was pandemic prevention. He donated to a lot of different political groups on the Democratic side, but much of it went to Protect Our Future, a political action committee that focused on candidates who prioritized heading off another COVID-19, which shut much of the world down for about two years.

We know from his activity over the prior couple of years, though, that there was something else he wanted very much. He wanted clear regulations for the cryptocurrency industry in the US, and mostly he wanted the Commodity Futures Trading Commission (the CFTC) to be FTX's main regulator.

Faiz Shakir, Bernie Sanders's 2020 campaign manager, told Politico that he thought pandemic prevention was an optimal issue for a crypto billionaire to use as a cover to go in and line up elected politicians who owed him favors such that he could leverage them when fights over how to make rules for digital money finally got real.

So which was it?

As people on the internet often say: Why not both?

"I think I probably started a little bit too late in taking a more proactive role in discussing how I view this," he told Politico. "There have been a lot of times when I have been a bigger supporter of Democratic candidates than Republican candidates. That's not—that's not an immovable fact about the world."

But that conversation only happened this year, as he started to look like he could be the Democratic party's next huge long-term funder. But when that *New York* story with the unfortunate photo came out, that was the first most people had heard about SBF or his political engagement.

And the truth is he stayed quiet there for a while.

Then over the summer the president got focused on passing his infrastructure bill, and it served as a wake-up call for the cryptocurrency industry.

During the weeks everyone was waiting for SBF to be arrested, they were all pointing at his past donations to President Biden as proof that he'd purchased a pass. But that supposed special dispensation from DC also hadn't prevented the Biden administration from adding language to his signature legislation that infuriated and activated the whole cryptocurrency industry.

In short, crypto people had gotten rich, and the Biden team and its congressional allies saw a pot of money they could access to fund reinvesting in the US economy.

That wasn't so much a problem, as sources of mine told me at the time; the problem was the language in the bill about who was expected to help the IRS find tax scofflaws.

To massively oversimplify it, the bill defined who was a broker in the cryptocurrency business, and it seemed to include miners and validators, the people who secure the blockchains. It's true these entities do finalize transactions, but all they really do is check them all as valid and then stamp them onto the record, making them real. One transaction is the same as any other to them, really.

They only verify that the wallet sending the assets actually has funds to send. Not their identity. Not their moral character. Not their compliance with local law. It's just: Do you have the money?

Validators aren't brokers any more than Bell South is a broker just because an investor uses a phone to ring his guy at the Lincoln Financial Group.

And, crucially, the strength of blockchains lies in part in the fact that lots of people are willing to do the work to secure these things. The more people who do the redundant work of validating, the harder it is for anyone to cheat.

But these folks don't want to do paperwork. If that became a thing in the US, hobbyists and small-time operators would just quit and the network would become less secure. It would swiftly centralize.

Because crypto hated the infrastructure bill language, lobbyists were hired, letters were written, and money was raised. There was fire. There was brimstone. There were tweets. Oh boy, were there tweets. There were so many tweets.

And, what do you know? The industry lost.

It completely, totally lost. The final language of the bill passed, and it was unchanged from what it had been.[1] But, the industry had a taste for how the whole process worked and what it could do. It came away wanting to fight more.

I covered it a bit at the time, and I know others who followed it more closely. It doesn't seem that FTX got very involved in the 2021 process, at least not publicly.

SBF did come out with a few big tweet threads on the legislation as it neared final passage in the Senate in August. Mostly he was explaining some nuances of amendments and things he found odd about the process to his followers.

But it was also amid the infrastructure bill fight that he articulated his conviction that the CFTC should be the regulator for exchanges that managed cryptocurrencies.

He highlighted a few legislators that he thought had been forward thinking about the industry, and then he asked: "Who *else* is taking a clear, constructive approach towards crypto regulation? Honestly, I think that the @CFTC has a pretty good track record here."

---

[1] The industry's DC foot soldiers would later put out the word that the Treasury Department wouldn't interpret the language overly broadly and come after the wrong types of entities. So far, there haven't been any outcries suggesting it has. But it hasn't been long, in Washington time, either.

He went on:

I know this isn't something I've made clear historically (among other things I think I was too pessimistic before!).
　　But the CFTC has:

a) made it clear that crypto, and crypto derivatives, can fit in their existing frameworks
b) Shown a good understanding of the industry
c) Provided guidance where appropriate, and otherwise shown interest in learning

Apparently, the US Securities and Exchange Commission hadn't shown much of an interest in learning, even though it had about six times more personnel. (For what it's worth, this squares with what a number of entrepreneurs have told me off the record.)

And that sets the stage for all the political spending SBF did in 2022, backing many young and unknown candidates in districts that were safe for their party. The idea here wasn't so much to tilt the balance of power but to get people in that would return his calls.

On the *80,000 Hours* podcast, he talks about why he focused on primaries. "The amounts spent in primaries are small. If you have an opinion there, you can have impact," he said.

His arguments in this conversation are striking. He was a campaign neophyte who seemed to believe he already saw the art of vote gathering better than the pros.

"I think often the state of the art is surprisingly shitty," he said of campaigns. "I agree it's better than a monkey would do. It's not literally random, but it's not super-impressive, given the stakes."

We don't know how many races he backed that ultimately won. A *Washington Post* analysis shows 14 candidates that Protect Our Future, the anti-pandemic PAC, supported as winning. Not a terrible start, though.

He had begun a nice list of electeds who owed him, at least a little.

That is until December 13, 2022, when the United States Attorney for the Southern District of New York charged him with conspiracy to defraud the Federal Election Commission and campaign finance violations. Those charges were made along with conspiracy to commit wire fraud, fraud, securities fraud, and money laundering.

He may have helped some folks get in for the first time, but it's unlikely now that he is going to be able to help again. They aren't likely to return his calls now.

Sources Referenced

"**The Mysterious Cryptocurrency Magnate Who Became One of Biden's Biggest Donors**," Wallace, Benjamin, *New York Magazine*, February 2, 2021.

"**Sam Bankman-Fried's First Interview After FTX Collapse**," Fong, Tiffany, @TiffanyFong, YouTube, Nov. 29, 2022.

"**FTX's Bankman-Fried donated about $40M this political cycle**," Stanley-Becker, Isaac, Chris Zubak-Skees, and Nick Mourtoupalas, the *Washington Post*, Dec. 14, 2022.

"**How the newest megadonor wants to change Washington**," Schneider, Elena, Politico, August 4, 2022.

"**Cryptocurrency CEO Donated Second-Largest Amount to Joe Biden's Campaign**," Sinclair, Sebastian, CoinDesk, Nov. 5, 2020.

"**Executive Order on Ensuring Responsible Development of Digital Assets**," The White House, March 9, 2022.

"**EXPLAINER: How cryptocurrency fits into infrastructure bill**," Gordon, Marcy, Associated Press, Aug. 10, 2021.

Sam Bankman-Fried, @SBF_FTX, Twitter, Threadreader, Aug. 7, 2021: https://threadreaderapp.com/thread/1424126908510392321.html.

Sam Bankman-Fried, @SBF_FTX, Twitter, Threadreader, Aug. 6, 2021: https://threadreaderapp.com/thread/1423529349828030467.html.

"**SamBankman-Fried on taking a high-risk approach to crypto and doing good**," Wiblin, Robert, and Keiran Harris, *80,000 Hours* podcast, April 14, 2022.

"**United States Attorney Announces Charges Against FTX Founder Samuel Bankman-Fried**," Southern District of New York, Department of Justice, Dec. 13, 2022.

"**FTX founder Bankman-Fried's campaign finance charges 'just the tip of the iceberg,'**" Manchester, Julia, The Hill, Dec. 13, 2022.

Chapter 37

House of Representatives

"It has been more productive interacting with regulators than I had expected that it would be,"

—SBF, FTX Podcast, November 2021.

From the vantage point of December 2022, SBF's failed as an advocate for winning crypto a better regulatory climate. But that simple statement doesn't capture it.

It's like saying that *Star Wars* fans have had mixed feelings about films made after the original trilogy. Or that Alan Greenspan's legacy was complicated by the events of 2008. Or that the political class miscalculated on the candidacy of Donald Trump. True on the face, but there's not really a way to express the depth in mere words.

Following FTX's collapse, SBF was fond of repeating the phrase "I fucked up," which would be tantamount to Grigori Rasputin going on TikTok to admit he could have done a better job of considering the best interests of the people around him or Robert Oppenheimer granting that his work had had some unforeseen consequences.

We can only guess at how far-reaching the distrust SBF has sown will go, but to understand the depths of this astounding policymaking blunder, we have to go to the heart of why FTX argued its exchanges should be treated differently than other players in the derivatives market.

SBF and his team said FTX was uniquely trustworthy because of the risk engine that its developers had built.

FTX argued that the best way to handle the crypto market was actually to bring everything under one roof. That way, it can function 24/7. This means that it can liquidate promptly when the market turns south, so customers' portfolios don't go into negative values, but it also means customers have access to their accounts at all times to top up their positions in order to avoid liquidations.

He also contended that the exchange should be the custodian of all users, crypto assets because this means that it has no counterparty risk when it needs to take possession of a client's assets.

SBF further argued that it's better to cross-margin collateral. In other words, if a user has $500 in bitcoin and $1,000 in ether, the exchange should treat them as having $1,500 to back margin trades. At the time, most exchanges would say the person could take two separate margin positions (one on $500 and one on $1,000). FTX disagreed.

Which brings us to the heart, the soul, the crux of what SBF argued made his exchange different. It offered a real-time risk engine that constantly assessed the risk of every customer's collateral position every 30 seconds. It assessed what it was taking positions on and it also assessed the risk levels of the different kinds of assets it was using for collateral.

So, for example, $1,000 as a dollar-backed stablecoin had more value as margin than, say, $1,000 of the cryptocurrency xrp.

And the crown jewel of FTX's approach to risk was this: it self-insured. FTX had a $250 million fund set aside to take losses if it ever failed to prevent a customer's account from going negative. FTX took that hit, not the other customers.

Fortunately for FTX, they hadn't had to tap it much. Or at least that's the story he told around DC.

FTX first presented the concept of his risk engine to Congress before the House Financial Services Committee on December 8, 2021. The event was an intro Q&A for legislators about this nascent but attention-getting sector. The *New York Times'* headline was: "Congress gets a crash course on cryptocurrency."

Margin trading

Here's a simple example of how margin trading works. Let's imagine you want to trade some asset that's worth $100 and you want to invest $100 to do so. So you have the money to buy one unit of the asset.

On an exchange like FTX, your $100 would stand in for the asset. It would be a synthetic asset.

Now, let's say that you wanted to make a 5X long margin trade. That would be effectively borrowing $500 from the exchange five units of the asset, with your $100 in the background, as collateral.

The exchange has "lent" that to you.

Since you're long, that means you are betting on the price going up. So if the price goes up $10, in this scenario you're up $50 (because you have 5 units).

If you were to close the trade there and then, you would still owe the $500. You don't get to keep that, but you do get to keep the difference between the value when you opened the trade and when you closed it (minus whatever fees).

So you'd exit with $150 (your collateral plus the gains).

But it also works the other way. In this scenario (let's keep it simple), the exchange would close your position down and take your initial investment away if the value of your asset lost $20 in value (because 5 × $20 is $100, which is all of your collateral).

That's all if you took a long position. You could also take a short, and bet an asset will fall in value.

On the back end, longs are paying shorts when assets are falling in value and shorts are paying longs when assets are going up. That's how it balances out.

Regulators and legislators are hesitant about letting too many people access this kind of trading because in booms idiots convince themselves they are geniuses and lose a lot.

The cryptoletariat loved Sam then. They were ecstatic watching this young guy talking about their weird industry in Congress alongside some of his least dynamic peers, such as the CEO of a stablecoin issuer and a tech company that serves crypto companies, represented at the hearing by an ex-regulator.

Those following along on Crypto Twitter became fixated on a photo someone took of Sam's shoes because they were badly tied.

This appearance was the first time his public had seen him in a suit. The suit didn't fit well. It looked cheap, and the shoes made it look like he didn't know how to wear it. This only made the people love the look more.

He was their hero, and his superpower was shabby tailoring. He wouldn't put on a decent pair of pants to sit next to Gisele, but he had gotten out the hotel's ironing board for Congress.

He told legislators, "To be sure, there are irresponsible actors in the digital-asset industry, and those actors attract the headlines, but FTX is not one of them and in fact has built a resilient, risk-reducing platform as a competitive advantage."

If SBF got impassioned at all in his remarks it was about stablecoins. He contended that everyone was better off if governments didn't put much friction on these new instruments. He made a point of saying that he felt less risk moving hundreds of millions of dollars of his company's money via stablecoins than he did through the banks.

But the SEC, in its December 2022 complaint against SBF and FTX, did not take note of his shoes or his thoughts on stablecoins at that hearing. They took note of his conclusion before the Congressional committee, which its legal staff quoted him as follows:

> And the last thing I will say is if you look at what precipitated some of the 2008 financial crisis, you will see a number of bilateral, bespoke, non-reported transactions happening between financial counterparties, which then got repackaged and releveraged again and again and again, such that no one knew how much risk was in that system until it all fell apart. If you compare that to what happened on FTX or other major cryptocurrencies in use today, there is complete transparency about the full open interest. There is complete transparency about the positions that are held. There is a robust, consistent risk framework applied.

Was there?

In his appearance before the House, his testimony would largely lump the CFTC and the SEC together, but at the end he would suggest that the former might be the better entity to provide primary oversight.

He would go before the Senate next, in February 2022, and take this slightly further. "The CFTC already has considerable experience and expertise in the regulation of digital assets, and FTX believes the Congress would be wise to leverage that expertise for the benefit of the public as well as the digital-asset industry," his written testimony said.

And he would mention the fact that "FTX is in discussions with the CFTC about expanding our derivatives offerings to US customers."

That wasn't the part that the CFTC would take note of, however. In its December 13, 2022, complaint against Sam and his companies, it would specifically point to the following statement in his testimony.

> As a general principle FTX segregates customer funds from its own assets across our platforms.

But this second conversation was somewhat overshadowed, though, by an event from the day before. The Department of Justice had announced that it had arrested a young, married Brooklyn couple: Ilya Lichtenstein and Heather Morgan. They were found to be in possession of more than 94,000 bitcoin, worth more than $4.5 billion at February 2022 spot market prices.

This bitcoin was, allegedly, the same bitcoin that had been stolen from Bitfinex in 2016, the cryptocurrency exchange that shares a parent company with the controversial stablecoin, tether, which we discussed in Chapter 12.

Morgan turned out to have an alter ego who made cringey hip-hop videos on YouTube under the name Razzlekhan. Razzlekhan also loved bedazzling. She gave talks about how to hustle people ("social engineering"). She published essays on *Forbes*'s website.

For a while there, everyone was obsessed with Morgan. With the market cooling and regulation coming, it felt like it was going to be a boring year. "The biggest news of 2022 might have just happened," is the kind of thing I would say about the Bitfinex couple at the time.

That was incorrect.

In March 2022, the White House would put out an Executive Order on regulating cryptocurrencies, though really all Biden did was ask a bunch of agencies to make reports and to let him know if regulation was needed.

In May, the CFTC would let Sam gather a bunch of representatives from the existing derivatives industry in a room and listen to him present on his application to bring his risk engine to the US and let him serve as the exchange, custodian, clearinghouse, and guarantor of derivatives trades all under one roof.

His presentation was made to a room dominated by older, comfortable men hyperventilating at this young upstart proposing a model that very clearly threatened to, eventually, one day, someday, put them all out of business.

But it was also hard not to believe him when he said he would be happy to make a $250 million bet that it worked better (the self-insurance fund) than the existing system if that's what American regulators needed him to do.

As the year proceeded, FTX got a lot more serious about lobbying. SBF was spending more time in DC, behind closed doors, trying to move legislation. A variety of bills were proposed, and again it seemed like a theme was emerging that legislators were starting to agree with: crypto markets needed a lead regulator, and perhaps that should be the CFTC.

Here's the thing to notice about all these efforts, though. He kept getting these spots to speak on behalf of the whole industry, but, when you read between the lines, it really seems like he was advocating for bespoke concessions made with FTX in mind.

★★★

It's a big world out there, but the truth is the ready money is in the United States.

The US particularly dominates in adventurous money. So the dominant crypto exchange needs to have access to consumers here, and both Binance and FTX had a similar approach to US customers.

For both, the main shop, the HQ, was global. It set up shop anywhere the local government didn't kick it out. Both also had a US affiliate that was more careful about the kind of tokens and instruments it let users trade, so as not to run afoul of cautious American regulators.

In both cases, they insisted, the US company and the global companies were completely different. Not even subsidiaries. No relationship!

But Binance and FTX were taking two very different approaches to that part of the business. CZ seemed to aim to get as much market share and brand awareness as he could get away with by setting up a US outpost, while SBF seemed to believe that he could use Washington to create a moat, suggesting he'd accede to any kind of rules, just so long as it gave crypto trading and futures trading a green light.

His bet might have been that he had the money to succeed in complying with almost any kind of regulatory regime. So he would comply, and he would get approval faster than any other exchange, allowing his company to succeed in establishing Facebook-like network effects such that no other exchange would ever be able to rival his.

In other words, he might have been shooting for regulations as a competitive advantage. CZ certainly seemed to think so. After FTX's fall, he would write in a tweet:

> We are not against anyone. But we won't support people who lobby against other industry players behind their backs. Onwards.

Sources Referenced

"**Cryptocurrency prices fall in December, and investors blame omicron, climate change**," Holland, Frank, CNBC, Dec. 29, 2021.

"**Episode 91: Sam Bankman-Fried founder of FTX and Alameda Research**," Yver, Tristan, *FTX Podcast*, published Nov. 30, 2021.

"**FTX's Unique Design**," FTX Crypto Derivatives Exchange, Help.FTX.com, WebArchive,Nov.10,2021,capture:https://web.archive.org/web/20211110081148/https://help.ftx.com/hc/en-us/articles/4404204316052-FTX-s-Unique-Design.

"**Testimony**," Bankman-Fried, Sam, Digital Assets and the Future of Finance: Understanding the Challenges and Benefits of Financial Innovation in the United States" Hearing Before the US House of Representatives Committee on Financial Services, December 8, 2021.

"**Congress gets a crash course on cryptocurrency**," Livni, Ephrat, the *New York Times*, December 8, 2021.

"**Testimony**," Bankman-Fried, Sam, "Examining Digital Assets—Risks, Regulation, and Innovation." Hearing Before the US Senate Committee on Agriculture, Nutrition and Forestry, February 9, 2022.

"*SEC v. Sam Bankman-Fried*," US Securities and Exchange Commission complaint before the US Court of the Southern District of New York, Dec. 13, 2022.

"**CFTC Charges Sam Bankman-Fried, FTX Trading and Alameda with Fraud and Material Misrepresentations**," Press release and complaint before the US Southern District of New York, Commodity Futures Trading Commission, Dec. 13, 2022.

"**Two Arrested for Alleged Conspiracy to Launder $4.5 Billion in Stolen Cryptocurrency**," Office of Public Affairs, Department of Justice, Feb. 8, 2022.

"**Testimony**," Bankman-Fried, Sam, "Changing Market Roles: The FTX Proposal and Trends in New Clearinghouse Models," US House Committee on Agriculture, FTXPolicy.com, May 12, 2022.

"**US Congress questions industry on merits and risks of FTX's non-intermediated model**," Reeves, Jeff, FIA.org, May 12, 2022.

"**FTX's crypto clearing plan needs scrutiny, says CFTC chair Rostin Benham**," Chan, Jeremy, *Financial News*, May 13, 2022.

CZ, @CZ_Binance, Twitter, Nov. 6, 4:49 p.m.: https://twitter.com/cz_binance/status/1589374530413215744.

Chapter 38

Senate

In October 2022, there was a bill being written by the offices of Senators Debbie Stabenow and John Boozman. No one knew for sure what it would say once its coauthors started pushing it; they just knew that SBF was very optimistic about its final language.

They also knew its name, the Digital Commodities Consumer Protection Act (DCCPA). The DCCPA felt like it could be the one that would guide the conversation going into the next Congress. If it wasn't a winner, it might be a bellwether.

That's when Sam did a very Sam thing. He published a blog post.

He had done this before his first appearance in the House in December 2021. Then, FTX had put out principles for regulating crypto trading platforms. No one had much cared.

In October 19, 2022, he went much further. He published a long blog post with the title "Possible Digital Asset Industry Standards." It did not go down well with those who had been behind him thus far.

This was a turning point for SBF in the public mind. It was as if people had come to see him as too rich and suspect that SBF was really just out to protect FTX, that he really wasn't on the side of normal people and maybe not even on the side of his industry peers.

Nathaniel Whittemore, the host of CoinDesk's podcast, *The Breakdown* (and then a member of FTX's comms team), picked this as the starting point for his version of events leading through to SBF leaving the company he founded.

On the first episode of his show after the bankruptcy, Whittemore said that he didn't see any good reason for SBF to publish this post. "It felt very main character syndrome to me," Whittemore said. "The only thing that did make sense was a personal ego attachment to being in the center of the debate."

He'd gone from December's quirky ally in the poorly tied shoes to October's attempted oligarch. He was starting to remind people of another young founder who had gone to Congress advocating for regulations: Mark Zuckerberg. SBF's crummy suits were starting to look like the prop cushion Zuck had aides slip onto his chair when he testified in April 2018, like a not-very-special effect.

Whittemore picked out two points that bothered all the folks SBF claimed to be advocating for.

In August, the Treasury Department had issued an edict that no American could use Tornado Cash, a smart contract on Ethereum that was designed to hide the sender and recipient of a transaction. This was viewed as a violation of people's right to financial privacy plus an executive branch overreach. Multiple entities are currently fighting it in court.

"There was a particular tone-deafness to the fact that Sam's position on this made no mention whatsoever of the OFAC Tornado Cash sanctions," Whittemore said.

SBF's blog post had just said that such sanctions should be "respected."

Then there was another point that irritated the degenerates toiling on the blockchains: his stance on decentralized finance. In his blog, he made a distinction between "*Decentralized code as speech*" and "Centralized GUIs and marketing as regulated financial activities."

GUIs are graphical user interfaces. Facebook is a graphical user interface running on whatever elaborate database the company has built that makes it work. Most things people do on the internet are through graphical user interfaces.

Not strictly so with crypto. A person can always interact directly with the blockchain (which is the database), but it takes technical skill to do it. So almost everyone uses GUIs, but another option is there. People can even make *other* GUIs.

The point SBF was making was that maybe crypto should consider embracing regulation (such as identity requirements) for users of GUIs in exchange for leaving the blockchains proper completely open?

A ferocious debate broke out online with many crypto users spinning into wild hypotheses about how SBF had done all his political spending to buy himself a willing legislature that would pass a bill that would allow him to foreclose on decentralized finance as a threat to his exchange.

So the guys at the Bankless media organization, a group that puts out educational and boostery content about Ethereum and DeFi, decided to convene a debate between SBF and the person on Twitter who had taken charge of the opposition to SBF's blog post, Erik Voorhees.

Voorhees has been around bitcoin and crypto since nearly the beginning. He founded a previously mentioned company called ShapeShift, which enabled some of the earliest cross-chain trading, but eventually succumbed to regulatory headwinds. When people say crypto has a libertarian streak, they are thinking of Voorhees.

The debate took place on YouTube.

"My core thought here is the following: I claim that the most important thing here at the end of the day is that smart contract validators remain open and free," SBF told Voorhees and the Bankless guys. "Because of that I am relatively willing to accept compromises."

He tried to make the case to Voorhees that by coming to the table with a proposal that showed he was willing to compromise, he was more likely to win the best possible world for the industry.

Voorhees, unlike SBF, had been around for a prior regulatory fight in New York state, over something known now as the BitLicense. In that, the industry had tried to cooperate, and it ended with a deal so bad several companies firewalled off the state for good.

In Voorhees view, it was too soon to even talk about DeFi. He urged SBF to just focus the conversation around exchanges like his own.

Voorhees had a calm and immovable presence through the conversation from beginning to end, a contrast to SBF's excited energy. "The political class, the regulators, are nowhere near ready to be regulating DeFi," Voorhees said in that steady tone of ideological clarity that characterizes him. "Whatever the appropriate regulations are for DeFi, this bill [the DCCPA] is not where they should be contemplated. We are not ready."

After the conversation, it started to feel like SBF had lost the room. He still sat atop a money-printing machine in FTX. He still was the darling of the EAs, and the Democratic fundraisers were warming to him, but the industry that brought him this far had started to turn.

FTX didn't last long enough to find out what would happen next.

Well, we do sort of know. The legislators won't pay much attention to the political infighting between crypto tribes, but they will look closely at the contrast between what SBF told them and what investigations under way now find.

Michael Safai is a cofounder of Dexterity Capital, a proprietary trading firm that does high-frequency crypto trading. When SBF was getting started running global arbitrages, Safai and his cofounder were finding similar inefficiencies in the trades among the bumper crop of new tokens being traded during the ICO bubble.

When FTX launched, he told me, "We obviously knew Alameda was out there and had seen them in the market. The idea of trading on an exchange that was backed by another prop shop seemed like a bad idea."

But eventually there was too much volume on FTX for them to ignore, so in 2021 they started using it. Dexterity's approach is one that sends tons of trades. Speed is very important.

The problem with FTX, he said, was there was just a little too much latency. The reason was the risk engine at the center of SBF's pitch to the CFTC and Congress. Every time it sent a trade the system had to recheck all of Dexterity's collateral positions and make sure the risks were right.

As Safai described it, a sophisticated shop that knows how to use the torrents of free data FTX provided can't quite see its competitors in the exchange, but they can get an idea about them. "We had seen evidence that someone had a faster advantage than us, which was pretty unusual," he said. "It was always my guess that Alameda was skipping the risk engine check, and the CFTC seems to think so too."

As charges were unsealed, hitting SBF with a variety of criminal charges, the CFTC brought a civil suit against FTX for precisely this violation.

In other words, this innovative risk management product that he spoke of as so promising that it gave consumers a better deal turned out to be a sham that enabled his multibillion-dollar enterprise to collapse in a week, taking a million or more customers' assets with it.

Policymakers are going to remember what he said about what his company does and what it actually did.

No one knows yet how bad SBF's mistakes are going to be for the blockchain business as their repercussions are revealed by political leaders in Washington, DC, but it looks worse every day.

In crypto slang, there are two fictional drugs: hopium and copium. Hopium is for optimists, and it's on clearance these days. Copium is for after the bad news is printed. It's sold out.

Sources Referenced

"**FTX Issues Key Principles for Market Regulation of Crypto-Trading Platforms**," FTX International, Cision: PR Newswire, Dec. 3, 2021.

"**Possible Digital Asset Industry Standards**," Bankman-Fried, Sam, FTX blog, October 19, 2021: https://web.archive.org/web/20221019211123/https://www.ftxpolicy.com/posts/possible-digital-asset-industry-standards.

"**Sam Bankman Fraud: Inside the Collapse of FTX's Hollow Empire**," Whittemore, Nathaniel, The Breakdown, CoinDesk, Nov. 14, 2022.

"**Ethereum's best known privacy tool falls under U.S. sanctions**," Dale, Brady, Axios, Aug. 8, 2022.

"**SBF vs. Erik Voorhees: How Do We Regulate Crypto?,**" Bankless, YouTube, streamed live Oct. 28, 2022.

"**FTX's Systems Gave Alameda Trades a Secret Speed Edge, CFTC Says**," Ossinger, Joanna, and Sidhartha Shukla, Bloomberg, Dec. 14, 2022.

Bankman-Fried, Sam, @SBF_FTX, Twitter, Nov. 10, 2022: https://twitter.com/sbf_ftx/status/1590709166515310593.

Chapter 39

About Securities

I n Robert Penn Warren's novel *All the King's Men* (1946), there is a quote by the character Willie Stark,[1] a powerful state politician who tells the book's protagonist that he's no lawyer even though he had practiced some law. Stark says:

> The law is like the pants you bought last year for a growing boy, but it is always this year and the seams are popped and the shankbone's to the breeze. The law is always too short and too tight for growing humankind.

I have thought about that line a lot while covering the ongoing collision between crypto and the state. An issue is bubbling under the surface of this whole book, of crypto tokens, coins, and the matter of whether or not they are commodities or securities and what that means about what agencies can tell which people about the kinds of extremely abstract businesses running inside overgrown spreadsheets.

---

[1] Stark is based on former Louisiana Governor Huey Long, a picturesque politician who died in 1935, aged 42, taken by assassination.

And also what that particular bit of legal minutiae means—and I'm not joking here—for our collective shot at a world that works better.

Once upon a time, too many guileless investors got screwed buying garbage investments, and the states and DC decided that investors needed to be regulated in order to protect regular people trying to bet on a better future. This led to the notion of the state having a duty to provide investor protection.

So I'm going to super-simplify the question of *why* this is an issue for crypto entrepreneurs.

There's a lot of talk about how tokens are this and aren't that but not *why* it matters. Even the crypto industry doesn't talk about this much. There's next to no discussion about what *could be*, because regulators don't understand that. They only understand what *has been*.

Lawyers I know who read this will probably lose their minds, but chill out, friends. I'm just trying to give readers a sense for what the fight here is, and it's a fight I've been slogging through since I started working this beat in 2017. So I think I can do the *Explain It Like I'm Five* version. You tell me.

So commodities are things that exist on their own in the world, and they have value. People want them, and so people trade them, but they function independently of any particular enterprise. Coffee is a commodity. Goldfish are a commodity. Honey is my personal favorite commodity. No one company controls such things. They just exist, we like them and so we trade them.

Anyone can own commodities, that's the key thing. How are you going to tell a guy he can't have coffee? Don't even try.

Bitcoin, as it happens, has also come to be seen as a commodity in Washington. Bitcoin just kind of runs out there. Yes, it needs people and machines to operate, but those people don't know each other, and they don't really work together (mostly). Nobody is in charge.

Bitcoin mostly just popped out of the worldwide web, and it appealed to a distinct group of people that loved to tell other people about it. Bitcoin is like the quinoa of the internet that way.

There's a big *financial market* around commodities because farmers and oil men and biofuel makers sell options on their output because it helps them manage cash flows. If you grew up in the Midwest like I did, you'd hear news anchors on TV talking about corn futures. That's a market where people bet on how much corn will cost down the road. They find this helpful; I don't judge.

That market is the concern of the Commodity Futures Trading Commission (CFTC). The CFTC handles commodities in the US (though really it handles the futures market for them). The Securities and Exchange Commission (SEC) handles the other thing: securities.

Commodities are simple. Securities are weird. It has been argued that securities are just about anything the SEC wants them to be.

Most arrangements that come about because some company is trying to make money are "securities." The security most people know about is equity. That is, shared ownership in a company. That is, stocks. While a company is still private, a small group of people own equity in it. Maybe just the founders. Maybe also some outside investors.

When a company gets big enough, it can spend piles and piles of money, jump through all kinds of hoops, and then the owners can sell a lot (or all) of the company onto the public markets, like the NASDAQ or the New York Stock Exchange.

When that happens, anyone can own a piece of the company. That is, they can own a security that represents partial ownership.

Securities were defined in a US Supreme Court case about orange groves. The definition is called "the Howey Test." It's one of those phrases like "rightsizing" or "solutions" or "both-and" that I wish I could unhear. In crypto, for now, the Howey Test is ever present, like movie remakes.

Because of our securities laws in the US, only fairly wealthy people can own them until they go on public markets like the New York Stock Exchange. You and I can't invest in new companies just getting off the ground, but big-shot lawyers can and hedge funds can and the tech elite can.

This is investor protection. Basically, the idea is that if people are allowed to buy and sell chunks of new, tiny companies, hustlers will take advantage of them.

And let's be clear: they definitely, definitely will. Watch *Wolf of Wall Street* (2014).

There are attorneys whose eyes are bleeding right now. *I'm so sorry. But for most of you*, this is *close enough* to right *often enough*. It is all "facts and circumstances," but we are where we need to be (unless you plan to go start a company, then please put down this book and hire a lawyer).

OK, so here's *the problem* crypto has. You can agree or disagree that this *is a problem* at all, but this is the heart of the concern for believers.

This is my point:

Crypto, the industry, thinks it can make new cool stuff that everyone will really like one day but also that governments need to let them spin up these things called tokens that are tradeable in order to fully maximize the indefinable but expected cool. There's a lot of things these things are good for, but let's just use a simple example (one that no one is doing).

Remember our decentralized Netflix story? If I want to start a new Netflix, right, but I want it to run itself autonomously on the internet one day, I might like to create a token for this purpose. Call it flix (FLIX), as we did before. Eventually, I want people to pay 1 flix token every month to access this new Netflix, and the market can figure out what a flix is worth in dollars. But maybe by then I, the creator, will be long gone.

By then, all kinds of people will contribute to the product that delivers the movies on this new Netflix so that they can earn flix (that they will sell on the market to people who want to watch movies).

Here's some stuff people might do to earn flix from this decentralized Netflix: some will create different interfaces that sort through the movies and help you decide what to watch (we all hate how Netflix does this, right? So what if there were multiple user interfaces sorting the available content different ways?). Some people will make movies or buy licenses of movies to publish on the service. Some people will make the digital pipes and storage systems that get the data to your house smoothly.

This Netflix would let anyone add movies to it, because it would also let anyone curate the movies. If bad movies get uploaded, the best curators would never even show them to you, so it wouldn't matter that they were there.

All those people (the curators, the data warehouses, the moviemakers, etc.) will split up your flix token every month based on how much you use their part of the service, and everyone will know the rules the system uses to decide how much of each flix everyone gets.

Some people believe this model could create an amazing future where lots more very cool stuff runs on the internet in an open, flexible, and transparent way that everyone can use. But it only works, they argue, *if they can make this flix token and other tokens like it.*

And *that* only works if anyone can hold such tokens and use them and trade them and plop them in to watch a month of movies.

But! Here's the sticking point that nobody ever talks about: How are you going to launch a service like this if *only rich people* can own the financial instrument, the token, that makes it all work?

How can you make the next Netflix if only rich people can get in and watch?

I could give you better examples than the flix token, but I want to keep this simple. I also want to end the pain of the lawyers reading this.

This *is* the basic problem: crypto wants to create a new class of service where contributors are decentralized. Blockchain entrepreneurs want to experiment with new kinds of coordination mechanisms online, and value (money) has always worked very well for coordinating people.

But they can't run these experiments if only a small class of people can participate, but under existing US securities laws, that's basically impossible. The regulators see these tokens as simply investments, and they are!

But they aren't *just* that. They are also (maybe) the keys to new kinds of services that can't exist in the world as it is permitted now.

Basically, DC seems to be saying that the potential of such new arrangements in the long term isn't worth the risk of investors losing money making bets on tokens like flix in the near term.

Having followed this issue for years, I've never seen any evidence that this facet of tokens has *ever even been considered* by the powers that be, beyond meaningless rhetoric about *enabling responsible innovation*. Tokens might make things work better. They also might not, but as far as I can tell, that potential has never been aired for actual discussion.

Regulators have a very hard time considering whether or not a new thing might introduce a new good. They are only really equipped to consider whether or not it might raise an old problem.

Sources Referenced

"**A Regulatory Classification of Digital Assets: Toward an Operational Howey Test for Cryptocurrencies, ICOs, and Other Digital Assets,**" Henderson, M. Todd, and Max Raskin, *Columbia Business Law Review* 444, Oct. 17, 2018.

Chapter 40

Departures

Pierre Rochard was not the only one who called problems at FTX before it went south. He just did it earlier and louder.

Ishan Bhaidani, a young hobbyist trader and marketing pro, also called it. He did it in October, a month before November's revelations. On October 5, 2022, he kicked off a 20-tweet thread about the problems he saw in the Samglomerate:

> Im taking all of my capital out of @FTX_Official and going short $FTT
> ☒ FTX has been swinging and missing all year long on so many activations
> AND
> Something shady is going on at FTX.

His chief complaints included lackluster product development on the exchange, failure to launch a stablecoin like the other big exchanges, SBF's insistence on chasing every hot trend, and also saying yes to every TV interview.

His 11th tweet had no text. It was just a quote tweet of someone else that had shared a photo of SBF with a goofy grin sitting next to supermodel Gisele Bündchen.

Bhaidani didn't even give lip service to the notion that Alameda and FTX were two different entities. He just threw its investment list in his thread, pronouncing it "Pretty underwhelming for an A Tier Brand."

Bhaidani and I spoke following the bankruptcy announcement, and he told me his short on ftt had been his best trade all year. He'd earned enough to pull his portfolio nearly back to homeostasis after months of bleeding.

But Bhaidani also made another point: it looked very bad that Alameda's Co-CEO Sam Trabucco, FTX US's CEO Brett Harrison, and FTX's chief of over-the-counter trading, Jonathan Cheesman, had each left over successive months (August, September, and October, respectively).

As Bhadani put it in his thread, "Either something shady is happening, or these guys are post-economic." (That is, too rich to feel motivated any longer.)

Case in point, Trabucco had announced he was leaving Alameda with a Twitter thread that began with "On happiness." Among other things, he mentioned that he had bought a boat. A month later he tweeted, "Why are journalists so excited to make my stepping down about something other than a desire to go fast over the nice water?"

On the *FTX Podcast*, Trabucco had been a bit less braggadocious. Without quite coming out and saying it, he seemed to suggest that Alameda was an exhausting place to work. For example, once Alameda started taking on external market making deals, they had to have staff on deck 24/7. It was grueling for a small team.

Trabucco, who'd taken on the co-CEO job the prior October, said that Alameda was a really fun place to be but also that he was burned out. This is fair. Basketball is also really fun, but no one wants to play it 16 hours a day, seven days a week.

FTX US's Harrison also announced his departure in a tweet thread. He wrote, "I don't doubt my experiences in this role will be among the most cherished of my career. Most of all I'm grateful to @SBF_FTX for the opportunity and trust he gave me during this period of FTX's history."

SBF went on Bloomberg TV to talk about Harrison leaving the day he announced. "It's not the kind of thing to go public were it not in the works for a while," he said. "I'm really excited about our leadership."

After Harrison's departure, the US arm would be stewarded by three different people, SBF included. Harrison had been there 18 months.

If there were a way to post a clip of SBF answering the first question from this interview, I would. He's more rambly than usual. He looks to be searching for what he wants to say. Bizarrely, he ends his response to the question about Harrison leaving by saying he's really excited about a potential headquarters for FTX US in Miami.

Around that same time, a memo was circulated among leaders in the company titled: "We came, we saw, we researched," according to the CFTC's December complaint against Sam. Authored by SBF, the memo contemplated shutting down Alameda. CFTC staff quote him as writing, "I think it might be time for Alameda Research to shut down. Honestly, it was probably time to do that a year ago."

He noted, among other things, that failure to hedge Alameda's bets properly "cost more in EV than all the money Alameda has ever made or ever will make."

SBF and I discussed this point, too. Remember when I explained expected value before and I wrote that risk was an actual liability on the balance sheet? You treat it as if it's a cost that you've incurred, though you haven't actually.

SBF explained that this is what he meant in that memo. It wasn't that Alameda had lost more than it would ever make, but that the risk was potentially that high.

As he put it:

> I wasn't saying that it was never going to make that. I wasn't even saying that it hadn't net made money historically. I think if you'd asked me, I would've said, look, there are a lot of ways to define that. I think mostly it has made money, but not by all of them, but that it was also in a leveraged position and, like, that leveraged position had real risk.

To the point that he had come to regret not shutting it down already. The risk was a potential cost. It was such a large risk that even if it were unlikely to be realized, the company had to factor in even a slim probability at that point. "I didn't think it was going to be realized, but like: That's how risk works. Even if you don't think it's going to be realized, maybe it will be," he said.

He didn't ever see Alameda as doomed. "Up until CZ's tweet on November 6, Alameda's fate was not written," he told me. Even then, he still thinks he might have saved it if he hadn't signed away his company.

Following Harrison, in October, Cheesman left quietly. The Block got the scoop from two unnamed sources, who said Cheesman was going back to a firm he'd founded, JCi Advisory Ltd. "Cheesman joined FTX in May 2021 and was tasked with bringing traditional financial institutions into crypto markets, having previously worked at HSBC, Goldman Sachs, and Barclays," the report said.

At that point, FTX only had five weeks left as a going concern.

Sources Referenced

Ishan Bhaidani, @Ishanb22 thread, Twitter, Oct. 5, 2022: https://twitter.com/ishanb22/status/1577699083808083969; Threadreader: https://threadreaderapp.com/thread/1577699083808083969.html.

"🦋 **Mum on bitcoin ETF**," Dale, Brady and Crystal Kim, Axios Crypto Newsletter, Axios, Nov. 16, 2022.

"**FTX's head of OTC and institutional sales has quietly left the firm**," Khatri, Yogita, Jeremy Nation, and Frank Chaparro, The Block, Oct. 3, 2022.

"**Sam Bankman-Fried Hands Control of Crypto Trading Firm Alameda to Two Deputies**," Nelson, Danny, CoinDesk, Oct. 12, 2021.

Sam Trabucco, @AlamedaTrabucco, Twitter, Aug. 24, 2022, https://twitter.com/AlamedaTrabucco/status/1562519114979356673; Threadreader: https://threadreaderapp.com/thread/1562519114979356673.html.

"**Alameda Co-CEO Trabucco Steps Down from Crypto Trading Firm**," Miller, Hannah, Bloomberg, Aug. 24, 2022.

"**The FTX Podcast #121—Sam Trabucco on Trading 2018—2022**," Yver, Tristan, *FTX Podcast*, deleted from internet, possibly released Sept. 8, 2022.

Brett Harrison, @BrettHarrison88, Twitter, Sept. 27, 2022: https://twitter.com/BrettHarrison88/status/1574782907876626433.

"**FTX President Brett Harrison steps down**," Yasmin, Mehnaz, Reuters, Sept. 27, 2022.

"**Bankman-Fried on Departure of FTX US President Harrison**," Bloomberg TV, Sept. 27, 2022.

"**CFTC Charges Sam Bankman-Fried, FTX Trading and Alameda with Fraud and Material Misrepresentations**," press release and complaint before the US Southern District of New York, Commody Futures Trading Commission, Dec. 13, 2022.

Interview, Sam Bankman-Fried, phone call with spokesperson, Dec. 30, 2022.

"**Former FTX Executive Brett Harrison in Talks with Investors for New Crypto Startup**," Ryan, Aidan, and Erin Woo, The Information, Dec. 2, 2022.

PART III

INFAMY

Chapter 41

Mango Markets

T he gods send warnings, but they are tough to see without the
benefit of hindsight.

One month before FTX entered its final act, something happened
that looked like a microcosmic allegory of what was to come.

How do you turn $10 million in stablecoins into just under
$50 million in a day? Market manipulation on a token that a DeFi
project has placed too much faith in. That's one way.

SBF pops up in the story of Mango Markets, though it has nothing
much to do with FTX directly, but its story illuminates both the flimsi-
ness of new token prices and the dangers of projects leaning operationally on an untested financial instrument.

Mango Markets is a money market and decentralized *perpetual swaps
exchange* that operates on the Solana blockchain (SBF's favorite chain,
from Chapter 26).

It has a token named mango (MNGO). Crucially, this decentralized
exchange allowed users to make leveraged trades using various crypto

assets as collateral. One of the assets users could post as collateral was its own token, mango.

How many similarities to FTX can we squeeze into one $100 million vignette?

So here's what happened. On October 11, a trader named Avraham Eisenberg funded two different wallets with $5 million in USDC stablecoins apiece.

Then he went on Mango Markets and made an offer for $5 million in long perpetuals on mango. His other wallet took the deal and bought the shorts on the other side. So now he's massively long and short on mango at once.

The price of mango is $0.03.

Next, on three different exchanges, Mango itself, Ascendex, and FTX, he bought between $1 million and $1.6 million in mango in all these markets, for a total of $4 million in mango purchased all at once.

This was a gigantic change in market activity for Mango. Typical volume for a given day prior to that had been between $200,000 and $300,000 on a token with a "market cap" of a bit over $40 million at the time. Eisenberg had just given mango a day of trading 13X larger than it normally was.

So the price leaps to $0.91, a 30X increase in a day. This is important, because Mango Markets would allow users to borrow based on how valuable their holdings were. Blockchains have to rely on software called oracles to know things that happen elsewhere. Eisenberg was executing an oracle attack.

Mango, as well as protocols such as MakerDAO and Compound, rely on oracles to let their smart contracts know how valuable deposits are. Based on what the oracles tell them, a given lending protocol will let users borrow more or less. It's one of the weakest parts of blockchains (everyone knows this), but mostly it works all right.

It helps to have caveats around oracle prices when they are used by robots on the internet to make important decisions, such as how much to let someone borrow. It also helps to put faith only in tokens that have some actual liquidity.

For example, following the Mango Markets attack, SBF would take to Twitter and use it to explain how FTX's risk engine was better than Mango's. He said FTX puts a time band around assets. So, for example, it won't count changes as "real" unless they are, *say*, more than 20 minutes old.

He concluded that thread by writing:

> It's why we started FTX in the first place.
>
> Tradfi had sophisticated (sometimes!), slow, manual risk models, and—in some FCMs[1]—fast, egregious ones.
>
> Crypto had fast, automated, broken risk models.
>
> There was an opening for a thoughtfully automated risk engine.

The SEC would specifically cite this thread in its complaint, by the way.

Regardless, without the benefit of FTX's foresight, Mango Markets "believed" that its token, mango, was worth 30X more than it normally was, due to the data oracles were reporting to it, which was due to very intentional market manipulation by Eisenberg.

So the long perp position Eisenberg had taken out went up wildly. That's when Eisenberg exited the position by borrowing against it, cleaning out all the tokens on the platform. Total take: $117 million in various kinds of cryptocurrency, all in deposits investors had made on the platform in hopes of earning yield.

At this point, Eisenberg could let his perpetuals be liquidated. It didn't matter. Those possessions would fall back to worthless shortly, but he had possession of assets with much less volatile value.

Remember, in crypto, there's no reversing a bad transaction. Once he had these assets, he had them, so Mango Markets became completely insolvent.

Investors had trusted that Mango Markets would responsibly steward their deposits, that it would only lend their assets against heavily collateralized positions, so they were "safe." That was the belief.

And, in fact, Eisenberg's borrows had been heavily collateralized. For a few minutes.

Here's where Eisenberg got bold: he went to the DAO and made a proposal. He offered to give back enough money to make all the users whole, but they had to let him keep the difference. He asked them to call it a "bug bounty." In exchange, the creators had to agree not to press charges.

---

[1] Futures Commissions Merchant.

On October 15, he tweeted, "I believe all of our actions were legal open market actions, using the protocol as designed, even if the development team did not fully anticipate all the consequences of setting parameters the way they are."

Still, he wanted assurances.

And. . . *he got them.*

Subsequent reports say the deal closed, and he walked away with $47 million in assets. The Block reported on October 14 that the attack cost him $10 million to execute. That's a nice return for a few days of work.

Subsequently, he has refused to talk about the deal he struck with Mango Markets.

Long story short: he found a project that let people place bets based on its thinly traded native token. He took one of those bets, intervened in the market, and managed to cause a temporary market blip that enabled him to exit his bet before equilibrium returned.

He's not the only one.

As I have explained before, founders have every incentive to make the token for their blockchain start-up go up in value. So they have also every incentive to *believe* it is valuable. Mango had let itself get into a situation where its own token was its vulnerability.

As we will see, FTX let Alameda leverage much too much largely based on its gigantic horde of FTX's ftt token, and that would be its undoing.

You can imagine, after Eisenberg's exploit, that Mango's team was shaking their heads, saying to themselves something much like what SBF wrote on Twitter on Nov. 16, after his own insolvency:

> I was on the cover of every magazine, and FTX was the darling of Silicon Valley.
>
> We got overconfident and careless.
>
> . . . And problems were brewing. Larger than I realized.
>
> [AGAIN THESE NUMBERS ARE APPROXIMATE, TO THE BEST OF MY KNOWLEDGE, ETC.]
>
> Leverage built up—~$5b of leverage, backed by ~$20b of assets which were . . . .
>
> Well, they had value. FTT had value, in EV! But they had risk.

That they did.

Epilogue: On December 26, Avraham Eisenberg was arrested for market manipulation in Puerto Rico. Charges against him were unsealed on the 27th in the Southern District of New York.

Sources Referenced

"**The Mango Markets Exploit: An Order Book Analysis**," Solidus Labs Team, Solidus Labs, Oct. 18, 2022.

"**DeFi Trading Platform Mango Markets Loses $117 Million in Hack**," Lodge, Michelle, Investopedia, Oct. 12, 2022.

"**Mango Markets DAO set to approve $47 million bounty for hacker**," Nwobodo, Christian, Cryptoslate, Oct. 14, 2022.

Joshua Lim, @Joshua_j_lim, Twitter, Oct. 12, 2022: https://threadreaderapp.com/thread/1579987648546246658.html.

Mango (MNGO), CoinGecko: https://www.coingecko.com/en/coins/mango/.

Sam Bankman-Fried, @SBF_FTX, Oct. 12, 2022, Twitter: https://twitter.com/SBF_FTX/status/1580170203664904195, Threadreader: https://threadreaderapp.com/thread/1580170218789253123.html.

"*SEC v. Sam Bankman-Fried*," US Securities and Exchange Commission complaint before the US Court of the Southern District of New York, Dec. 13, 2022.

"**EXCLUSIVE: The Man Who May Have Milked $100+ Million from Mango Markets**," Burnet, Chris, Karlstack, Oct. 12, 2022.

"**Mango Markets community set to approve $47 million deal with hacker**," Copeland, Tim, The Block, Oct. 14, 2022.

Avraham Eisenberg, avi_eisen, Twitter, Oct. 15, 2022: https://twitter.com/avi_eisen/status/1581326197241180160?s=20&t=7SAT6UacQ8GUOtz0V9llEw.

"**Mango Markets exploiter comes clean, claims all actions were legal**," Avan-Nomayo, Osato, The Block, Oct. 15, 2022.

"**Repay Bad Debt #2**," Mango DAO, Oct. 2022: https://dao.mango.markets/dao/MNGO/proposal/GYhczJdNZAhG24dkkymWE9SUZv8xC4g8s9U8VF5Yprne.

Sam Bankman-Fried, @SBF_FTX, Twitter, Nov. 16, 2022: https://twitter.com/SBF_FTX/status/1592958061341474817.

"**U.S. charges fraud in Mango crypto manipulation case**," Stempel, Jonathan, Reuters, Dec. 27, 2022.

United States v. Avraham Eisenberg, Letter from Damian Williams to The Honorable Katharine H. Parker, United States Magistrate Judge, Southern District of New York, Dec. 27, 2022.

"*United States of America v. Avraham Eisenberg*," Racz, Brandon, Special Agent, FBI, Southern District of New York, Dec. 23, 2022.

Chapter 42

Nine Days in November

Ian Allison published a story in CoinDesk, and from that moment on, Sam Bankman-Fried had fallen off a metaphorical yacht of start-up mega success and he was swimming in a vast ocean of personal fault, alone, outmatched by the sea. In the first moments, he thought he could swim. He was swimming, in fact, but he couldn't see that he'd been caught in an enormous but slow-moving whirlpool. It had him trapped, he just couldn't tell. He couldn't see the shore and he didn't know he wasn't getting any closer. But he swam and swam.

He might as well have just treaded water and watched the stars in the sky.

It was already over.

The title of Allison's post was, "Divisions in Sam Bankman-Fried's Crypto Empire Blur on His Trading Titan Alameda's Balance Sheet." The original version, before they updated it with an extraneous quote and a no-comment from Alameda, ran only about 450 words. The CFTC would specifically cite it as the first event under "November 2022 Collapse of FTX Trading and Alameda" in its complaint.

Name a single dispatch that's had more impact on the industry this year, on the business world this year. I can't. It might be the most impactful single post in all of the news in some time.

The story came out on Wednesday, November 2. By Friday, November 11, it was all over. Very nearly the whole of SBF's empire was in bankruptcy, and another man was CEO. FTX as he'd known it was finished, and it started with a tiny story on an industry news site.

The substance of the CoinDesk story was simple: Allison[1] had gotten his hands on what looked like Alameda Research's balance sheet.

Allison simply reported what he found there. The company had $14.66 billion in assets, but most of this was crypto. The biggest line item was $3.66 billion in FTX's own ftt token, *marked to market*.

They also had over a billion dollars in Solana's sol, but most of it was locked. It had a bunch of Sam coins, $134 million in cash, $2 billion in equities, and some other stuff.

And that was the whole post—*kaboom*.

It has been, to say the least, very hard to get insiders' perspectives on FTX since the company fell apart, especially on the record. But we all got a very good one in the form of Nathaniel Whittemore's podcast, *The Breakdown*.

Whittemore was an FTX employee on the marketing team. He joined the company when it acquired the crypto app Blockfolio, in August 2020, and stuck around. He says on the podcast that he was one of the folks behind that Superbowl ad with Larry David.

On November 14, after SBF was out, he published his first episode of the podcast since the bankruptcy, and he went through the whole process step-by-step, giving an insider's account and all of his personal opinions.

Whittemore is a commentator, not a journalist. His thing is analyzing the larger narratives that drive the crypto industry. The focus of his take was from the perspective of a member of FTX's communications team. In this case, that's a good perspective.

---

[1] Ian and I overlapped at CoinDesk and we were on the same team for a year or more, and he always got the biggest scoops. Primarily, he focuses on big businesses, like PayPal or Barclay's. Or he covers the more institutional crypto firms, such as Fireblocks, Paxos, or Anchorage—the straightlaced stuff. It's not at all surprising that CoinDesk's biggest scoop of all time came from Ian.

So after Allison's post, Whittemore explains, the market was shaken by the fact that there was so much ftt and other Sam coins on its balance sheet. As he says and I have written, everyone knows you just can't sell that much of a token like that without making it plummet in value.

Which meant that Alameda's portfolio was in fact worth a lot less than advertised.

Because of that, FTX was processing more withdrawals than normal following Allison's story.

Jason Choi is a venture investor, now part of a fund he cofounded, but formerly with The Spartan Group. Choi had written a long Twitter thread after the crisis started explaining why Spartan had taken a pass on FTX's venture funding round but also admitted that for years he had wondered if passing had been a mistake.

We spoke, and I asked him why people started withdrawing money from FTX when Alameda's balance sheet was exposed. "I think the assumption people had was Alameda and FTX had a commingled balance sheet," Choi said.

That might sound like hindsight being 20/20, but that's also why Spartan hadn't invested. It made partners nervous seeing FTX open its doors with effectively an in-house market maker. His later FOMO was because it appeared, in hindsight, that the arrangement had actually worked well. And it had! Until it didn't.

But Choi emphasized something that might not be obvious to non-traders: there's basically no reason for a trader feeling at all skittish not to remove assets from an exchange. There's no cost to exit. So, at first, many traders using FTX were just getting ahead of it, de-risking.

If everything turned out to be fine, they could easily return. The only opportunity cost would be a few days of missed trading, but the markets stunk in early November anyway.

The same is not true in our world. Imagine someone with $10 million in cash in a bank that's looking shaky. What do they do? It's complicated. As cash, that would take up a ton of space and feel dangerous. Bank transfers take forever.

With crypto, it's a breeze. They pop it off the exchange and onto a blockchain address whose key is on a thumb drive they keep inside a safe inside another safe in their penthouse. Their lawyer even has a copy of the drive in case their client's building burns down.

The crypto trader doesn't actually even have to remove the thumb drive to make the deposit! That's what public keys are for. It takes up no space. It's done in minutes. It could not be easier.

So why hesitate? Traders who were at all worried just withdrew funds. A lot of them.

"It wasn't till Sunday [November 6] that things got really gnarly," Whittemore said. From here, things move fast.

Binance and FTX were about to feud. "Privately it felt to me like something must have gone down" between Binance and FTX when the two split up in 2021, Whittemore said.

Indeed, when I asked Sam in Spring 2021 if there were a person in crypto he viewed as his opposite number in the market, he hemmed and hawed, but finally he said "Binance." He didn't say "CZ," but the answer came close enough.

When I asked him about this again in December, he said that FTX had arranged to buy out Binance's stake because "it was clear that they had transitioned from thinking of us as a portfolio company to thinking of us as a competitor."

At first, he said, it seemed like both sides agreed that it was time for a split, but "it was a very acrimonious negotiation," SBF said. Bad feelings lingered on both sides, and they seemed to come out in November 2022.

Kicking off that Sunday at 9:32 a.m. on the U.S. east coast, Alameda CEO Caroline Ellison tweeted, "A few notes on the balance sheet info that has been circulating recently: - that specific balance sheet is for a subset of our corporate entities, we have > $10b of assets that aren't reflected there."

About an hour later, Binance's CEO, CZ, tweeted a thread that included this key sentence: "Due to recent revelations that have come to light, we have decided to liquidate any remaining FTT on our books."

In the next tweet, he wrote, "We will try to do so in a way that minimizes market impact."

Whatever they tried, though, it didn't work.

Ellison replied shortly thereafter, "If you're looking to minimize the market impact on your FTT sales, Alameda will happily buy it all from you today at $22!"

She had made it worse. "This tweet basically single-handedly set a price target for the entire market to go and attack ftt and very transparently so," Whittemore said.

After Ellison was charged by the DoJ, CFTC, and SEC alongside SBF and FTX cofounder Gary Wang, the SEC would cite this tweet as an example of market manipulation.

The SEC wrote, in its updated complaint, that Ellison would have had to know that "Alameda would have to draw down additional funds from FTX itself, further extending its line of credit, or obtain funds from third-party lenders without disclosing its own tenuous financial condition."

Before the tweets back and forth that day, ftt had been trading between $22 and $24, but then traders saw weakness, as Whittemore and many other commentators have noted. By Tuesday, ftt would dive down to around $15.

"At this point people in FTX were getting uncomfortable," Whittemore said. "Sam's communications were—shall we say—less than inspiring."

At a little before 1 p.m. New York time, after CZ and Ellison's exchange, SBF did a Twitter thread about a new exchange feature, and he tacked on a note that "we're all in this together."

Later that day, CZ tweeted again, this time comparing ftt to luna. Luna had been the year's biggest disaster. In the moment, that seemed to be unfair to many, including Whittemore.

Whittemore was stunned to see one CEO threatening the solvency of another that was systemically important to the whole industry. "As CZ moved in for the kill, and Sam tweeted platitudes about coming together and working together, the industry was frantically asking for real answers from FTX, answers that we would not give," he said.

FTX's VIP guy Tackett told me much the same thing. He said he was internally "screaming" at SBF to speak up.

As Whittemore says, these things work differently in this industry. If money is leaving a bank, all you know is what other people tell you about it. On blockchains, though, when funds leave an exchange, that's visible. People know the wallets exchanges do withdrawals from.

"By late Sunday night, all of our biggest clients were frantically asking for answers as well," Whittemore said. "They wanted to know we were solvent, and they wanted to know we don't lend out our customer assets."

Meanwhile, some FTX employees were trying to speak up for the company where SBF wasn't. "There were rumors of insolvency," Tackett told me. Since Tackett's job was to interface with the biggest clients on the exchange, he was trying to reassure them that a weak Alameda was no threat to FTX.

"I was like, guys that's silly." He was out in public saying there was no reason Alameda unwinding should hurt the exchange, because it was just another customer. He really believed that, then. His take at that point was: "We're an exchange. One client going insolvent doesn't impact us."

Tackett practiced what he preached. He told the *Wall Street Journal* that he had kept 80% of his net worth on FTX. He's now out a life-changing amount of money just like many of the exchange's customers.

But on Monday, November 7, looking at the internal dashboards that FTX staff had access to, it hit him that the company might have let Alameda go too long on spot margin. He told me once he saw that, his assessment was: "Worse comes to worst, we have a $2 billion hole we need to fill."

But "even if that's the case, we'll be able to plug that," he said he thought at the time. "And then it comes out that fucking $10 billion is missing? Jesus Christ, Sam. And there was no way that could have happened via the spot margin market."

Tackett didn't know what those above him in the company had already realized. According to the CFTC's complaint:

> Bankman-Fried and other key personnel of FTX and Alameda acknowledged internally that this shortfall was not merely a matter of having sufficient liquid funds on hand to cover customer withdrawals in the short term; rather, FTX customer funds were irrevocably lost because Alameda had misappropriated them.

If he knew it, though, SBF wasn't ready to say it. "Instead of going out and being like, 'No, we're fine,' Sam just stayed quiet," Tackett said. "And the problem is: Anybody that wants to defend you, if you're not defending yourself, they can't go out there and defend you as well. So our silence was pretty damning."

But then November 7 would be the day that SBF would go on Twitter and tweet a message he would later delete (but has been preserved in CFTC's documentation, and I definitely saw it while it was still up). He wrote (among other things):

> A competitor is trying to go after us with false rumors.
>   FTX is fine. Assets are fine.

It also said that FTX does not invest clients' assets. As the CFTC notes, insiders "expressed concerns" about the accuracy of that message.

Meanwhile, Whittemore said the internal Slack channels were getting increasingly desperate, especially coming from the folks facing the largest clients, such as Tackett.

Other employees, Tackett said, were coming to Sam's side, talking about reserves that remained. But to Tackett it wasn't enough.

In the CFTC's account, FTX leaders were already out looking for more money to plug the hole at that point, but Whittemore and Tackett didn't know and couldn't know. Their calculations for the shortfall at that time grew quickly from $1 or $2 billion to as much as $8 billion.

"Numerous parties declined to bail out FTX regardless of the favorable terms being offered," the complaint alleges, but it does not explain how it knows this. More, no doubt, will come out when this case goes to court.

The CFTC wrote that FTX presented potential rescuers with a balance sheet for its fundraising, the one that the *Financial Times* published on November 12. "Most notably, the balance sheet included an $8 billion negative balance from a 'hidden, poorly internally labeled "fiat@ftx. com" account,'" the CFTC noted.

As we've described in Chapter 14, this was the Alameda (and North Dimension) bank account that FTX used to get customers' non-crypto money onto the exchange, at least until FTX had its own banking relationship in August 2020. The thing is, the CFTC said, the money in this account never moved to FTX's bank account, and Alameda made use of it.

On Tuesday, November 8, it was Election Day. I'm a crypto reporter, but my company, Axios, has its roots in politics. I expected to spend my day finding some kind of angle on politics and crypto. Maybe something about all those donations that SBF had made?

Since I cowrite a daily newsletter about the crypto business, my first course of action would be getting the day's issue out, and then maybe we'd look into some of SBF's candidates? I don't really remember what I was thinking. The day's events wiped a lot away.

As I was getting started, one of my coworkers, Felix Salmon, flagged a story in The Block, with the headline, "FTX appears to have stopped processing withdrawals, on-chain data show."

Withdrawals stopping was the worst-case scenario. I confess I found this extremely hard to believe. I was not an SBF fanboy, but as I said at the beginning of this book, I basically believed he had a good head on his shoulders.

Whittemore saw it differently. "Now for me, by this point, it was clear that the game was over," Whittemore said.

At 9:29 a.m in New York. I would write in Slack, "I guess this whole thing should be the topic of tomorrow's newsletter." I wasn't getting it. My other coworkers were. They were teaching themselves at the last minute how to read Ethereum's blockchain using Etherscan, and honestly, this one was a pretty easy read because nothing was happening.

Meanwhile, the CFTC contends, fundraising was not working, so FTX went to Binance, and Binance agreed to an acquisition pending due diligence. The two CEOs would tweet out the arrangement, which would be the first that FTX employees would learn about.

At 11:03 a.m., SBF would tweet: "Hey all: I have a few announcements to make. Things have come full circle, and FTX.com's first, and last, investors are the same: we have come to an agreement on a strategic transaction with Binance for FTX.com (pending DD [due diligence] etc.)."

As Whittemore notes, language in SBF's subsequent tweet all but admitted that FTX had holes in its balance sheet. This wasn't going to be the topic for the next day's newsletter. We were starting over, and this was the news.

Later that day, on Slack, Whittemore said, SBF would post a reassuring message that reassured no one.

Later yet, Jon Wu, from the growth team at crypto privacy project Aztec, would tweet a perceptive thread. "The prevailing narrative of FTX-Alameda had been one of brazen corruption: FTX gives Alameda priority orderflow, allowing its sister hedge fund to front-run other traders," he wrote. "But FTX isn't Alameda's data source. FTX is Alameda's piggy bank. Sam uses a highly profitable exchange as a source of capital for a wildly profitable trading operation."

Mostly right. Now we know, though, that FTX was Alameda's piggy bank; it's just that Alameda hadn't been all that profitable lately.

On November 9, Binance's main account would tweet at 4 p.m.: "As a result of corporate due diligence, as well as the latest news reports regarding mishandled customer funds and alleged US agency investigations, we have decided that we will not pursue the potential acquisition of http://FTX.com."

Ellison, the *Wall Street Journal* would report a few days later, had gathered some of her staff together Wednesday, November 9, to talk. The *Journal* reports:

> In a video meeting with Alameda employees late Wednesday Hong Kong time, Alameda CEO Caroline Ellison said that she, Mr. Bankman-Fried and two other FTX executives, Nishad Singh and Gary Wang, were aware of the decision to send customer funds to Alameda, according to people familiar with the video.

The CFTC would provide further details about this meeting in its amended complaint of December 21, but the important detail was in the *WSJ*'s original version: "Shortly after this meeting, most of Alameda's staff resigned."

Also on Nov. 9, bitcoin would post its lowest price of the year, $15,742, down 77% from the all-time high in November 2021.

For many, many global FTX employees that lived in places with weak financial systems, this meant their money was gone, because they had been using FTX as their bank as well as their employer, Whittemore said.

"It wasn't just that Sam and those about him perpetrated fraud," Whittemore said. "Every single ounce of their effort went into self-preservation. They continued asking their team to lie for them publicly, even knowing it could expose those people to legal ramifications. It was callous, cruel, and utterly devoid of any human consideration."

SBF had said again and again that FTX kept customer funds sacrosanct. The CFTC report now very much alleges that wasn't true, as does a complaint by the SEC and an indictment from the DOJ.

Jordan Fish, better known as @Cobie on Twitter, formerly @CryptoCobain, tweeted his impression later that day.

"In my decade of crypto, think this exchange rug is by far the worst ever," he wrote. "The rumours for this blowup seem so egregious and unnecessary to me. I can't imagine running an exchange that does mid 8 fig PER DAY in revenue and thinking 'how can we leverage this for more?' . . . Cheers Sam."

On Thursday, November 10, FTX and FTX US both halted all trading and withdrawals. The Securities Commission of the Bahamas would also announce that it was freezing the assets of the FTX entities over which it had authority. We would later learn that FTX Digital Markets CEO Ryan Salame had contacted them to tell them what he knew.

Around 4 a.m., SBF would sign over control of the company, authorizing another CEO to be appointed.

At 9:13 a.m. he would post a twitter thread that began with, "I'm sorry. That's the biggest thing. I fucked up, and should have done better."

On November 11, at 9:14 a.m., FTX's Twitter account posted a statement that said 134 related companies had filed for bankruptcy and that John J. Ray III, known for stewarding the unwinding of Enron,[2] had taken SBF's place as CEO.

Hundreds of millions of dollars in crypto would slip out of FTX's accounts that day. At the time, it was estimated at $600 million worth. By late December, that estimate had fallen to $370 million.

It will likely be some time before we really understand what happened there. It could have been some mix of insider or insider-adjacent hack or the authorities in the Bahamas seizing funds in the due course of their securing of the exchange. Or it could be all of one or the other. We may never know.

On December 30, authorities in the Bahamas would put out a statement saying that it had been able to seize $3.5 billion worth of crypto assets controlled by FTX (at November prices).

For a month before the collapse, Tackett told me he had found that the spot margin dashboard wasn't working. He wasn't allowed to look at Alameda's balances, either. It was tagged the same way employees'

---

[2] I said Enron would pop up again, and there it is.

accounts were (so that FTX staff couldn't spy on each other). Tackett could see the accounts of other customers but not Alameda.

So his estimate of the worst case for spot margin borrows assumed that all the spot margin borrows on the platform had been Alameda's, but of course that wasn't the case.

"Do you at all wonder if that admin page wasn't working because they didn't want it to be working?" I asked him.

"Yep. That was one of those things looking back that I'm curious if that was a red flag," he said, but he also knew the company was short on developers. Lots of dashboards didn't work.

More mysterious than internal transparency, to Tackett, was trading an exchange with enormous potential for a mere proprietary trading firm. "Why didn't they just let Alameda die and keep this insanely profitable money-printing machine that they had up and running?" Tackett asked.

Sources Referenced

Sam Bankman-Fried, @SBF_FTX, Twitter, Nov. 5, 2022: https://twitter.com/SBF_FTX/status/1588965167827935232.

"Divisions in Sam Bankman-Fried's Crypto Empire Blur on His Trading Titan Alameda's Balance Sheet," Allison, Ian, CoinDesk, Nov. 2, 2022.

"CFTC Charges Sam Bankman-Fried, FTX Trading and Alameda with Fraud and Material Misrepresentations," press release and complaint before the US Southern District of New York, Commodity Futures Trading Commission, Dec. 13, 2022.

"Sam Bankman Fraud: Inside the Collapse of FTX's Hollow Empire," Whittemore, Nathaniel, The Breakdown, CoinDesk, Nov. 14, 2022.

Interview, Jason Choi, mobile call, Dec. 11, 2022.

Sam Bankman-Fried, interview, phone call with spokesperson, Dec. 30, 2022.

Caroline Ellison, @carolinecapital, Twitter, Nov. 6, 2022: https://twitter.com/carolinecapital/status/1589264375042707458.

Changpeng Zhao, @cz_binance, Twitter, Nov. 6, 2022: https://twitter.com/cz_binance/status/1589283421704290306.

Caroline Ellison, @carolinecapital, Twitter, Nov. 6, 2022: https://twitter.com/carolinecapital/status/1589287457975304193.

Changpeng Zhao, @cz_binance, Twitter, Nov. 6, 2022: https://twitter.com/cz_binance/status/1589374530413215744.

"SEC Charges Caroline Ellison and Gary Wang with Defrauding Investors in Crypto Asset Trading Platform FTX," US Securities and Exchange Commission, press release and updated complaint, Dec. 21, 2022.

"**FTX balance sheet, revealed**," FT Alphaville, *Financial Times*, Nov. 12, 2022.

"**FTX appears to have stopped processing withdrawals, on-chain data show**," Khatri, Yogita, The Block, Nov. 8, 2022.

Interview, Zane Tackett, video conference, Dec. 5, 2022.

"**FTX's Collapse Leaves Employees Sick with Anger**," Osipovich, Alexander, Caitlin Ostroff and Gregory Zuckerman, *Wall Street Journal*, Nov. 16, 2022.

Sam Bankman-Fried, @SBF_FTX, Twitter, Nov. 8, 2022: https://twitter.com/SBF_FTX/status/1590012124864348160?s=20&t=2ofLgcSTq3SVy1kmmGxf6g.

Jon Wu, @jonwu_, Twitter, Nov. 8, 2022: https://twitter.com/jonwu/status/159009970329878280.

"**FTX Tapped Into Customer Accounts to Fund Risky Bets, Setting Up Its Downfall**," Huang, Vicky Ge, Alexander Osipovich and Patricia Kowsmann, *Wall Street Journal*, Nov. 11, 2022.

"**Alameda, FTX Executives Are Said to Have Known FTX Was Using Customer Funds**," Michaels, Dave, Elaine Yu and Caitlin Ostroff, *Wall Street Journal*, Nov. 12, 2022.

Binance, @binance, Nov. 9, 2022: https://twitter.com/binance/status/1590449161069268992.

"**Securities Commission of The Bahamas Freezes Assets of FTX**," press release, Securities Commission of The Bahamas, scb.gov.bs, Nov. 10, 2022.

Jordan Fish, @cobie, Twitter, thread, Nov. 9, 2022: https://twitter.com/cobie/status/1590188580483497985.

"**A top FTX exec blew the whistle on Sam Bankman-Fried's moves just 2 days before the crypto exchange's collapse**," Glover, George, Markets Insider, Dec. 15, 2022.

Sam Bankman-Fried, @SBF_FTX, Twitter, Nov. 10 9:13 AM: https://twitter.com/SBF_FTX/status/1590709166515310593.

FTX, @FTX_Official, Twitter, Nov. 11, 2022: https://twitter.com/ftx_official/status/1591071832823959552.

"**FTX starts bankruptcy proceedings and Bankman-Fried resigns as CEO**," Kim, Crystal, Axios, Nov. 11, 2022.

"**'FTX Has Been Hacked': Crypto Disaster Worsens as Exchange Sees Mysterious Outflows Exceeding \$600M**," Ligon, Cheyenne, and others, CoinDesk, Nov. 11, 2022.

"**US Probes How \$372 Million Vanished in Hack After FTX Bankruptcy**," Benny-Morrison, Ava, Bloomberg, Dec. 27, 2022.

"**Securities Commission of The Bahamas Seeks Court Direction Regarding Disclosure of Information**," Media release, Securities Commission of The Bahamas, Dec. 29, 2022.

"**Regulators in the Bahamas Are Holding \$3.5 Billion in FTX Customer Assets**," Reynolds, Sam, CoinDesk, Dec. 30, 2022.

Chapter 43

Alameda and the ftt Shuffle

After the troubles at FTX, lots of firms came out to offer real talk about how they had had concerns about FTX and/or Alameda Research from long before. They just hadn't made them public. For all its tough talk about rebellion and adversarial thinking, the truth is that the blockchain industry is a tiny world, and most of its bigshots don't like to offer negative opinions about anyone but the worst possible actors. There are lots of projects that few successful crypto entrepreneurs have any respect for, but good luck getting them on the record before suspicions resolve into certainties.

For example, Orthogonal Credit was a small institutional credit company built on an Ethereum-based protocol called Maple Finance. The idea of Maple Finance was to extend unsecured or undersecured credit to very good borrowers (hedge funds, well-resourced traders, etc.). Maple did this by onboarding firms such as Orthogonal who would do the work of vetting the companies that borrowed its capital.

In a thread released the same day that Binance announced it would not acquire FTX, Orthogonal Credit's official account tweeted:

During our Alameda due diligence earlier this year, the team identified a number of key weaknesses: a) declining asset quality, b) unclear capital policy, c) less than robust operational and business practices, and d) an increasingly byzantine corporate structure.

Orthogonal Credit, as it happens, was an independent subsidiary of Orthogonal Trading, a hedge fund similar to Alameda, which operated out of Australia. Orthogonal Trading stood by the work of its subsidiary, though, in that its stake in loans made by the credit subsidiary was also the first to take losses.

The subsidiary had approved *one* loan to Alameda from Maple's pool of usd coin, the stablecoin from Circle, but it got out of the tranche in the second quarter and foreclosed the possibility of approving more deals.

"We were a big lender to them, and we had very economic reasons to continue to be a lender, but we decided to take the longer term, responsible decision and cut commercial ties. That looked great, and so we had a lot of inbound inquiries about how we made that decision and what our risk management process is like," Sefton Kincaid, Orthogonal Credit's chief, told me in an interview.

In other words: Orthogonal Credit hadn't said anything, but it had *done* something.

Orthogonal was Kincaid's first full-time crypto gig. He'd previously managed corporate bonds in the tech sector in the traditional way, and he brought a similar approach to this DeFi attempt at institutional lending.

Orthogonal and Maple were different from the lenders I discussed in Chapter 35 because its arrangements were on chain. Everyone could see how much it had to lend and how much companies like Orthogonal had responsibility for.

His dealings with Alameda were always different than his dealings with other counterparties, he told me in an interview. Other applicants for loans didn't fight due diligence from Orthogonal, at least not like Alameda had. "I came into the room late and they were just a bunch of chuckleheads. My relationship with them was adversarial from the start because they thought that their shit didn't stink," Kincaid said.[1]

---

[1] It's a different kind of business, but Harry Halperin of Nym described a similar attitude when his company explored taking on Alameda as an investor in 2021. As Halperin put it in a Nov. 29, 2022, phone call, "Alameda were the only ones who believed that they were so intelligent and so amazing we should allow them to do whatever they want to us."

Throughout the process, Kincaid's small team kept asking to speak to the compliance director. "Alameda repeatedly stonewalled us on that request," he said.

Its risk management appeared "reckless," he said. He found the whole engagement alarming and was relieved to close off any business with them early in the year. "They were pretty unprofessional from the start," he said.

After FTX and Alameda fell apart, blockchain data analytics firm Coin Metrics started combing through data for clues.

The first thing they noticed was that Alameda-associated wallets seemed to be very active in ERC-20 tokens late in 2021. ERC-20 tokens are everything represented on Ethereum that isn't ether. They are tokens that correspond to different projects that rely on Ethereum to operate.

Everything from well-established tokens such as aave to weirder tokens such as ribbon (RBN) and shiba inu (SHIB) are ERC-20.

The bull market had peaked in late 2021. Crypto was sputtering and gasping at an unnatural high through May 2022. It was running on momentum, but momentum runs out.

The fact that Alameda was passing through a lot of ERC-20 tokens might suggest they knew this and that staff were just looking for a few final outsize wins.

On-chain data

Much is made about the openness of data on blockchains, particularly Ethereum. It's true, but the data can be very hard to sort out. It's a torrent. It's confusing. And it's hard to be sure which addresses correspond to which people.

On-chain data is kind of like kids at a big picnic. Everyone thinks someone is watching all of them, but sometimes no one is looking at the right one when they need to be seen.

This story is one of those where what happened on-chain was no more hidden than anything else, but apparently no one had thought to look into it before.

When we spoke in early 2021, SBF would explain a philosophy to me that makes it credible to believe that the firm might have gone big even while it seemed everything was going south.

"Being able and willing to turn on a dime, and turn massively on a dime . . . that's the thing that's come to most define Alameda in a lot of ways and make it most different from a lot of the other trading firms in the area," he told me in February 2021. "Given how much and how weirdly and how unpredictably the space rotates, you do lose out on most of the value if you're kind of too dogmatic about what you're doing."

Which helps put some context on what the Coin Metrics research team observed.

The research team writes, "In our view, the timing and magnitude of funds deployed leading up to the market peak partially explains why Alameda would incur enormous losses as the crypto market collapsed over the first half of 2022."

Notably, they might have been hit very badly as the new year started.

But SBF objected to this characterization, calling on-chain data "close to useless" for evaluating Alameda in late 2021. All that would show, he explained, would be when Alameda was finding arbitrages between DEXes and centralized exchanges.

However, he said, Alameda did most of its business and made most of its money trading on centralized exchanges. So looking at its wallets wouldn't be that revelatory, in his opinion.

But it was real money. "Cross-chain outflows sum up to at least $9.5B. Surprisingly, the largest flows from Ethereum were to Avalanche, Fantom, and Polygon," Coin Metrics found (those are three other minor chains, alternatives to Ethereum).

As we know, Alameda had become convinced that it paid to bet big on farming opportunities. Over on the Avalanche blockchain (which was like Solana, but never as big) there was a project called Wonderland-TIME, which had been huge. It's not worth explaining its logic: there wasn't any. Wonderland was a mid-80s straight-to-VHS horror flick of massively multiplayer online delusion.

That said, folks who got in early and got out made a lot.

Wonderland collapsed in January, surprising absolutely no one. If Terra seemed too experimental, Wonderland was like one of those labs in comic books run by a scientist operating from a hideout in Paraguay to pursue biological research no academic university would ever let pass an ethics board.

Bizarrely, a larger version of Wonderland persists on Ethereum, called Olympus. Somehow, it has not evaporated, though it has diminished considerably.

I asked SBF in December if he thought Alameda had made bets on Wonderland or Olympus, and he said, "I'm gonna be honest, I have no idea."

Lucas Nuzzi, from the Coin Metrics team, started looking on-chain and found something that seemed weird. On September 28, $8.6 billion in just ftt moved that day.

Nuzzi wrote in a November 8 thread, "That was by far the largest daily move of FTT in the token's existence and one of the largest ERC20 daily moves we ever recorded at Coin Metrics."

Of that, $4.19 billion was ftt that had just unlocked, it was 173 million ftt. Backing up: a lot of times when new tokens are launched, many more tokens are created in the smart contract than are released onto the market. I talked about this in Chapter 28, "Sam Coins."

Once you look under the hood, though, this big move was expected. The token had been launched with half the supply locked for three years. That ended July 2022. SBF confirmed that this was the correct interpretation. And, remember: Alameda got the locked up ftt.

The report from Nansen that I discussed in Chapter 15 also deals with this. Half the tokens unlocked over three years, but if they weren't claimed, they stayed put. As I wrote before, these belonged to Alameda, and up until then it seems that Alameda did not see a good reason to bring more ftt onto the market. However, as summer changed to fall in 2022, that situation started to change for reasons that seem more understandable now.

But the weird part is that the deployer sent the token to what Coin Metrics had tagged as an Alameda address, a wallet identified on Etherscan (a site for reading the Ethereum blockchain) as "Alameda Research 24." It seems to be the address that all the past disbursements have gone to.

Of the $8.6 billion that Nuzzi found moved that day, $4.19 billion in tokens hit Alameda's wallet, and then the hedge fund sent it to FTX.

Which might mean it was a loan repayment, or perhaps a collateral deposit. Both firms had probably been counting on this disbursement to get through.

As November revealed: the market didn't want ftt. A major liquidity event for ftt turned out to be a disaster for FTX, so if it had ever tried to turn that ftt into something more substantive, like bitcoin, ethers, or actual dollars, it could have sunk the company just as easily as CZ's tweets had.

The exchange token really only seemed to serve the two firms as a fiction, an asset they could list on their balance sheets when they needed to impress a potential backer.

One of the most surprising features of ftt was that it could be used as collateral for margin positions, and that feature might have been crucial in allowing ftt to put the exchange in as much danger as it did, so I asked SBF if he regretted permitting his own exchange's token to be used that way.

"I like the idea of it being useful as collateral for small size. I don't think it should have been useful for collateral for giant size, in retrospect," he said.

I learned after the FTX bankruptcy, with everyone else, that many investors had passed on opportunities to invest in FTX out of concerns about its risk management or concerns that Alameda and FTX were too cozy.

Orthogonal Credit had never publicly spoken about its discomfort with Alameda as a customer for Maple, but anyone paying attention would have noticed that no more loans were approved to Alameda from Orthogonal's allocation of Maple's assets.

But there is a twist in this subplot.

Orthogonal's parent company had been a heavy user of FTX. It just so happened that the day that Kincaid and I spoke Maple Finance had revealed that it was cutting both Orthogonal Credit and Trading off from its platform.

The reason: unbeknownst to the credit subsidiary, Orthogonal Trading had a large amount of funds stuck on FTX when the company cut off withdrawals. Orthogonal Trading had a $36 million loan stewarded by M11. M11 was a company that did the same sort of work for Maple that Orthogonal Credit did.

(I know this is confusing. Think of it like this: imagine if a rich guy had a lot of money that he wanted to lend out, but he couldn't be bothered. So he hired a few other smart people to act as agents and go out and find borrowers. He gave them each a stack of money and just said, "Try to make me more than you lose." That's the situation here.

Orthogonal Credit was one of those. M11 was the other. *It's made weirder* by the fact that Orthogonal Trading *owned* one such agent, while also borrowing from another. But it's like a brother and sister marrying another brother and sister—it feels weird, but it's really not.)

In response to the default of Orthogonal Trading, Maple Finance released a statement saying that it had been "operating while effectively insolvent."

The statement continued, "The decision to cut the relationship with the Orthogonal Credit team is not taken lightly," it said. "Orthogonal Credit has grown a lending book to originate $850M with a 1.2% default rate in a volatile market."

Nevertheless, "Maple will not work with bad actors or with firms that misrepresent their financials or business operations," the statement read.

So this is the irony: even though Kincaid's part of the business, Credit, had resisted the temptation to make more money off Alameda and got out of business with it, it still took a massive hit from the collapse of Alameda and FTX.

The incident captures just how incestuous the tiny crypto market had become and just how much an excess of leverage made its market crash more painful than it had to be.

Sources Referenced

Interview, Sefton Kincaid, Orthogonal Credit, phone call, Dec. 5, 2022.

Interview, Sam Bankman-Fried, via videochat/Telegram call, Feb. 8, 2021.

"Issue 181," CM Staff, Coin Metrics' State of the Network, Nov. 15, 2022.

"Issue 182," Lee, Christine, Christian Brazell, and Matías Andrade, Coin Metrics' State of the Network, Nov. 22, 2022.

Orthogonal Credit, @OrthoCredit, Twitter, Nov. 9, 2022, https://twitter.com/OrthoCredit/status/1590328422542495744.

Sam Bankman-Fried, @SBF_FTX, Twitter, March 17, 2021, https://twitter.com/SBF_FTX/status/1372250887222030337.

Lucas Nuzzi, @LucasNuzzi, Twitter/Thread reader, Nov. 8, 2022, https://threadreaderapp.com/thread/1590122590206824448.html.

Interview, Sam Bankman-Fried, phone call with spokesperson, Dec. 30, 2022.

"DeFi Lender Maple Finance Cuts Off Orthogonal Trading for 'Misrepresenting Its Financial Position,'" Kelly, Liam, Decrypt, Dec. 5, 2022.

Chapter 44

New Boss, First Day

Iirst-day declarations in bankruptcy cases, I am told by a coworker who has covered many bankruptcies, are supposed to come out on the first day.

FTX's came out six days later, on November 17. A summary of it written by Axios quoted a piece of a paragraph that has been quoted again and again since. New FTX CEO John Ray, III, writes:

> Never in my career have I seen such a complete failure of corporate controls and such a complete absence of trustworthy financial information as occurred here. From compromised systems integrity and faulty regulatory oversight abroad, to the concentration of control in the hands of a very small group of inexperienced, unsophisticated and potentially compromised individuals, this situation is unprecedented.

And Ray has seen some things. He's overseen the unwinding of some very big companies. Most notably, Enron, the crash of the energy company that came right after the DotCom boom crumbled, when it felt like the US economy couldn't catch a break.[1]

Before the public could hear from Ray, though, we would hear from SBF. Vox.com would publish excerpts from an extensive interview over Twitter DM that Kelsey Piper conducted with him.

I mostly haven't mentioned other reporters by name in this account (you can see their bylines in the chapter notes, though), but it's worth mentioning Piper because this incident turned personal. She's one of the reporters on the "Future Perfect" project at Vox, which reports from the perspective of the Effective Altruist movement. Tagline: "Finding the best ways to do good." She covers the world from that "philanthropic, data-oriented" perspective.

SBF would later say he thought he was chatting with a friend, only to find the whole thread published. In other words, he basically accused Piper of misleading him. Piper would later say on Twitter: "I emailed Sam from my work email to confirm our talk . . . (first ever DM interaction, because I have had very little interaction with Sam outside an interview for Vox conducted eight months ago)."

To say that Sam was someone who had had a lot of experience with the media is an understatement.

In the interview, SBF reads like a person over the edge. He comes off like he's imploding, yet people are treating it like it's the steely confession of a stoic come to terms with fate. To me, it seems clear he was spiraling.

Go find it yourself and see what you think. The internet will never lose this post, so whenever this book finds you, you can find it. As long as everyone else is making much of the conversation, though, I'll highlight what most strongly confirms the view of SBF that writing this book has brought me to see.

Piper asked:

so the ethics stuff—mostly a front? People will like you if you win and hate you if you lose, and that's how it all works?

---

[1] For what it's worth, the crypto crash that culminated in FTX this year is being called Web3's DotCom bust. Personally, I suspect the equivalent of the DotCom crash is still to come, but we'll see.

To which he replied:

> yeah. I mean that's not all of it. but it's a lot.
> the worst quadrant is "sketchy + lose"
> the best is "win + ???"
> "clean + lose" is bad but not terrible!

Here's what he meant by "quadrants." People playing with game theory will assess combinations of two sets of outcomes like this.

↓ Ends \ Means →	Sketchy	Clean
Win	Sketchy win	Clean win
Lose	Sketchy loss	Clean loss

In other words, the best quadrant is whichever way one comes out winning. At that juncture, he was saying it didn't really matter to Sam. *Mainly* he wanted to win.

This was also the first place where we got this story he would repeat again and again. He told Piper that he could have fixed everything if he had just waited a little longer.

Based on a November 11 tweet from Bloomberg reporter Tom MacKenzie, Justin Sun was likely one of the parties here. Sun is a controversial figure. The Tron blockchain is the basis of much of his wealth.

In our December interview, SBF confirmed for me that Sun had been one of the parties, but he said there were several others, but he wouldn't name any more of them.

He also confirmed that the "balance sheet" reported on by the *Financial Times* shortly after the bankruptcy was one version of the holdings that FTX had been showing to a variety of interested parties. "Some of them were close to a hundred percent. I mean, some of them had already given an offer, but most of them were in negotiation," he told me.

Piper checked in the morning via email that she'd really been talking to him the night before, and he confirmed.

Ray's declaration made it clear he had seen the interview and was unimpressed. However, before he could express that, he laid out his plan for restructuring FTX.

Ray would break the Samglomerate up into four silos. He would begin instituting corporate controls. Accounting, human resources, security, regulatory compliance, etc.

He would break these into four pieces:

- The WRS Silo. Basically, the companies that might be worth a decent amount still, such as FTX US and LedgerX.
- The Alameda Silo. That is, Alameda, the mess, but one that probably had some good venture purchases in it.
- The Venture Silo. Other corporate entities that had made venture bets and other investments. There were a ton of these. It was anyone's guess what the stuff in it was worth.
- The Dotcom Silo. FTX international and companies that operated as it had.

Directors were appointed to head the boards of each silo.

At that point, Ray couldn't place a lot of faith in what anything was worth. "The FTX Group did not maintain centralized control of its cash. Cash management procedural failures included the absence of an accurate list of bank accounts and account signatories, as well as insufficient attention to the creditworthiness of banking partners," he wrote.

In a subsequent filing, the new FTX would report that its staff had found a billion dollars' worth of cash and assets across various accounts.

One of my sources with knowledge of FTX told me it was a firm in which everything happened on Slack. This sounds like a case in point: "The Debtors did not have the type of disbursement controls that I believe are appropriate for a business enterprise. For example, employees of the FTX Group submitted payment requests through an on-line 'chat' platform where a disparate group of supervisors approved disbursements by responding with personalized emojis," Ray's declaration said.

The same source who told me about Slack also told me that the other main vector of communication was the messaging app Signal. It's a messaging app, like iMessage or WhatsApp, in which all messages are encrypted, even from the people who made Signal. If you're not familiar, Signal makes it easy to set your chat records to auto-delete.

Signal is likely what Ray is referring to when he writes, "One of the most pervasive failures of the FTX.com business in particular is the absence of lasting records of decision-making. Mr. Bankman-Fried often communicated by using applications that were set to auto-delete after a short period of time, and encouraged employees to do the same."

And then Ray zoomed out, to comment on his predecessor (where he writes "the Debtors," he's referring to FTX and related companies).

"Finally, and critically, the Debtors have made clear to employees and the public that Mr. Bankman-Fried is not employed by the Debtors and does not speak for them," Ray wrote. "Mr. Bankman-Fried, currently in the Bahamas, continues to make erratic and misleading public statements."

Sources Referenced

"**Sam Bankman-Fried tries to explain himself**," Piper, Kelsey, Vox.com, Nov. 16, 2022.

Kelsey Piper, @KelseyTuoc, Twitter, Nov. 16, 2022: https://twitter.com/KelseyTuoc/status/1593031254076977152.

Sam Bankman-Fried, interview, phone call with spokesperson, Dec. 30, 2022.

"**Revealed: FTX's emergency fundraising term sheet**," FT Alphaville, *Financial Times*, Nov. 15, 2022.

"**Declaration of John J. Ray III in support of Chapter II Petitions and First Day Pleadings**," FTX Trading LTD., US Bankruptcy Court of Delaware, Chapter 11 Case No. 22-11068 (JTD), Nov. 17, 2022.

"**FTX Finds $1B in Hundreds of Company Bank Accounts**," Haig, Samuel, The Defiant, Dec. 21, 2022.

Interview, unnamed source, mobile, Dec. 18, 2022.

Chapter 45

A Flood of Pure SBF

When I wrote in Chapter 1, "I am drowning in Sam," I was here, at this point in the story. I was then. I still am, but the tide is going out. I'm not back on land yet, but I know if I rest and I don't fight it, the land will find me. I don't need to find the land.

Unlike SBF after CoinDesk's Ian Allison released his post about Alameda's balance sheet, I can see the shore from where I am.

In late November and early December SBF would not leave the public eye. He was in magazines. He was in the *New York Times*. He was doing interviews on YouTube. He was on Twitter Spaces.

YouTube gadfly Coffeezilla was chasing him.

NFT influencers were chasing him.

TV reporters were chasing him.

A goofy token shill I will not dignify by naming chased him.

Everyone thought if they could just get one more interview from him, it would make sense. They were all playing into Sam's hands.

Many who felt betrayed believed that his media tour was working to his benefit, that he might actually get away with losing $8 billion (or was it $10 billion?) in customer money. They saw large media companies as complicit in helping to burnish his image.

But then he was arrested, and as I write this, he's sitting in the sick-bay of an overcrowded prison in the island nation his company had recently made his home.[1]

Looking back on it, there is not a lot of value to say about all these many appearances. We were all just tea bags soaking in the flavors of a collective stew we had boiled up together, a swirling potion of shifting sadness, outrage, intrigue, schadenfreude, and mockery.

SBF appeared in many places, but to my mind, these were the key media appearances:

- Axios interview on Nov. 29. A few pieces were published with different parts of the interview. Where he first said he was down to $100,000.
- The first recording from Tiffany Fong's phone call with SBF, released on YouTube Nov. 29.
- The *New York Times* Dealbook Summit, Nov. 30.
- *Good Morning America*, Dec. 1.
- *New York Magazine* interview on its Intelligencer site, Dec. 1.
- *The Scoop* podcast, Dec. 5.

There were others. People really like the grilling scam vigilante Coffeezilla gave him, too. Eventually, though, listening to these things was like watching one of those YouTube videos of skateboarding accidents: it was a lot of the same thing over and over.

He was sorry, there was an accounting artifact, he should have had better risk management, he shouldn't have given up his company, etc., etc., etc.

Were anyone to go through the above accounts and more from that month in a two-day marathon session like I did, I think they would eventually discern a strategy. What appeared to be a series of open conversations had become, to my ears, talking points.

I wrote the same for Axios at the time, but I don't actually think the talking points are all that interesting anymore now that he's been arrested.

---

[1] At the end of December 2022, he would be back in his family home, under house arrest, his passport taken, and wearing an ankle monitor.

Once those handcuffs went on, the public relations campaign became irrelevant because it was something designed to prepare himself if his lawyers succeeded in keeping him out of jail.

As I wrote in the beginning, as new facts and circumstances arise, the set of possible explanations and futures shrink. Before the handcuffs, it seemed almost likely he might get away with the company's failure. Once he went to jail, it's hard to imagine how we ever even saw that possibility.

Because they failed to keep him out of jail, the talking points matter very little.

Except one point, which I think is worth highlighting. The fact that Alameda was drawing customer funds from FTX to cover losses on investments hasn't been verified by a court yet, but it has been alleged in multiple accounts by different government organizations who seem to have had a look at the books.

That cash (in cryptocurrency form) had moved from FTX to Alameda to meet margin calls, make loans, make investments, and even to make political donations. This is, in my estimation, considerably more nefarious than the way SBF described the hole's origins in his media tour.

In all of his appearances, he described Alameda as having an excessive *margin* position. For example, in *New York Mag*, he said:

> A client on FTX put on a very large margin position. FTX fucked up in allowing that position to be put on and in underestimating, in fact, the size of the position itself. That margin position blew out during the extreme events over the last few weeks. . . . I feel really bad about that. And it was a large fuckup of risk analysis and risk attention and, you know, it was with an account that was given too much trust, and not enough skepticism.

In other words, FTX let Alameda's bets *on FTX* get too big. We were to imagine Alameda was, *I don't know*, 12X long $500 million on bitcoin and 20X long $200 million in ether or something.

All secured by the ftt token. And ftt went bad, and now they were out a bunch of money.

When FTX first fell apart, I went into Slack and explained my understanding of the whole debacle to one of my coworkers this way:

Step 1.

Launch a trading desk. Make piles.

Step 2.

Decide you want to make more piles, so open an exchange that prints
   money off retail trades and use that money to lend to trading desk.

Step 3.

Lend retail money to trading desk in hopes of quadrupling all gains.

Step 4.

Trading desk loses borrowed money.

Step 5.

But SBF was trying to spin it as if it had all stayed inside the house.
It was just big bets, but funds hadn't left FTX. This is still bad, but more
negligent, less outright theft.

Jason Choi had been with Spartan Capital when FTX was raising
money, and he'd declined to invest because he didn't like the Alameda/
FTX relationship. He explained all this on Twitter after the exchange
collapsed. We spoke before complaints had been made against SBF, and I
asked him whether he thought it mattered if Alameda had an outsized
margin position or had taken customer funds out of the exchange.

"I think functionally they are the same," he said. "It implies that
Alameda is able to run things into seriously negative positions."

In other words, in terms of what people have lost, each outcome
arrives at the same place.

But it does matter in terms of how to understand the decisions
made. If funds were taken out and handed to Alameda to use elsewhere,
people had to green-light those moves, knowing that they were against
the terms of service and against the many assurances that the company
had made to the public and their users.

It's not negligent. It's willful. Legality aside, it just feels different
ethically.

However, for what it's worth, when SBF and I last spoke he stuck by
this explanation: the hole in FTX's balance sheet was from a margin
position Alameda took out. It had failed to adequately hedge, and it had
gotten much too long on the wrong collateral.

Before he was arrested, that's how he described the problem. That's still how he describes it. He agreed, when we spoke, that it would be different if FTX had been sending actual customer assets to Alameda to use in other ways, but he says that wasn't happening.

The government is claiming that it did happen, and to do so it's drawing attention to loans made to SBF and other cofounders, loans they used to make venture investments, to buy stock in Robinhood, political donations, and to purchase real estate.

This points to a part of the story that I didn't really understand until the complaints started coming out.

When it's said that someone is a "billionaire," that doesn't mean that they have billions of dollars *in cash*. It doesn't mean, necessarily, that they can even spend that much money. That doesn't even mean that they *can* access billions of dollars in cash, or even many millions.

If someone's billionaire status is tied up in a stake in a private company, it can be very difficult to turn that value into spendable money. If their status is tied up largely in thinly traded, extremely new crypto tokens, it might be even harder.

In the complaints by the SEC and the CFTC and the DoJ, they allege loans from the Samglomerate, using customer funds, to enable investments, property purchases, political donations, and more. All of these things take actual cash. SBF and his cadre had very high net worth, but it hadn't occurred to me that they wouldn't really have access to that much cash until those complaints came out.

Of course SBF, Wang, Singh, and others could borrow money somewhere, and maybe more sophisticated readers than me presumed it was borrowed from banks. Or maybe it was borrowed from some of the new crypto lenders (many of which fell into dire straits, as described in Chapter 35). But these various agencies allege something else: the funds were borrowed from FTX customers. And the customers didn't know. Further, they had no upside. Only downside.

And the downside is here now.

"I thought at the time and still do think that, the size of those loans was substantially less than the profit, than like the liquid trading profit that Alameda had made," he told me in December. In other words, he denies that the loans were made using FTX user funds.

The whole story of what happened is confusing and dripping in finance jargon and involves a level of mathematics few of us have contemplated recently. It may be that SBF's story here has been a bet that he was smart enough to cast a spell and convince us all that all the mistakes were only made inside the casino.

And if he had done that well enough, the sting of the error might fade, and if he evaded an arrest and conviction, he might be able to rehabilitate himself in the public eye and apply his considerable gifts, once again.

He might still have won, but then he was arrested.

So in that case, these appearances might really have just been about enjoying that last moment in the spotlight. For some, it's better to be hated than ignored. But it's also worth noting that he hasn't given up on this story.

As I wrote in the prologue: he doesn't believe the evidence of crimes is there. He seems as eager to reopen the books at FTX and Alameda. He wants everyone to get from 20 percent of the story to 80 or 90 percent. And maybe we will. And maybe the fact that he seems to want that as much as anyone will prove to be a sign that he was right.

But trust me, if you haven't seen the many media appearances of November and December 2022, you don't need to. This chapter gives more than you need to know about what he had to say before they put him in a Bahamas jail.

Sources Referenced

"**Exclusive: Sam Bankman-Fried says he's down to $100,000**," Shen, Lucinda, Axios, Nov. 29, 2022.

"**Sam Bankman-Fried Interviewed Live About the Collapse of FTX**," *New York Times Events*, YouTube, Nov. 30, 2022.

"**FTX founder Sam Bankman-Fried denies 'improper use' of customer funds**," Stephanopoulos, George, *Good Morning America*, Dec. 1, 2022.

"**Sam Bankman-Fried's First Interview After FTX Collapse**," Fong, Tiffany, YouTube, posted Nov. 29, 2022

"**What Does Sam Bankman-Fried Have to Say for Himself? An interview with the disgraced CEO**," Wieczner, Jen, *New York Magazine*, Dec. 1, 2022.

"**2-hour sit-down with Sam Bankman-Fried on the FTX scandal**," Quinton, Davis, and Frank, Chaparro, *The Scoop* podcast, The Block, Dec. 5, 2022.

Jason Choi, interview, mobile, Dec. 11, 2022.

"**The SBF media blitz's key messages**," Dale, Brady, Axios, Dec. 8, 2022.

Interview, Sam Bankman-Fried, phone call with spokesperson, Dec. 30, 2022.

Chapter 46

Arrest

The Miami Heat cut ties with FTX so fast it was almost as if the basketball team never had any genuine interest in the cryptocurrency business.

Companies that have funds stuck on FTX that seriously compromised them included Galois Capital, Ikigai Capital, Orthogonal Trading, and Multicoin Capital. Multicoin was heavily exposed to the SBF galaxy of token projects. Those investments are worth considerably less than what they were last year.

The *New York Times* reported on November 11: "FTX's list of investors spans powerful and well-known investment firms: NEA, IVP, Iconiq Capital, Third Point Ventures, Tiger Global, Altimeter Capital Management, Lux Capital, Mayfield, Insight Partners, Sequoia Capital, SoftBank, Lightspeed Venture Partners, Ribbit Capital, Temasek Holdings, BlackRock and Thoma Bravo."

BlockFi went into bankruptcy after its lifeline from FTX was broken. Voyager Digital went looking for a new buyer.

The Royal Bahamas Police force with SBF as he is extradited to the United States. Royal Bahamas Police Force/Handout/Reuters

Genesis Trading paused withdrawals and as of mid–December it has not opened them back up again. Questions are swirling around the health of its parent, the Digital Currency Group, one of the largest and oldest crypto funds out there. Accounts of Genesis troubles appear to be more linked to May's troubles rather than November's, though as the bad news from FTX pushed crypto prices lower, that may have been more stress than Genesis could stand up to, at least without a fresh injection of capital.

The Block, a news organization that has been doing very good reporting on FTX, turned out to have been secretly financed by its subject in a way that only the company's CEO, Michael McCaffrey, knew about. For what it's worth: I believe the editorial team when it says they were not aware of this arrangement and received no pressure to be soft on FTX. Still, it's taken a reputational hit.

There's a narrative that a lot of small start-ups, especially in the Solana ecosystem, had their treasuries on FTX. That said, I don't understand why so few have come forward.

Ren Protocol, which enables people to trade bitcoin on other chains, first announced that it is decentralizing to dissociate itself from FTX, which had acquired the team. Now, it just seems to be shutting down. Serum users also announced a hard fork of the exchange (a copy, basically) because the underlying smart contracts remain in FTX's control.

The *WSJ* reported that 300 people worked at FTX until the bankruptcy. Some are still employed there, helping Ray's team, but it's unknown how many.

A nonprofit organization in Chicago, Equity and Transportation, was told that a $600,000 grant promised by the FTX Foundation would not be fulfilled. SBF's father, Joseph Bankman, emailed the organization to say that he would have funded at least part of the grant out of his own pocket, but "I'll be spending substantially all of my resources on Sam's defense," according to a November 22 story in the *New York Times*.

Over a million people are said to have funds stuck on the exchange, including many former FTX employees.

SBF's name no longer appears on the website of The Giving Pledge, though it did in June.

CoinGecko says that the market cap for all of crypto was over a trillion on November 2, the day of Ian Allison's CoinDesk post. As I write this, in mid-December, it's at $844 million. Market caps are nonsense, but those numbers aren't putting anyone in a good mood. It's unlikely to get better for a while. Anyone who says they know when the market will turn around is just glad to be filling time in a TV segment.

On December 9 I got this message on Telegram from an account that showed up as @iillliiill:

> Hey Brady, someone shared with me your contact. I'm a former trader at alameda and as you're aware, there are a lot of uncovered stories regarding the relationship between alameda/ftx. I'd be happy to share more of these details for a negotiable fee. (Pending contractual agreements after viewed by respective attorneys) let me know if this is something that your firm would be interested in.

Reporters don't pay sources, so I said no. When I suggested it might be good to speak simply to help the world understand what really happened, my interlocutor was unmoved.

Whoever they were, they replied, "Obviously you can also think of this fees as potential legal fees that I will personally face for speaking, even in an anon capacity, as well as my time and effort in speaking and coordinating with my attorneys."

I suspect that the supposed trader—if he was real at all—was going to reveal the things now alleged in the CFTC's complaint.

In the end, SBF had succeeded in having high impact, at least—just not the kind he had hoped for.

His efforts took a heavy toll, including on himself. "It was really shocking seeing Sam's transformation over the years," Frankel told me. When she met him, he was slender and young-looking. By the end, she said, "His face was like. . . so aged."

There has been some resolution in the story. The US filed charges against the Alameda and FTX founder, and he was arrested in The Bahamas on December 13. The indictment by US Attorney Damian Williams charged him with wire fraud, commodities fraud, securities fraud, money laundering, and violation of campaign finance laws. Charges were later made against cofounder Gary Wang and Caroline Ellison.

It should be emphasized that these are only charges. We haven't seen the evidence. A court still needs to rule. It's all alleged.

It should also be noted that I didn't say hardly anything about Wang, or fellow cofounder Nishad Singh or former Alameda co-CEOs Trabucco and Ellison. Part of that was a function of time but also because in covering this story I became convinced that everything really did in the end come back to SBF.

It seems that the others just didn't matter a lot. The trial may disprove this, but that's where I'm at right now, so this narrative focuses on him.

He is, of course, innocent until proven guilty.

The judge who considered bail for SBF in The Bahamas didn't want to grant it. In his first hearing before the court, CoinDesk reported that she told his attorneys that she'd seen many defendants skip cash bail when she'd let them go free. Judge Ferguson-Pratt said in the hearing.

The creole expression is 'allez'. They never came back.

The arrest prevented the former CEO from making a final appearance before the cameras, via video, before the House Financial Services Committee.

On the occasion of his arrest, Committee Chairwoman Maxine Waters (Dem., Calif.) issued a statement:

> The American public deserves to hear directly from Mr. Bankman-Fried about the actions that've harmed over one million people. The public has been waiting eagerly to get these answers under oath before Congress, and the timing of this arrest denies the public this opportunity.

No doubt Committee members were eager. Were Americans? I was not. If you were eager for the informed questioning of elected members of Congress, though, I'm sorry.

When there are trials, however, all of us will hear much more.

★★★

It has seemed to me, in retrospect, that John Ray's statement from the first-day declaration about the disarray at FTX has been one that crystallized the story for many of those following along, especially for my fellow journalists. As in it's one thing to do the wrong thing, but it's another to do it from a poorly run business. His statement became a sort of double bottom line, making it hard to conceive of a scenario in which SBF and his companies hadn't betrayed customers.

So I asked SBF about Ray's "never in my career" comment. I asked him this after he had been arrested, perp walked through the Bahamas, held in Fox Hill Prison, taken in handcuffs to an airplane, extradited to the US, and then finally released to his parents' home on bail wearing a monitoring device.

Through most of our conversation he had been his typical self. Fast talking and energetic, but in a level way, as if we were just continuing the conversation we had begun in early 2021. But when I asked him about Ray, however, he became furious.

"I don't fucking know how he could have any clue about anything when he said that. He is so fucking incompetent that to this day he has no idea what is going on at FTX or whatever it has. To my knowledge, he still has not figured out how to get substantive information from the database. He cut off all access to anyone else from a month and a half ago. To this day, they seem to be fumbling around, unable to safeguard any assets," SBF told me. "The only information he could possibly have had to go on when I said that was basically perjurious testimony given by a scared FTX executive covering his own legal ass after he'd lost his mind."

As SBF has said previously, several times before, he believes that he could help Ray recover much of the information he needs to do his work, but Ray will not respond to his messages or return his calls.

Sam said, "He shut down all access to all internal data, didn't know how to get it back, and refused to ask or even respond to messages from anyone who had been involved in running the company and could have trivially told him where the records of such things were."

In public, he'd been apologetic. To me, he was defiant.

Sources Referenced

"**Miami Heat to cut ties with bankrupt FTX, rename arena**,"Windhorst, Brian, ABC News, Nov. 11, 2022.

"**Multicoin LPs are frustrated over its Solana bet,**" Dale, Brady, Axios, Nov. 21, 2022.

"**Crypto Fund Galois Capital Has Half of Its Capital Trapped on FTX**," Kessler, Sam, CoinDesk, Nov. 12, 2022.

Travis Kling, @Travis_Kling, Twitter, Nov. 14, 2022: https://twitter.com/Travis_Kling/status/1592198107734876160.

"**Which Companies Are Exposed to FTX?**," Reiff, Nathan, Investopedia, Nov. 17, 2022.

"**Investors Who Put $2 Billion into FTX Face Scrutiny, Too**," Griffith, Erin, David Yaffe-Bellany, the *New York Times*, Nov. 11, 2022.

"**Crypto lender BlockFi files for bankruptcy**," Lawler, Ryan, Axios, Nov. 28, 2022.

"**Genesis crypto lending unit halts services, adding to FTX contagion**," Kim, Crystal, and Brady Dale, Axios, Nov. 16, 2022.

"**Exclusive: SBF secretly funded crypto news site**," Fischer, Sara, Axios, Dec. 9, 2022.

"**Inside Sam Bankman-Fried's Quest to Win Friends and Influence People**," Vogel, Kenneth, Emily Flitter, and David Yaffe-Bellany, the *New York Times*, Nov. 22, 2022.

"**FTX's Collapse Leaves Employees Sick with Anger**," Osipovich, Alexander, Caitlin Ostroff, and Gregory Zuckerman, *Wall Street Journal*, Nov. 16, 2022.

Interview, Tamara Frankel, Dec. 13, 2022.

The Giving Pledge, Pledge Signatories, Archive.org, captured June 15, 2022: https://web.archive.org/web/20220615072621/https://www.givingpledge.org/pledgerlist.

"**Former FTX CEO Bankman-Fried arrested in Bahamas after U.S. files charges**," Ward, Jasper, Luc Cohen, and Angus Berwick, Reuters, Dec. 13, 2022.

"**Bankman-Fried is ready to 'face the music,' prison official says**," Villegas, Paulina, the *Washington Post*, Dec. 17, 2022.

"**Inside Sam Bankman-Fried's First Bahamas Court Hearing After His Arrest**," Ligon, Cheyenne, CoinDesk, Dec. 13, 2022.

"**Exclusive Transcript: The Full Testimony SBF Planned to Give to Congress**," Ehrlich, Steven, *Forbes*, Dec. 13, 2022.

"**Sam Bankman-Fried Released on $250M Bail Secured by Parents**," Napolitano, Elizabeth, and Jesse Hamilton, CoinDesk, Dec. 22, 2022.

Interview, Sam Bankman-Fried, phone call with spokesperson, Dec. 30, 2022.

Conclusion

A source who made it decently high in the ranks of FTX before self-extricating ahead of the immolation—but who, nevertheless, does not want to be identified because, well, because of everything—told me the following at the end of a conversation we had on the same day that I finished writing the first draft of this book:

> A lot of people are finger-pointing and asking how did these people not know. Politicians. VCs. Employees. Etc. I think when you put it all together and you realize that Sequoia, BlackRock, President Biden . . . Katy Perry, all these different people, had absolutely no idea about what was going on. [It] is not about a failure of any one of these people.
>
> It's about, that. . . Sam was a genius at covering up his fraud.
>
> He was just the best.
>
> He was able to tell the story to everyone, including from the very earliest days that we all started working here, there were things going on. He clearly was just a masterful liar and a masterful storyteller. And I think that's what people need to understand to move on.

★★★

An adjective that gets used a lot in the reporting on FTX is that it was "unregulated."

But keep in mind that the mechanisms of the 2008 financial crisis were built by a slew of well-regulated entities. And governments propped up those same entities in the crisis' aftermath, rather than simply unwinding them in an orderly fashion. Those institutions remain. One has to wonder if any lessons were really learned.

One can use FTX as an example of the dangers of dealing with unregulated financial systems and, by extension, the dangers of the blockchain industry, but it's not a fair conclusion.

Crypto assets that exist on open blockchains are well regulated, by transparency and readable code.

Think back to the story of MakerDAO and Black Thursday. One day in March 2020 the granddaddy of decentralized finance apps was shown that its risk management had failed. At the end of a sharp shock to the price of its collateral, the blockchain had seized up, it wasn't possible to unwind positions fast enough, and the system came up short approximately $4 million.

Far from this damning DeFi, it's commendable. There will never be a financial system without risk, and there has never been a financial system that made a shortfall known so quickly and precisely.

Users immediately knew the system was underfunded. Leadership assured users it was moving to resolve the situation, both in the immediate term and the long term.

No one tried to hide the hole, and they couldn't have hidden it if they tried.

That's what DeFi promises. Not a regulatory system where companies with something to hide bury their troubles in complex and opaque financial statements, overseen by technocrats who are just biding their time while they wait to take a job with the same companies they've been keeping an eye on.

DeFi promises a world where financial systems can't get into serious insolvency because the holes can't be hidden. In other words: no one needed to write a law for DeFi to work this way. This is just how DeFi works.

To paraphrase the blogger Scott Alexander, one can dismiss DeFi as relearning the same lessons that traditional finance had already learned, except DeFi is doing it *a different way*, with an openness to scrutiny never contemplated by traditional finance.

Traditional finance is secretive. It's closed. It reveals no more than it has to. In the same way, FTX was a closed, centralized company, just like many others that have gotten into financial trouble.

"This is really just old-fashioned embezzlement," John J. Ray, the CEO of FTX after the company entered into bankruptcy, said before the House Financial Services Committee the same day that SBF's indictment was unsealed in New York.

★★★

Let's imagine it's 2042. SBF never let his machinations get so out of hand in 2022. Instead, he made piles of cash that he gave away well. He never saw the inside of a Bahamas jail. In fact, maybe he heard about how bad it was and built the nation a new, nicer one? To reduce human suffering.

He owns a very nice penthouse in Manhattan he bought for, say, $22 million in 2028, lives off an annuity that's many decimal places smaller than what he could have afforded and largely devotes his time to stewarding a foundation and a political fund, both of which he endowed long ago.

He's on stage at the Kennedy Center in DC at some event, being interviewed by whoever is the 2042 equivalent of Lester Holt, and he gets thrown a softball: "What was it about cryptocurrency in 2017 that made you so sure it was the place to go that you could make a difference?"

And he says, "Has it been long enough that I can admit now that I think I probably screwed a lot of those early blockchain degenerates on the way to curing malaria?"

Everyone laughs.

EA espouses a voluntary transfer of wealth from the rich world to those in need. Institutionally, it definitely does not, it should be said, advocate robbing from the rich and giving to the poor.

But one can imagine how someone singularly ambitious, steeped in such a worldview, might convince themselves that they weren't precisely being unethical as they started to get a bit unethical. And then it could all get away from them.

It is easy right now to disdain crypto people. They are rich. They are weird. They are pushy. They are intemperate.

And probably no one would hold it against someone if—in the service of some generally agreed upon greater good—they didn't so much *manipulate* crypto degens but maybe took a little advantage of the fact that they were all just so eager to make money.

★★★

Peter Singer's speech that he gave at TED2013, "The How and Why of Effective Altruism," is a very good speech. It should jog the conscience of any normally functioning person.

But giving money to save a life isn't the same as saving a child whose life is in danger right in front of you. In the first place, because in the case of that child in that situation, you are the only one who can do it. It's a matter between you and the child.

In the matter of those who are in need, many more can. It's between the many and the many more.

But it's also different because in that moment you know you can save that child and you will also know if you don't. Perhaps I can't fit this into a logical model that would satisfy Bertrand Russell, but I can stop right there, and most readers will already know that I'm right. I don't need to write another word.

It's different.

Not only is this how we function, this is how we must function.

You probably should support some good causes, but you definitely should feel guilty for the rest of your life if you let another person die right in front of you if you could have prevented that death. This is obviously true. The moral difference is clear.

The awful truth is that no one can ever really know that they saved anyone when they give to save. They can know it's likely they did, but they can't know. They can hope they did. They can credulously read reports from the nonprofit that took the money reassuring them that they did. But they can never know.

If someone is in mortal danger right in front of you, and you successfully intervene, you know.

And in that way, Singer's model is a helpful model, but it's also a toy model.

The Life You Can Save (the title of Singer's 2009 book) is a very strong statement.

Probably You Will Save Some Lives is the best I think anyone could justify and the best I think anyone can do. *You Might Save Some Lives, And It's Good to Try* would be more honest still.

SBF comes from an ideology that pushes people to consider that the abstraction (the statistical likelihood of saving someone via directing a certain amount of money toward vetted interventions) is equivalent to the fact (actually knowing you saved a person with your own hands).

It's a nice way to nudge people's hearts into the right place, but SBF looks to be a cautionary tale of what happens when it goes too far.

Haseeb Qureshi, a crypto investor and an EA, pushed back on me very hard but very perceptively when I told him I thought SBF's encounter with EA is wrapped up in some way in this disaster. That said, he granted this:

> His risk profile was very much shifted by his engagement with EA ideas and utilitarianism. I think that's definitely true. He learned, through his engagement with EA, that most people have far too low of a risk appetite. That the downside of a lot of forms of failure are much less bad than a lot of people think.

Qureshi feels the same. "But," he said, "that does not get you to commit fraud and hope you get away with it."

Qureshi objects to a story he's seen told in the press, that EA caused Sam to commit the crimes he's alleged to have committed, because he had come to believe the ends justify the means.

"If that were true, why only Sam?" Qureshi objected, many people have encountered these ideas and not gone this far.

And I said, "I feel like most people who are adherents of a philosophy understand that any framework is only good up to a point, but if you take it all the way, everything's nuts. But if you're a megalomaniac, a philosophy is the way you justify doing what you already want to do."

This seemed to mollify Qureshi, and I hope it mollifies EAs reading this. EA is dangerous in the wrong hands, but all compelling philosophies are dangerous in the wrong hands. "It was so much a part of his public persona," Qureshi said. "It has to be part of the story now because that's how stories work. The gun you put on the table in the second act and blah blah. . . and EA is the gun. You've got to talk about it."

I agree.

What if the means EA provided was enough allies to get started and later it provided a cover story, one where he wasn't "winning," one where he was "helping."

In our culture, it is true (and often remarked upon) that criminals who hurt people through abstractions (white-collar criminals) get treated more leniently than street criminals, who do less harm overall but whose crimes are more visceral. Street criminals do direct harm. White-collar crime is in spreadsheets. It's mediated. Street crime is direct, and society reacts more strongly.

Street crime taps into a primal fear, but that's unfair. Harm is harm.

That dichotomy is an injustice, wherein lies the elegant justice if SBF is found guilty and convicted. This alleged embezzler and fraudster, in abstract ways, made use of another grand abstraction—a social movement—to justify his means.

And this master of abstractions may in fact become a rare example among his like to face real consequences for harms committed to many people far from him, whose names and faces he never knew nor will know.

★★★

Chuck Klosterman has a whole book called *I Wear the Black Hat* about villains. The thesis of the book is that the villain is the one who knows the most and cares the least. He supports it well, but there is also the villain who knows the most and cares way too much.

Righteousness is distorting. Righteousness combined with actual power is blinding.

People love the revolutionary Che Guevara because he died fairly young. They might have loved Fidel Castro the same way if he had too, but old Fidel was hard to love. Doing a bit of wrong for idealistic reasons has a pernicious way of morphing into just doing wrong.

In 1951, Albert Camus published *The Rebel*. It was a book-length essay about the suffering that a revolution will probably bring and the utopia it probably won't. It was a pointed critique of the ends-justify-the-means ethics of Marxists in his time.

In response, Jean-Paul Sartre wrote an open letter to Camus, "Our friendship was not an easy one, but I shall miss it."

But knowing what we know now, I hope most readers can agree that Camus, looking back, had been right. History has vindicated him. Sartre, the great man, was wrong about Europe's Communists. He was wrong about "the revolution" in Russia. Harm committed on the path to justice can't be justified, *because* you can't actually know that justice is coming after the harms.

The revolutionary might just find he's invented a whole new genre of injustice.

The life you save is only imagined. The injustice you end is only a vision. The suffering you reduce is speculative. *People are welcome to try, but they can't know.*

No one can know what the ends will be when they commit some harm in the name of a greater good, though we do have some idea. History has told many stories of how it didn't work out.

The trouble is when you do so much work to know that you actually start to believe you know. Maybe you're a part of a whole group of people trying very hard to quantify the good they do, reinforcing your budding confidence with social rewards for making it look more and more as though you do know something that you can never really know.

Maybe eventually you lose track of the model as a motivating moral allegory, and it becomes dogma.

And maybe you do so much of this work of knowing outcomes of actions here and what they do there that before long you believe you can know all kinds of things you can't know. Maybe you generalize this imagined knowing.

Then, you've lost track of the humility that made this toy model helpful, and that makes it a problem. It's become the bridge you've crossed over to hubris.

Altruism isn't so bad, but overconfidence about its effectiveness can be.

SBF seemed confident about something. And he seemed to grow more confident as he went, piling up more money and power and fame.

What we do know from this story is that people who seem extremely confident that they know what's best and make a compelling case can get it very wrong. If that's true of SBF and if it were true of Sartre, it might be true of Singer and his successor, Will MacAskill, too. It might be true of anyone who tells a good story and makes people want to follow.

But that's less concerning because it's rare for leaders of social movements and philosophers to accrue as much wealth as Sam once had.

Ideas are always dangerous, but ideas atop a huge pile of money are a much larger threat. And that's why cryptocurrency will always be a lot more dangerous than other ideas, because it's an idea that became money.

Sources Referenced

"**Anyone Seen Tether's Billions?**" Faux, Zeke, Bloomberg, Oct. 7, 2021.

"**Tether's Impact on Bitcoin Price Not 'Statistically Significant,' Study Finds**," Dale, Brady, CoinDesk, Sept. 21, 2018.

"**The why and how of effective altruism**," TED, TED 2013, https://www.ted.com/talks/peter_singer_the_why_and_how_of_effective_altruism?language=en.

"**Why I'm Less Than Infinitely Hostile to Cryptocurrency**," Alexander, Scott, Astral Codex Ten, Dec. 8, 2022.

I Wear the Black Hat: Grappling with Villains (Real and Imagined), Klosterman, Chuck, Scribner, 2013.

The Rebel, Camus, Albert, 1951.

Index